W9-APZ-527

INTERREGIONAL MIGRATION IN THE U.S.S.R.

STUDIES IN SOCIAL AND ECONOMIC DEMOGRAPHY

General Editor

GEORGE C. MYERS, Director,
Center for Demographic Studies, Duke University

---

1. Joseph J. Spengler, *Facing Zero Population Growth: Reactions and Interpretations, Past and Present*
2. Joseph J. Spengler, *France Faces Depopulation: Postlude Edition, 1936–1976*
3. Peter J. Grandstaff, *Interregional Migration in the U.S.S.R.: Economic Aspects, 1959–1970*

INTERREGIONAL MIGRATION IN THE U.S.S.R.

ECONOMIC ASPECTS, 1959–1970

Peter J. Grandstaff

Duke University Press   Durham, North Carolina   1980

L.C.C. card number 78-57233
I.S.B.N. 0-8223-0413-9
Printed in the United States of America

Cataloging in Publication Data

Grandstaff, Peter J 1942–
Interregional migration in the U.S.S.R.

(Studies in social and economic demography; no. 3)
A revision of the author's thesis, Duke University, 1973.
Bibliography: p.
Includes index.
1. Migration, Internal—Russia. 2. Migration, Internal—Economic aspects—Russia. I. Title. II. Series.
HB2067.G7 1980 304.8'2'0947 78-57233
ISBN 0-8223-0413-9

CONTENTS

LIST OF FIGURES

Figure

PREFACE

The present work is the outgrowth of a doctoral dissertation done in the Department of Economics at Duke University. Its chapters 2 and 6 are basically from the dissertation as it was accepted in 1973. Chapter 3 appeared in an abbreviated form in volume 9 (1975) of the *International Migration Review*. The estimates of chapter 4 are now appearing for the first time in their entirety. Chapter 5 was presented at the 1977 meeting of the Population Association of America. The ideas of appendix C were earlier presented in volume XVI (1974) of the *Bulletin of the Association for Comparative Economic Studies*.

Vladimir G. Treml provided essential direction, George C. Myers provided a valuable reading and Murray Feshbach made the library and data of the U.S. Department of Commerce's Foreign Demographic Analysis Division available. Robert A. Lewis and Reynolds Smith were also very helpful later on. I thank them and others for their help and of course remind the reader that they have no responsibility for errors contained in this work. While at Duke University I was enrolled in the then Population Studies program (under the direction of Joseph J. Spengler) which was supported by the National Institutes of Health. I am grateful for the support received there.

Tables presenting data, to which references are made in the text, are grouped together starting on page 127. This slight inconvenience for the reader allowed a substantial reduction in type-setting costs.

University City, Mo. PETER J. GRANDSTAFF

INTERREGIONAL MIGRATION IN THE U.S.S.R.

1

INTRODUCTION

This research examines the interregional migration of persons in the Soviet Union between the censuses of January 15, 1959, and January 15, 1970. Its primary concerns are to identify the migration that took place, view the economic consequences, and study the significance of economic factors in motivating migrants, though also of interest are the determination and effectiveness of Soviet policy on migration. A definitive work on these questions would entail extensive study and is impossible at the present time without the assistance of the Central Statistical Administration of the Soviet Union. Sufficient data do not exist to treat the topic in great detail. The aim here is to study those aspects on which data are available.

THE PROBLEM IN THE CONTEXT OF ECONOMIC SYSTEMS

Comparisons are often made between the economic system of the Soviet Union and the economic system that has evolved from the Anglo-American experience of Britain, Canada, and the United States. (In this work the latter system will be referred to as the market system.) Differences between the two economic systems have been strongly emphasized, but in recent years some students of economic systems have identified enough similarities in terms of direction of development to advance a "convergence thesis," suggesting that the systems are developing somewhat similar economic mechanisms. The questions studied here provide insights concerning recent experiences in the Soviet Union compared with the substantial work on migration of human population in market economies.

There are obviously differences in population distribution, settlement, and migration among societies, and differences between the current Soviet system and the market economic systems are easily found. In Soviet pronouncement and thought two main views exist, one associated with Marxian theory and dogma and the other with economic planning in its spatial aspects.

For an example of the Marxist–Leninist view one may turn to the current secondary school text on economic geography of the U.S.S.R. by A. Lavrishchev.[1] The laws which govern the distribution of population are said to be a

1. A. Lavrishchev, *Economic Geography of the U.S.S.R.* (Moscow: Progress, 1969).

function of the mode of production; this, Lavrishchev tells the student, was shown by Marx and Engels in their study of the distribution of population under the conditions of premonopoly capitalism. Lenin updated Marxian study by including the age of imperialistic capitalism. At this point, however, further reading of Lavrishchev is not enlightening. By the socialist law of population, Marxian theory and dogma seem to mean only that all able-bodied persons can and will be used in socialist production—a notion familiar to everyone. The socialist law of population, when combined with the "law" of proportional development of the economy, supposedly implies something about the distribution of population. What that is, however, is not made clear.[2]

Lavrishchev does make clear the problems of population distribution experienced in the West and attributes them to capitalism. A basic problem is the opposition between town and country. In the Marxian dynamic the notion of the increasing concentration in the ownership of capital is a familiar one but, Lavrishchev states, we may not appreciate that this concept accounts for the geographical concentration of capital in urban settlements. Capitalism is the cause of urban overpopulation, with all its real and imaginable ill consequences, and has fostered increasing gross internal migration and net international emigration. These developments result from "relative over-population," that is, the unemployment caused by the familiar dynamic. The implicit idea is that the relative employment opportunities for the proletariat are important considerations in decisions about migration. But how decisions to migrate are made in the socialist system—in contrast to the market system—is, somewhat characteristically, unspecified.[3]

Another Soviet view of their presumed differences from market economic systems, specifically differences in the distribution, settlement, and migration of population, derives from recent thought concerning the planning of economic activity in its spatial aspects. Surprisingly, this view contradicts the conclusions and tenets of Marxian theory and dogma. The conclusions of the Marxian paradigm are that urbanization beyond the optimum, as well as high levels of both gross internal migration and net international emigration, occur in the market system. The presumption is that these phenomena do not appear in the Soviet system. Of course, substantial net emigration has not occurred in the Soviet Union for obvious reasons. But two principal problems encountered by Soviet location economists have been the rural-urban balance of population and labor turnover, both of which are related to the process of migration. Concern with these problems has resulted from genuine difficulty in operating the economy, not mere academic interest.

An article by the Chairman of the Council for the Study of the Location of Productive Forces *(Soviet po Izucheniiu Rasmeshenii Proizvoditel'nykh Sil)* of GOSPLAN, the State Planning Commission, is illustrative.[4] Two subjects are

2. Ibid., pp. 130ff.
3. Ibid.
4. N. N. Nekrasov, "Man, Industry and Nature," *Soviet Union* (No. 1, 1971), pp. 5–7.

discussed in the article: the question of rational distribution of productive forces throughout the U.S.S.R. and the problem of the developed, central regions. According to the author, continued development of the resource-rich East is desirable. Attention is called to the maldistribution of the country's population and to the historical and contemporary requirement for the redistribution of population to the East. The principal requirement necessary for redistribution is attractive wage levels and living conditions. The problem of employee turnover and often concomitant gross migration rates higher than desired is skirted in the short article. A number of extensive labor turnover studies have appeared in recent years showing that high levels of gross migration, supposedly a phenomenon of the market economic system, are at present a problem for the Soviet economic system too.

Concerning the problems of the developed central regions of the Soviet Union, the author discusses energy use and conservation, and urban agglomeration beyond the optimum. Although Soviet dogma attributes the problem of oversized cities to the capitalist system, recent popular discussion in this article and scholarly discussion elsewhere indicate the Soviet system has experienced the same problems—at least in some individuals' views. The author leaves no doubt about his view; he details a list of problems of urban centers familiar to students of cities in Western industrialized nations.[5]

RECENT SOVIET EXPERIENCE

Recent Soviet experience, defined in this study as the period between the January 15, 1959, and the January 15, 1970, population censuses, is unique in Soviet history for several reasons. During this interval the Soviet Union considered as a whole escaped the influence of cataclysmic events such as famine, war, and collectivization; pursued a chartable population policy; allowed the operation of a relatively free labor market; and provided some information about population processes. The coincidence of these developments makes this study possible and the methods used at least superficially plausible.

The presence of war and civil strife has been the most important consideration in Soviet demographic history. It is only the generation born after World War II and now involved in family formation that has escaped the direct influence of these historical upheavals. The approach used here to explain migrants' behavior derives from microeconomic theory; the migrant is thought to weigh the present value of locations with a variety of factors contributing to the value of different prospects. To apply this approach to an experience dominated by war and civil strife is basically inappropriate since rational conduct may not be taken in such situations or since single factor considerations may dominate.

To some extent the acts and effects of population policy can be followed. Throughout the Soviet period, state policy with regard to fertility has been

5. Ibid., pp. 6–7.

poorly considered; two inconsistent tenets have been held simultaneously. The first tenet is each family has the right to choose as many children as it wants, and the second is advocation of a pronatalist policy. Current de facto contradiction arises from the contemporaneous existence of declared pronatalist policy providing family allowances, social medicine, and recognition of high-parity mothers and an undeclared antinatalist policy of keeping housing scarce and female labor participation high.

Migration policy is most quickly grasped in the general context of the post-Stalin liberalization and in specific consideration of changes in labor law that made a Union-wide labor market possible. The most important labor law change was the abolition in April 1956 of penal liability for quitting a job; thereafter, the only requirement for quitting became the provision of two weeks notice to employer. Only job changes that are unauthorized terminations or disciplinary firings are regarded as constituting labor turnover; appointments by enterprises or the government and transfers of a similar nature are not labor turnover. With the issuance of the 1956 decree, labor turnover became more an economic and less a legal problem. This development was a radical departure from the preceding Soviet practice. Nevertheless, many restrictions on the operation of the labor market remain. Important ones are wage rigidity due to central regulation and guidance; the placement of school graduates in directed, first assignments; and, the use of organizational pressure to influence workers to take certain jobs.

Recent Soviet experience is also distinguished in general by greater publication of data, including information about population. Michael Kaser describes the personal influence with regard to the availability of statistics of V.N. Starovskii, former Head, Central Statistical Administration (Tsentral'noe Statisticheskoe Upravlenie, TsSU) who was appointed to his position in 1940.[6] The essence of the story is that only grudgingly, but nevertheless significantly, have Starovskii and the TsSU followed the liberalizing changes in Soviet society that have developed since Stalin's death. Investigators now have annual regional total population estimates, some annual regional crude rates of natural increase, some gross migration statistics, and will soon have three population censuses. The situation is again different from the experience of earlier years.

INTERREGIONAL MIGRATION

Much of interest to students of migration during this period is excluded by limiting this study to interregional migration. The Soviet Union is a vast country; its expanse is divided for political purposes into fifteen Union republics and for purposes of rather limited economic administration into eighteen major economic regions.[7] Only migration between Union republics and be-

6. Michael Kaser, "The Publication of Soviet Statistics," in Vladimir G. Treml and John P. Hardt (eds.), *Soviet Economic Statistics* (Durham, N.C.: Duke University Press, 1972), pp. 45–47.

7. In this study boundaries as of January 15, 1970, are used, and Moldavia is considered a

tween major economic regions is being studied here; thus, what may be termed intraregional migration, including most short-distance moves and much of the rural-to-urban flow of recent years, is excluded. Also excluded is international migration involving the U.S.S.R.

Estimation

Distinguishing between gross and net streams in the study of interregional migration is important. Gross migration is measured by the total number of moves during a period of time while net is defined in terms of change of population as a result of the difference of numbers moving in and out of an area. One view of migration is that it is "an arrangement for making the maximum use of persons with special qualifications."[8] Looking at migration in this light, an economic planner would regard a migration act as a cost. If he were interested in redistributing population from point i to point j, he would desire a net in-migration rate from i to j that is high relative to the gross migration rate between i and j. The data generally available to students of recent Soviet migration allow only the use of methods that provide estimates of net migration. Less frequently, some data are provided that give gross migration totals; comparisons of these totals with estimates of net migration is of interest.

The identification of selectivity among migrants is an important aspect of migration study. Generally it has been found that migration is selective (that is, not random) with regard to age, sex, intelligence, ethnicity, and occupation. Determination of the selective aspects in recent Soviet experience are of interest, but data sufficient for this study are not generally available. A valuable document for study of this aspect of migration is a population register. The Soviet Union does have registers of population of rural soviets *(sel'sovety)* as well as municipal registration of arrivals and departures of persons. Neither of these systems, however, can help us on the question of selectivity of migrants for the reasons indicated later in connection with the sources of recent Soviet demographic data. Although some data presented in summary form in Soviet studies can be used to evaluate findings in this area, unfortunately, the overall data limitations will not allow any original work on this question.

Streams of migration are a traditional area of interest for migration studies. Population registers again are the best source of data for study of streams of migration between specific points. Data for only 1967 and 1969 were published.

Causes

Repeatedly in Soviet discussion of recent migration one encounters the judgment that its basic cause has been economic. It is most likely correct that

major economic region, contrary to Soviet practice. Information on these political and administrative divisions is given in Appendix A.

8. Donald J. Bogue, *Principles of Demography* (New York: John Wiley, 1969), p. 487.

workers did move on net account to areas where living conditions were more agreeable and working conditions were more attractive. According to this view, potential migrants continually evaluate the present value of their existing life circumstances and of other possible living situations and choose to remain or migrate depending upon which option proves most attractive. This seems a strong assumption from which to proceed, but it may not be as confining as it appears. The "economic" factors entering the calculation of present value may be broadly construed. "Psychic" income benefits can be monetized, at least conceptually, so that things like enjoyment of climate, acquaintances, and leisure enter the calculation. Locational inertia is not inconsistent with this hypothesis, since it can result merely from extraordinarily high personal valuation of present circumstances or lack of information about possibilities elsewhere.

Simple tests of the importance of economic opportunities in the explanation of migration are possible. The "push-pull" approach divides the factors that cause migration into "push" factors from origin and "pull" factors to destination. One may use a simple linear regression model to test the significance of such factors. Differences in wages, unemployment, and living conditions and distance usually have proven to be significant explanatory factors.[9]

Another way of viewing the decision to migrate is to concentrate on so-called stimulants to migration during an individual's life. Stimulants may be divided into two general classes: those associated with an individual's life cycle and those associated with major social and economic change. Both entry and exit from schooling, marriage, military service, labor force, and a social class have implications for migration. As long as the population under consideration is relatively stable (that is, has the property of unchanging percentage age distribution), it is probably safe to neglect consideration of life cycle in estimating and predicting the volume of migration. Data allow only the study of total number of migrants. If the Soviet population were stable or nearly stable, consideration of life cycle could be neglected, but since this was not so, it is necessary to consider life cycle stimulants.

The second class of stimulants, those associated with major social and economic change, include war, disaster, persecution, windfalls, economic collapse, and government policy. As indicated, recent Soviet experience has been relatively free of this class of stimulant. It is necessary, however, to be alert to government policy, both with respect to migration specifically and location of productive forces in general. Sometimes government policy has been explicit in intent and formulation while at other times it has not. In the case of the Soviet Union there exists contemporary and historical expression of location policy. It is necessary to determine the extent to which theory and dogma, on the one hand, and scientific thought, on the other, were given attention in the actual political formulation of policy.

9. See Ira S. Lowry, *Migration and Metropolitan Growth: Two Analytical Models* (San Francisco: Chandler, 1966) and other works to which references are made in chapter 5.

Effects

Knowledge of the economic, demographic, social, and psychological effects of migration is incomplete; although perhaps more is known about the economic and demographic effects of migration. In this study the economic effects will receive primary attention. The clearest demographic effect of migration is that it changes the composition of populations at points of departure and arrival of migrants. If streams of migrants in and out of a locality are not balanced, the size of the local population changes. The degree to which composition, as distinguished from size, changes depends upon how selective the migration streams are. Since migration is usually age-selective in the sense that young members of the labor force migrate most frequently, a persistent flow sometimes causes a losing population to grow older and a gaining population to become younger. Most of the economic effects of migration derive from the demographic effect of changing population compositions. Changes in population composition usually alter the ratio of able-bodied persons of working age to persons unable to work. Changes also require quantitative and qualitative adjustments in the capital stock of an economy receiving or losing substantial numbers of migrants.

One important economic effect occurring somewhat independently of the mechanism of composition is the neoclassical economic effect in labor markets. A long-standing notion is migration in response to geographical differences in wages eliminates the differences. But this need not always follow. One of the interests of this study is to outline the likely consequences of migration for the Soviet labor market.

DEMOGRAPHIC DATA[10]

Sources

Population censuses were taken at the beginning and ending points of this study. The first census, taken on January 15, 1959, was published in 1962 with a volume for each Union republic and a summary U.S.S.R. volume. For large political units (oblasts, krais, and republics),[11] age and sex distribution data, total population counts (for individual cities and for urban and rural areas), figures detailing rural-urban patterns of settlement, and data on education, ethnic composition and family composition are available. Unfortunately, there were no life tables for large political units of even Union republics published following the census. The absence of regional mortality data prevents the age-specific projection of the 1959 population for comparison with the population enumerated in 1970 to indicate the extent of age-specific net migration.

10. Many of the ideas of this section were first expressed by the author in a paper "Economic Aspects of Interregional Migration in the U.S.S.R., 1959–70" presented to the 1972 meeting of the American Association for the Advancement of Slavic Studies. The material as it appears here has benefited from the criticism of those who heard the paper.

11. A brief description of political geography may be found in Appendix A.

The 1970 census was taken on January 15 exactly eleven years later.[12] In general much of the same kind of information provided by the 1959 census is contained in the 1970 reports. In addition, however, a 25 percent sample of the population answered questions about length of continuous location, previous residence (for persons with less than two years continuous residence), and reason for change of residence (for the same persons). Tabulations of these migration data, which appear in a separate volume, are quite interesting, but their value for the present study is diminished by their focus on movement during just 1968 and 1969 and by some questions about their reliability. Extensive information concerning population numbers, age distributions, and ethnic compositions for Union republics, major economic regions, and large political units are used in conjunction with census-survival techniques to estimate net migration into various areas.

In addition to the two censuses, other information is available. Data that would be valuable and their availability on a regional basis are shown in Table 1.1.[13] Multiple sources for the same data are listed in order of currency, completeness and convenience for use. To complete some series of data, it was necessary to use sources not indicated. For example, for the year 1967, volumes commemorating 50 years of Soviet power were issued instead of the annual *National Economy Yearbook (Narkhoz)*; this created a gap in some of the series requiring the use of other sources. Other series indicated as complete are only nearly so. For example, population estimates for some large political units on January 1, 1960, had to be interpolated.

The 1970 census volume VII contains information on place-to-place movement within the U.S.S.R. during 1968–69. The *Narkhoz* series typically provides about 30 pages of total population data with rural-urban classification (down to large political units and cities), crude rates of natural increase (down to Union republics or major economic regions), and all-Union marriage and divorce rates. *Naselenie 1973* contains long time-series on arrivals at and departures from urban areas deriving from the population registration system. *Vestnik statistiki* typically publishes two or three series a year usually dealing with characteristics of female population, the number of total population, and the crude rates of natural increase for the U.S.S.R. and Union republics, along with age-specific, all-Union measures of fertility and mortality.

Accuracy and Collection

The accuracy of the last two Soviet censuses is difficult to assess. Persons interested in the demography of countries like the U.S. and England are familiar with the usual discussions occurring during a census about how many people

12. TsSU, *Itogi vsesoiuznoi perepisi naseleniia 1970 goda*, 7 vols. (Moscow: Statistika, 1972–73.)

13. In most instances statistical data in the tables have been reworked by the author. Where data have been taken directly from Soviet sources a notation to this effect is included in the table.

have been missed in the enumeration; it is well known that the calculated margins of error have been large. Soviet officials and demographers have not publicly discussed such matters; foreign observers must speculate as to how Soviet demographers adjust for incomplete enumeration. However, the motivation for Soviet censuses and the methods used for the 1970 enumeration are known.

State planners feel that accurate information about population composition and characteristics can be obtained only through censuses of population which need to be taken frequently.[14] The Central Statistical Administration, wanting an accurate count, started making preparations for the most recent census four years in advance. The Soviet Union had planned to take the census in 1969 but in April 1967 without explanation postponed the count until January 15, 1970. Official pronouncements notwithstanding, it appears incomplete plans and lack of data processing equipment were important reasons for delaying the census. The procedures used in enumerating the population also demonstrate a desire to obtain an accurate census. Average workload for enumerators was planned to be 675 persons in urban areas and 575 in rural areas. Enumerators were to visit all households twice. The first visit was primarily for the arrangement of a time for the enumeration and presumably to survey the designated tract; the second was for the actual enumeration. Finally, it was planned that half the households would be visited a third time to check the accuracy of the count.[15]

The reliability of answers to questions 16 through 18 of the 1970 census concerning migration during 1968 and 1969 are a topic of special interest. The history of censuses, and more generally survey research, is replete with instances of the collection of inaccurate information when respondents have been asked to recall past actions or have been questioned concerning acts or circumstances which the state seeks to control or tax. It is the author's judgment that these influences in certain instances undermine the reliability of the recent results on the migration; this view is developed at some length in Appendix C.

Soviet intercensal population estimates and registration of births, deaths, and migration probably are inaccurate in many instances. A hypothetical example of how the population estimates are reached is shown in Table 1.2. It is merely a components of change scheme that distinguishes between rural and urban populations. To obtain accurate population estimates in a components of change scheme, complete and correct registration of births, deaths, and migration is necessary; accordingly, it is desirable to learn how the registration systems operate.

Births and deaths in cities and *raiony* (county-like units described in Appendix A) are registered by the Civil Records Office (Zapis' Aktov Grazhdanskogo Sostoianiia, ZAGS); in agricultural localities and settlements of

14. For example, see Murray Feshbach, "Observations on the Soviet Census," *Problems of Communism*, XIX, No. 3 (May–June 1970), pp. 58–64, and TsSU, *Posobie po statistike dlia raionnykh i gorodoskikh inspekturov* (Moscow: Statistika, 1970), p. 360.

15. Feshbach, "Soviet Census," pp. 59–60.

urban type they are recorded by the soviets *(sovety)*.[16] Working deputies of the rural soviets have the responsibility of collecting all the statistics concerning the soviets; the ZAGS bureaus have a more narrowly defined function. If specialization engenders competence, it is likely that the ZAGS bureaus accomplish more complete registration than the rural soviets. In addition, it is probably true that the interest of administrators in the statistical reporting system, as perceived by the rural soviets, lies more with various economic and agricultural reports than the registration of events of population change.[17]

Soviet law requires the registration of births not later than a month after occurrence and of death not later than the third day. The month-long period for birth registration extends longer than seems necessary and may conceivably lead to a failure to register births and deaths occurring during the first month of life. A handbook for statistics inspectors hints at this possibility when it mentions the need for special attention to instances having the greatest probability of not being registered, still-births and deaths occuring soon after birth.[18] A Soviet demographer recently suggested that many instances of unregistered births could be eliminated by filling out ZAGS birth records at the hospital or maternity home before the mothers leave.[19] Factors that contribute to relatively complete registration of births are the small payment and related bonus and stipend systems for higher parity births. They probably act most strongly in poor and rural areas where the change of nonregistration may be greatest. But significant numbers of births probably go unregistered. The U.S. Foreign Demographic Analysis Division estimates that births throughout the U.S.S.R. were underregistered by 3.1 percent during the early 1960s and by 1.6 in later years of the decade.[20]

Observers have noted death rates at old age are extraordinarily low and have suggested a possible cause may be incomplete registration.[21] Soviet specialists

16. TsSU, *Posobie po statistike*, p. 349.

17. James W. Brackett, "Demographic Trends and Population Policy in the Soviet Union," in U.S., Congress, Joint Economic Committee, *Dimensions of Soviet Economic Power* (Washington, D.C.: U.S. Government Printing Office, 1962), p. 500.

18. TsSU, *Posobie po statistike*, p. 350.

19. A. Matveeva, "Nekotorye voprosy analiza dannykh perepisi naseleniia 1970g.", *Vestnik statistiki* (No. 9, 1973), p. 17.

20. U.S., Department of Commerce, Foreign Demographic Analysis Division. *Estimates and Projections of the Population of the U.S.S.R., by Age and Sex: 1950 to 2000*, International Population Reports, Series P–91, No. 23 (Washington, D.C.: U.S. Government Printing Office, 1973), p. 6.

21. D. Peter Mazur, a leading Western student of Soviet demography, has recently investigated mortality differentials among ethnic groups in "Expectancy of Life at Birth in 36 Nationalities of the Soviet Union: 1958–60," *Population Studies*, XIII, No. 2 (July 1969), 225–46. In a rejoinder to a comment, Mazur makes clear that reported death rates must be regarded as unreliable. In general, Mazur's work is important to anyone studying recent Soviet fertility and mortality. Other references are: "Birth Control and Regional Differentials in the Soviet Union," *Population Studies*, XXII, No. 3 (November 1968), 319–33; "Fertility Among Ethnic Groups in the U.S.S.R.," *Demography*, IV, No. 1 (December 1967), 172–95; "Reconstruction of Fertility Trends for the Female Population of the U.S.S.R." *Population Studies*, XXI, No. 1 (July 1967), 33–52. See also very important work by James W. Brackett: "Demographic Trends," pp. 487–589. U.S.,

have responded by asserting that differential mortality by cause-of-death has produced the extraordinary death patterns, but this hypothesis is untestable with the mortality statistics available. The comparison in Table 1.3 of recent Soviet age-specific death rates with those of Sweden and the U.S. illustrates the low Soviet rates at old ages.

The rates in Table 1.3 marked by the letter "a" were calculated by the author. On page 38 of the *Narkhoz* cited, rates are given for five-year intervals beginning from 0 to 4 and ending with 65 to 69; on page 39 corresponding l_x figures continuing beyond ${}_5l_{65}$ (that is, persons aged 65 to 69) are listed. The last death rate on page 38 is for the open category of persons older than 69 years, but the corresponding life table runs (at five-year intervals) up to 100 years and can be used to derive death rates for the five-year intervals if an assumption is made about the distribution of deaths. Assuming an even distribution of deaths understates the rate. However, assuming a constant force of mortality may overstate the rate. Rates reported in the *Narkhoz,* rates resulting from assuming an even distribution of deaths, and rates resulting from assuming a constant force of mortality are shown respectively in the following columns A, B, and C.

Age Interval	A	B	C
60–64	17.4	17.4	17.4
65–69	25.9	25.8	25.8
70–74		40.3	40.5
75–79		61.5	62.0
80–84	66.1 (70 and over)	89.2	90.7
85–89		129.4	134.2
90–94		157.8	166.8
95 +		206.1	227.9

Series C, the high series, was used for the U.S.S.R. in Table 1.3. If these rates are approximately correct, they demonstrate the extraordinarily low mortality experience in the U.S.S.R. One can only speculate as to why death rates for old ages are not presented in Soviet demographic series; perhaps the Central Statistical Administration seeks to avoid the issue of their accuracy.

How migrants are registered would be of great interest if the data were made generally available. Since 1967 the Central Statistical Administration has increased the tabulation of the returns from registration. For example, records of arrivals and departures at urban points during 1968 have been tabulated by cause of movement, occupational class, age, sex, and nationality of mover; however, the tabulations have not been made public. For 1967, 1969, and 1970 special studies of migration streams *(migratsionye potoka)* for urban and

---

Bureau of the Census. *Projections of the Population of the U.S.S.R., by Age and Sex: 1964–1985*, Interational Population Reports, Series P–91, No. 13 (Washington, D.C.: U.S. Government Printing Office, 1964).

urban-type settlements were undertaken and summary results were published in *Vestnik statistiki*.[22] They represent the only publication of migration registration data for the 1959–70 period of which the author is aware.

Workers at offices of housing management in urban areas and in settlements of urban type, and the working deputies in rural *sovety* register acts of migration. Movements for permanent change of residence, for seasonal or nonseasonal change of job, for study (excepting short courses that are less than 30 days in rural areas or 45 in urban areas, and for field trips (that is, business or organizational trips lasting the same number of days) are registered as migration while vacation trips, admissions to (and discharges from) medical and social institutions, and movements within the same population point are not.[23] Acts of migration are registered in a book of address forms having detachable portions which serve as the source documents for statistics about migration. They are turned into the local ministry of internal affairs of the region or city and a government inspector collects them. The inspector verifies that the slips should have been filled out and were completely correctly. He conducts spot checks of the registration process and instructs persons doing registration in correct procedures.[24]

A major defect in the system of registration is incomplete registration in rural areas. According to V. V. Pokshishevskii, a leading U.S.S.R. population geographer, "Direct registration of population movmement . . . has not yet been perfected (especially in rural areas)."[25] The tabulations of these data for 1967, 1969, and 1970 presented in *Vestnik statistiki* give information collected exclusively from the slips filled out in cities and settlements of urban type, presumably because the information from rural areas was incomplete. In 1965 two Soviet specialists found systematic nonregistration of migration and late reporting in areas where personal passports were not required (that is, much of the rural area).[26]

It is the author's judgment that out-migration is systematically underregistered relative to in-migration. The registration of in-migration is usually connected with obtaining housing and beginning work, activities of immediate interest to many migrants. Thus, not only legal requirements, but also self-interest motivate the settler to register. In addition, the simple influence of continued presence in an area of in-migration (as opposed to subsequent absence from an area of out-migration) and human curiosity concerning new inhabitants act to insure more complete registration of in-migration. In 1967 P. G.

22. *Vestnik statistiki* (No. 10, 1968), pp. 89–95; *Vestnik statistiki* (No. 3, 1971), pp. 74–83; and *Vestnik statistiki* (No. 11, 1971), pp. 77–87.

23. *CDSP*, XVII, No. 35 (November 22, 1965), 3. *CDSP* denotes *Current Digest of Soviet Press*.

24. TsSU, *Posobie*, p. 357.

25. V. V. Pokshishevskii, "Migration of Population, U.S.S.R.," in U.S., Joint Publications Research Service, *Translations on U.S.S.R. Resources*, JPRS 49279 (November 19, 1969), p. 55.

26. *CDSP*, p. 3.

Pod'iachikh, then Deputy Director of the Central Statistical Administration, verified that in certain situations the registration of out-migration of population is quite deficient. Pod'iachikh stated that although the registration at both destination and origin of migrants moving between cities was quite accurate in 1966, the same could not be said of registration of out-migration from urban settlements to rural settlements and from rural settlements to urban settlements. In 1966, registered arrivals at urban settlements from rural settlements exceeded the measurement of the same flow made at the point of departure by 152,000 and, similarly, the registered arrivals in rural settlements from urban settlements exceeded the measurement of that same flow made at point of departure.[27]

The Importance of Migration in Population Estimates

For annual population estimates for regions in the Soviet Union to be accurate, it is necessary that the registration of migrants be accurate, since migration was often the largest component of population change. To see the relative size of the migration components of population change, one may check various 1967 rates as shown in Table 1.4. The accurate registration of migration is most important for precise annual estimates of population in regions where gross migration rates (arrivals and departures per 1000 inhabitants) are highest. But even in regions like Transcaucasia where migration rates were very low, they still exceeded rates of birth and death. Thus, when studying migration, the accuracy of annual estimates of population is crucial as large errors in estimates may indicate, by themselves, that migration was an important component of population change.

One check of the accuracy of annual estimates of population is to compare the regional population estimates reached independently of a census with the numbers actually enumerated in the census. Specifically, if the 1970 census gave accurate data in comparison with registration systems, the deviations of enumerated from expected regional populations indicate the direction and magnitude of errors in registration systems. Of course, the comparison of count estimates may not reveal some errors and may misstate the magnitude of other errors due to the possibilities for offsetting and amplifying combinations of error. Prior to the 1970 census the Central Statistical Administration last estimated regional populations for January 1, 1969. To obtain estimates for January 15, 1970, consistent with those of the preceding years, the author assumed the 1970 estimates might be approximated by:

$$P^r_{1\text{-}15\text{-}70} = P^r_{1\text{-}1\text{-}69} \times e^{\left[\frac{380}{365} \times (\ln P^r_{1\text{-}1\text{-}69} - \ln P^r_{1\text{-}1\text{-}68})\right]}$$

Thus, the rate of population growth during 1968 was applied over the interval beginning on January 1, 1969 and ending on the date of the census; on these

27. D. I. Valentei et al. (eds.), *Problemy migratsii naseleniia i trudovykh resursov* (Moscow: Statistika, 1970), pp. 123–24.

bases, the percentages by which the 1970 census enumerations exceeded the 1970 estimates for the various regions were calculated and are presented in Table 1.5.

It is interesting to speculate on the reasons for these divergences. The effects of the various kinds of error that could have occurred in the registration systems are shown in Table 1.6. The possibilities resulting from overregistration of births and deaths may be neglected, since in the absence of widespread prospect for extraordinary gain from fraudulent registration of events (births and deaths), there is no reason to believe overregistration occurred. The argument concerning the relative preponderance of migration among the components of population suggests that migration ought to be the first component checked in examining deviations. Thus, the large positive divergences listed for the Central Region (containing Moscow) and the Northwest Region (containing Leningrad) could very likely have resulted from clandestine, unregistered in-migration, since restrictions on settlement in the largest cities may have meant for some that they could settle there only if they circumvented restrictions designed to exclude them.

The "new" or eastern regions of economic development (the two Siberian economic regions, the Far East, and Kazakhstan) and the Urals, known in recent years to be areas of substantial out-migration, fit (with the notable exception of East Siberia) a general pattern of the census numbers falling substantially short of the numbers expected on the basis of the preceding annual estimates. Again considering the preponderance of the migration component and the possible motivations of migrants, its seems failure to register out-migration might have been a very important factor in the total situation in these regions.

Since the migration component of population change was relatively small in the Transcaucasian and Central Asian regions, concentrating exclusively on it as the source of error in estimates of population is probably a mistake. The rates of death in these regions have long been the object of frequent comment, either noting their extraordinarily low level[28] or openly questioning their reliability.[29] In Table 1.5, the Transcaucasian and Central Asian regions have negative deviations (again with an egregious exception, in this case, Armenia); underregistration of deaths or out-migration or both could have produced such a result. Failure to register one death per thousand per year over an eleven-year period would have led to a census count approximately 1 percent too low.

Regardless of the causes of error, it is clear that no one was satisfied with the accuracy of the systems; Pod'iachikh's remarks show this, as do the revised postcensus annual estimates of republican populations during the 1960s.[30] The percentage revisions for each republic having at least one annual revision that

28. For example, see D. Peter Mazur, "Expectancy of Life at Birth in 36 Nationalities of the Soviet Union: 1958–60," pp. 231–32.

29. For example, see Brackett, "Demographic Trends," p. 500.

30. *Vestnik statistiki* (No. 2, 1971), pp. 85–86.

exceeds by 1 percent in absolute value the originally reported population are shown in Table 1.7. The revisions in the population figures for Uzbekistan and Tadzhikistan are noteworthy since they reduce the variation in the high annual rates of growth previously reported. The appearance of Latvia and Estonia, showing sizable upward revisions, may be the result of unregistered migration into these regions while unregistered out-migration is verly likely to be of significance in the downward revision of annual estimates for Kazakhstan.

From this review several conclusions emerge concerning the demographic data used in this study. First, the reported crude rates of death are low, and age-specific mortality at old ages fall well below rates observed in other developed countries. It seems likely that substantial numbers of deaths go unregistered. This would appear to be the case particularly in rural areas. Until it is possible to learn why age-specific death rates at old ages are so low, it seems reasonable to be somewhat skeptical of the accuracy of the data. Belorussia and Moldavia in the West, Uzbekistan, Kirghizia, and Tadzhikistan in Soviet Central Asia, and Kazakhstan and Georgia are Union Republics having rather high percentages of rural population and thus may be areas in which deaths are being underregistered.

Second, reported levels of birth in the U.S.S.R. appear to fall short of actual levels by 1 to 3 percent. Conceivably, the underregistration of both births and deaths could yield accurate data on natural increase (births less deaths), but it is more likely that in areas where births are much more numerous than deaths, that is, where rapid population growth is occurring, the calculated levels of natural increase may be too high. This circumstance would impart any upward bias to residual estimates of net migration since too little of the observed population change would be attributed to natural increase. The Transcaucasian and Central Asia regions are ones in which this difficulty may be encountered.

Third, registration of migration is, in part, unreliable. It is incomplete in rural areas, and in all areas the registration systems appear to do a better job recording in-migration than out-migration. Since migration is such an important component in population change, annual estimates of population depend to a large extent upon the accuracy of migration registration. High levels of migration and inaccurate registration will combine to produce unreliable annual estimates of population. In this regard figures reported during the 1960s for some regions and republics are suspect.

2

STATE POLICIES

This chapter examines the general problem of planning the location of economic activity, the major factors determining location policy, specific measures used to allocate labor, and other policies affecting interregional migration in the U.S.S.R. during the 1959–70 period. Recent state labor policies differ sharply from those of earlier periods. During the collectivization drives of the early 1930s many rural inhabitants were exiled. From 1940 on into the early 1950s the imposition of military discipline (used here to denote the powers to transfer labor, to call up persons not participating in social economy, to deny the freedom of quitting a job, and to use criminal punishment for infractions of discipline) was the basic tool for controlling industrial labor. It appears that a de facto labor market operated in the 1959–70 period; actions taken to allocate labor interfered with the operation of a completely free market.

THE MARKET FOR LABOR

Distinguishing between formal principles and actuality is always important in Soviet economic planning, particularly in the area of wage determination. State policy during this period intended that enterprises pay all industrial workers for their work according to its quantity and quality in accordance with existing governmental norms.[1] Formal principles suggest that the worker producing normal output (according to norms of quantity and quality) under normal conditions received pay according to his base rate *(stavka)* for his narrowly defined occupation and according to the schedule *(setka)* of occupational skill levels. However, incentive systems applying the "socialist" principle of "from each according to his ability, to each according to his labor" have been the rule ever since Stalin's 1931 dictum against "petty bourgeois egalitarianism," and they, in general, have modified labor remuneration substantially. Although a variety of schemes have existed, generally the system of piecework adjusted wage payments upward (proportionately or progressively) for production in excess of norms. The piecework calculations were made according to individual or collective performance in relation to the norms. In addition, various

1. N. G. Aleksandrov et al. (eds.), *Trudovoe pravo* (Moscow: Sovetskaia Entsiklopediia, 1969), p. 138.

ad hoc targets of production continued to be an important part of the "to each according to his work" system of compensation. More recently, the gradual introduction of the 1965 reform has led to payments from the profit-financed fund for material stimulation of workers on the basis of enterprise performance.

With some exceptions that are unimportant for the study of migration in the 1959–70 period, wage scales were set centrally, not at the enterprise level. Nevertheless, the rules or the spirit of the rules were violated by various means, most frequently by abuse of the piecework system and artificial upgrading of workers. By "abuse of the piecework system" the author means the setting of norms at levels that depart significantly from actual average production; such abuses typically led to average wage payments larger than those specified by the tables of wage rates for the average worker in a particular job category and at a particular skill level. "Artificial upgrading of workers" means nothing more than the classification of workers at skill levels higher than they actually have, thereby qualifying them for higher rates of pay leading to larger wage payments. These actions are the necessary consequences of the simultaneous existence in the U.S.S.R. of a labor market and central wage-setting.

Migration may be viewed as a possible consequence of a decision to change employment. While inappropriate in times of war or other calamity, this assumption, which the author uses here, has proven valuable in a variety of institutional settings under normal conditions. Thus, choice of employment becomes the central problem. To pass the test of empirical explanatory power any theory of choice in labor markets must follow Adam Smith's dictum of concentrating on "the whole of the advantages and disadvantages of the different employments of labor."[2]

The extent to which Soviet commentators on labor problems recognize the existence of a market for labor and the freedom of job choice is somewhat surprising to persons accustomed to distinguishing between Western economic systems and the Soviet economic system on the basis of methods used for allocating resources. One may presume that the mechanism of administrative direction dominated in the allocation of labor in the 1959–70 period simply because it was very important for labor direction during Stalin's rule and remains important today for allocating other goods and services. But such a presumption would be incorrect. Several quasi-official pronouncements may be cited to show the existence of a labor market.

In *Trudovoe pravo (Labor Law)*, a handbook for administrators, enterprise officials, and students of labor law, migration is defined as

> the process of territorial movement of cadres [by which] in the U.S.S.R. workers are able with comparative ease to find suitable work in any region.

2. Adam Smith, *An Inquiry into the Nature and Causes of the Wealth of Nations* (New York: Random House, 1937), p. 99, as identified by Simon Rottenberg, "On Choice in Labour Markets," in B. J. McCormick and E. Owen Smith (eds.), *The Labour Market* (Baltimore: Penguin, 1968), p. 50.

> The primary influence in determining streams of migration is, not regional requirements for labor, but rather the worker's unrestricted self-interest.[3]

The entry on migration next notes that study has revealed the failure of actual migration streams to correspond with those desired by planners to such an extent that it must be regarded as a first-order national economic problem.[4] Of course, in prominent sources it is still the case that in general: "In contrast to the spontaneous *(stikhiinye)* migration associated with the presence of mass unemployment found in capitalism, socialist society provides governmental-organized recruiting *(nabor)* of labor."[5] It seems unrealistic to expect much candor from conspicuous sources concerning the operation of the market in the U.S.S.R. Nevertheless, even the source just cited hints at the existence of a Union-wide market for labor by saying that in its labor-channeling the state must solve a whole complex of difficult problems, most importantly the inter-regional regulation of wages and the creation of better living conditions for resettlers.[6] It seems reasonable to infer from the importance of these problems that there is considerable freedom for workers to move and choose location on the bases of wage levels and living conditions.

There are even studies of the labor market efficiency in the Soviet Union, although investigators and correspondents would never label them as such. In a 1965 report, *Izvestiia* correspondents discussed how the man seeking a job and the enterprise seeking a worker get together, and they explicitly excluded from consideration the placement of recent graduates and the organized recruitment of workers for remote regions of the country. Their story is that typically the job seeker goes out into the street to survey numerous, standard "help-wanted" or "needed" announcements posted on bulletin boards and elsewhere, queries friends to learn of opportunites, and listens to the municipal radio station to hear its announcements of job openings until work is found. More specifically, a study quoted by the correspondents showed that in the city of Gor'ky the length of transitional unemployment for newly hired workers had been distributed as follows:

0 days	9 percent
1 to 3 days	15 percent
4 to 10 days	33 percent
11 to 15 days	15 percent
16 to 30 days	16 percent
over 30 days	12 percent

The correspondents also talk about the social costs of this kind of unemployment and develop the argument for more coordinated job-placement services.[7]

3. Aleksandrov, *Trudovoe pravo*, p. 248.
4. Ibid., p. 249.
5. B. Smulevich, "O sovremennom Mal'tuzianstve," *Vestnik statistiki* (No. 6, 1971), p. 39.
6. Ibid.
7. *CDSP*, XVII, No. 52 (January 19, 1966), 8.

These circumstances are not new. Their development began following World War II, and continued after Stalin's death and the important change in labor law in 1956. At the Twenty-Second Party Congress (in 1961) Khrushchev asserted that there was needed a whole system of carefully worked out measures "for the planned redistribution of manpower on a purely voluntary basis and with strict observance of the principle of material incentive. Suitable living conditions and cultural facilities [had to] be provided to encourage people to move to jobs in other regions."[8]

Additional evidence of a Union-wide labor market and of freedom to choose any single employment among several opportunities is provided by the now substantial, Soviet literature on the problem of labor turnover. Job changes that result from voluntary quitting or from firing by the enterprise make up turnover *(tekuchest')*. In the early 1960s these studies focused on the regional aspect of the problem; rates of labor turnover were found to be very high in eastern and northern regions. For example, in Siberia, it was found that the numbers departing from Siberian cities for other regions divided by the numbers arriving were sometimes quite high. This may be seen in Table 2.1.

Since the early 1960s much interest has been shown in surveys of stated causes of labor turnover. The Institute of Labor conducted the first such study of labor turnover in 1958–59, but the first detailed survey noted in the West was the city-wide survey taken in Leningrad during the first ten days of April 1963.[9] Other surveys, now well known, were taken at Krasnoyarsk and throughout the U.S.S.R. by the Institute of Labor. The percentages of workers leaving work for various reasons according to these surveys are shown in Table 2.2. More recently, labor turnover studies concerned with motivation have become more sophisticated, and researchers now discuss at some length the problems that survey research poses and particular steps to cope with them. Thus, in a recent survey of labor turnover in Novosibirsk, when the distribution of motivational responses showed "change of place of inhabitance" to be the most frequent response, the investigators candidly admitted that little could be concluded from this response. Many people had chosen it to avoid listing actual motives as evidenced by its predominance among workers leaving enterprises in comparison to workers arriving at enterprises. In this study the most frequent responses as to principal cause for quitting were the following:[10]

Change of place of inhabitance	26.9 percent
Dissatisfaction with wage pay	12.7 percent
Lack or absence of living quarters	10.0 percent
Dissatisfaction with occupation	8.9 percent

8. *CDSP*, XIV, No. 26 (July 25, 1962), 6.

9. Murray Feshbach, "Manpower in the U.S.S.R.: A Survey of Recent Trends and Prospects," in U.S., Congress, Joint Economic Committee, *New Directions in the Soviet Economy* (Washington, D.C.: U.S. Government Printing Office, 1966), p. 727.

10. E. G. Antosenkov (ed.), *Opyt issledovaniia peremeny truda v promyshlennosti* (Novosibirsk: Nauka, 1969), pp. 66–67.

Dissatisfaction with or absence of child care facilities	6.7 percent
Remoteness of work from home	6.2 percent
Health reasons	5.7 percent

As interesting as the motives for quitting, is the extent of turnover. In general, however, there are no overall figures available. It has been estimated that in most regions and industries, rates of labor turnover ranged from 3 to 4 percent during 1961.[11] The Institute of Labor reported in 1963 that monthly turnover was low, but that at some enterprises it ranged from 1.5 to 2.0 percent of labor force.[12] In 1962, 30 percent of all separations were classified as turnover in the Ukranian Ministry of Trade, and in Moscow 67 percent of all separations were so classified in 1963.[13] The same percentage figures are available for the industrial sector of Union republics in 1965 when the all-Union figure was 62 percent with little variation among the republics, except for rates in the 70s for the Kazakh, Tadzhik, Turkmen, and Uzbek republics.[14]

PLANNING THE LOCATION OF ECONOMIC ACTIVITY

Recent advances in the economic theory of location, the reemergence of economic analysis in the Soviet Union, and progress in the field of computers combine to create some possibility for the solution of the problems of optimal macroeconomic planning, including its spatial aspects. The difficulties of optimal planning within and without the Soviet context have been the object of much attention concerning problems of pricing, information, motivation, and computation.

More important in this study than existing technical problems in planning is the problem of choosing the objective of the plan. There arises the possibility that the problem of locating industrial production is not conceived in terms of maximizing anything, since party officials and state planners with some frequency make statements like "[Efficiency is only obtained when] the industrial output for the entire country is maximized, industry developed equally in all republics and regions, and the country's defense is strengthened."[15] Certainly, maximization of industrial output, equalization of industrialization in all regions, and the maximization of military strength must be competing goals,

11. R. Fakiolas, "Problems of Labor Mobility in the U.S.S.R.," *Soviet Studies*, XIV, No. 1 (July 1962), 18–21, as identified in Emily C. Brown, *Soviet Trade Unions and Labor Relations* (Cambridge, Mass.: Harvard University Press, 1966), p. 34.
12. Brown, *Soviet Trade Unions*, p. 35.
13. Feshbach, "Manpower in the U.S.S.R.," p. 727.
14. Murray Feshbach and Stephen Rapawy, "Labor and Wages," in U.S., Congress, Joint Economic Committee, *Economic Performance and the Military Burden in the Soviet Union* (Washington, D.C.: U.S. Government Printing Office, 1970), p. 81.
15. Attributed to Soviet economists in I[wan] S. Koropeckyj, "Industrial Location Policy in the U.S.S.R. during the Postwar Period," in U.S., Congress, Joint Economic Committee, *Economic Performance and the Military Burden in the Soviet Union* (Washington, D.C.: U.S. Government Printing Office, 1970), p. 244.

since there must be trade-offs associated with changes in the level of each. If all three goals are to be pursued, planning only becomes possible when the relative importance of each goal is specified, or the absolute importance of one, with minimally acceptable levels of attainment for the others, is declared.

It is also possible that political considerations of the Communist Party leadership dominate administration of the economy. It may be that the "ultimate goal for the leaders must be to retain power in their hands, and if possible, to expand it"[16] and that "all aspects of national life are subordinated to this objective."[17] When a particular location decision coincides with political considerations in the above sense and at the same time is economically efficient, there arises no problem; but when the economic and political objectives are in conflict, it may be that politics takes precedence over economics. The center and subordinate territorial divisions often have divergent interests so that changes of voluntarism (*voliuntarizm,* the adoption of policy not in the interests of social welfare as defined by the center) and localism (*mestnichestvo,* the adoption of policy strictly on the basis of prospective local benefit) have been expressed frequently during recent years in the journals and papers of central administrative organs.

Thus, not only concerning the technical problems of planning, but also with regard to specifying what is to be maximized, has there been little prospect for achieving optimality. It must therefore be realized that recent location thought by Soviet economists is somewhat irrelevant. More important for the present study is the examination (in subsequent sections of this chapter) of actual state policies derived from considerations of political leaders of the Soviet Union. Nevertheless, it is of value to survey briefly the origins and development of Soviet thought on location and examine recent ideas on the subject.

Origins and Development of Soviet Thought[18]

The works of pre-Soviet Marxians are distinguished by the absence of prescriptions and designs concerning how to run socialist economies. In the writings of Marx and Engels one finds little that is directly relevant to the problem of industrial location in the socialist economy, the one possible exception being the ideal of proportional distribution of industry to eliminate the contradiction between rural and urban areas found in capitalism. Thus, the *Communist Manifesto* proposes: "Combination of agriculture with manufacturing

16. I[wan] S. Koropeckyj, "Industrial Location Policy in the U.S.S.R. during the Postwar Period," in U.S., Congress, Joint Economic Committee, *Economic Performance and the Military Burden in the Soviet Union* (Washington, D.C.: U.S. Government Printing Office, 1970), p. 283.

17. Ibid., pp. 283–84.

18. The remarks that follow draw heavily on the valuable surveys: Holland Hunter, "Soviet Locational Objectives and Problems," in *Soviet Transportation Policy* (Cambridge, Mass.: Harvard University Press, 1957), pp. 21–38; and Iwan S. Koropeckyj, "The Development of Soviet Location Theory before the Second World War: I and II," *Soviet Studies,* XIX (July and October 1967), 1–28, 232–44.

industries, gradual abolition of the distinction between country and town, by a more equitable distribution of population over the country."[19] Lenin and the Bolsheviks upon ascent to power received little help from Marxist thought, and the regime had only its own devices to deal with the location problem. In the early years of the consolidation of political power it does not seem as if industrial location could have been considered important, yet as soon as April 1918 in "Draft Plan of Scientific and Technical Work" Lenin (of course, long a student of the distribution of productive forces in capitalistic Russia) directed attention to the problem. He identified the desiderata of industrial concentration, industrial location near raw materials, and the economical (with regard to transport costs) development and use of energy sources (implying the development of electricity and fuels of light weight). Thus is seen, even this early, a somewhat characteristic contradiction between contending objectives (in this case, the equal distribution of industry of the *Manifesto* and the economies sought by Lenin). The planning policies of the first years of the Soviet state drew heavily from the experience of the German wartime logistical direction and control of its industry.[20] With regard to the location of industry the state drew from German experience in a somewhat different sense. The work of Alfred Weber,[21] the German location theorist, influenced Soviet location decisions and thought greatly in the 1920s and, despite its repudiation at the end of that decade, is still the basis for much of today's approach.

The principle of weight-losing of commodities assumes a central position in Weber's approach. It states that productive processes which have high ratios of weight of commodity input to weight of final commodity output should be located near the sources of inputs, while processes which have low ratios of weight of commodity input to weight of final commodity output should be located near points of the consumption of the finished good. The validity of the principle is established by the strong assumptions Weber made concerning uniform environment, fixed sites of consumption and raw materials, geographically immobile yet infinitely elastic supply of local labor, and the nature of transportation costs.

Whether the approach is valuable depends upon the extent to which the assumptions are realistic. While it may be judged in general that Weber's assumptions are unrealistic, the vastness of the Soviet Union and its level of development may have mitigated substantially the general disparity between assumptions and reality. The assumptions made by Weber result in his approach focusing on transportation costs which, in view of the long distances involved in the logistics of input supply and distribution of products in the

19. *Communist Manifesto*, as identified by Koropeckyj, "Location Theory before the Second World War," p. 16.

20. Vladimir G. Treml, "Interaction of Economic Thought and Economic Policy in the Soviet Union," *The History of Political Economy*, I, No. 1 (Spring 1969), 189.

21. Alfred Weber, *Über den Standort der Industrien* (Tübingen, 1909) and the same translated, *Alfred Weber's Theory of the Location of Industries*, trans. Carl Joachim Friedrich (Chicago: University of Chicago, 1929).

Soviet Union, should have been, but were not always, an important consideration in decisions concerning the location of economic activity.

Recent Approaches

Contemporary Soviet location economists advocate the pursuit of efficiency; but political considerations, informational problems, and naive benefit-cost calculations are so much a part of actual decision-making that one must be skeptical whenever it is maintained that certain location decisions are clearly efficient. Nevertheless, the prospect for reaching economically efficient decisions has been enhanced by attempts to refine benefit-cost calculations and the use of modern optimization techniques.

Representative of the refinement of the benefit-cost approach is a recent monograph by M. Vilenskii, "Determining the Efficiency of Territorial Distribution of Production."[22] Vilenskii makes the correct, elementary distinction between capital and operating costs. Costs of construction, capital expenditures for energy, transportation, and accompanying sectors, losses caused by location, investment for labor's comfort, and land costs are identified as capital expenditures to be included in calculations. The operating expenses that he includes are enterprises' costs of material factors of production, labor, and transportation. Vilenskii points out that it is marginal costs that matter in these calculations and that it is important to include the correct opportunity cost for land. In short, the monograph is a neat, valuable summary of how to conduct a benefit-cost analysis. Interesting, moreover, are Vilenskii's complaints about the difficulties involved in practical application. He says that the cost data with which planners work are incomplete, that some of the capital costs specified above are not included in calculations, and that prices do not represent socially necessary costs.[23]

The introduction of optimization techniques in location planning has consisted mainly in the use of linear and nonlinear programming. The greatest use of programming in regionalization occurs in the solution of limited industrial problems like the location of industrial branches, scheduling of freight flows, and identification of areas of agricultural specialization.[24] When attention is turned from the practical applications in planning to the theoretical exposition of problems of location, extremely widespread use of programming formulations is found.

The value of the programming formulation is appreciated when one learns of the simple, crude measures of efficiency that undoubtedly are used in the evaluation of competing proposals for the location of economic activity. A 1969 volume on economic regions and regionalization by the Moscow Institute of

22. M. Vilenskii, "Determining the Efficiency of Territorial Distribution of Production," in Murray Yanowitch (ed.), *Contemporary Soviet Economics* (White Plains, N.Y.: International Arts and Sciences Press, 1969), pp. 117–28.

23. Ibid., pp. 120–25.

24. L. P. Al'tman, "Economic Regionalization of the U.S.S.R. and New Methods of Economic-Georgraphic Research," *Soviet Geography*, VI, No. 9 (November 1965), p. 49.

National Economy gives some indication of the quantitative measures of productive structure of regions and of efficiency in various locations that are used by planners.[25]

The economic specialization of regions is judged by the coefficients of localization and of product per capita. The coefficient of localization, K_L, is defined as:

$$K_L = \frac{\textit{percent of sectoral output in the region of total output in the region}}{\textit{percent of sectoral output in the U.S.S.R. of total output in the U.S.S.R.}}$$

The coefficient of product per capita, K_D, is defined as:

$$K_D = \frac{\textit{percent of sectoral output in the region of total national sectoral output}}{\textit{percent of population in the region of total national population}}$$

The K_D index is calculated by using either value or natural units. Values greater than one indicate specialization. To indicate the comparative efficiency of specialization the index of current costs is used, defined by:

$$J = \frac{\textit{unit expense of production in given region}}{\textit{unit expense of production in compared region}}$$ [26]

The well-known coefficient of relative efficiency of investment, K_E, is also used in decisions concerning the location of capital. It is defined as:

$$K_E = \frac{C_2 - C_1}{I_1 - I_2}$$

with I_i being the capital invested and C_i being the current cost of production under option i. It shows the rate of current cost savings gained by adopting a more capital-intensive option. A series of indices exist for special purposes such as indices of regional support of sectors of specialization, of efficient use of labor, of regional satisfaction of consumer demand, and of development of products in great national demand.[27]

The most important organ for regional planning appears to be the Council for the Study [of the Location] of Productive Forces (Soviet po Izucheniiu Razmeshenii Proizvoditel'nykh Sil), but assessing its actual influence is not easy. In this regard it must be noted that the Council, although part of GOSPLAN since 1960, has an extremely long tradition of scientific study, rather than state planning, so that it may be more properly regarded as a research activity of GOSPLAN than as an operational department. If it has become more operational in character, such a development would represent a change in its historically defined function.

It is the author's judgment that the Council has indeed become more operational and that it would be a mistake to dismiss its importance in decisions

25. Moskovskii Institut Narodnogo Khoziaistva. *Ekonomicheskie raiony S.S.S.R.* (Moscow: Ekonomika, 1969).
26. Ibid., pp. 26–29.
27. Ibid., p. 29.

concerning the location of economic activity. The Council has concerned itself with long-range problems of location of economic activity and has been principally involved in the calculation of the various measures mentioned above. N. N. Nekrasov, its chairman in 1964, that year identified regional, sectoral, and synthetic aspects involved in planning an optimal long-range scheme of economic location. The regional aspect involves determination of the potential for regional specialization and economic integration by ascertaining natural conditions, resources, and economic development to assess the possibility of developing productive complexes. The sectoral aspect involves the study of industrial sectors to identify factors that are most important in determining economical operation. In very general terms, sectors may be characterized as power-oriented, raw material–oriented, or market-oriented. The synthetic or national aspect involves the survey of broad national problems like the use of manpower, energy, and natural resources.[28] Work of this nature has led to documents with the translated title of *The General Scheme of Development of Macro-Regions of the Economy*.[29] The first such document was for the period 1966–70, and the second is for the period 1971–80. The documents contain the main principles of location for the Soviet Union and calculations of the various indices used.

Based on its analytical work, the Council proposes investment projects which are considered along with the proposals of ministries, bureaus, territorial entities, and other councils. One example of direct influence on investment seems to be the development of industry in small- and medium-sized cities. The Council has designated certain small- and medium-sized cities as sites for investment and has controlled further location and investment in developed regions.[30]

TWO MAJOR ISSUES AFFECTING INTERREGIONAL MIGRATION

In this section two issues of Soviet national life that may have affected streams of interregional migration during the 1959–70 period are discussed: the development of economic activity in the regions of Siberia and the Far East along with contiguous areas of northern Kazakhstan and problems posed by tension with the People's Republic of China. The state policies formulated to cope with these issues or to meet goals articulated in connection with them were not meant to have principal impact on migratory streams. The policies may be regarded as macroeconomic (or macrosocietal) factors affecting migration and as such may be distinguished from state policies having the specific

28. N. N. Nekrasov, "Scientific Principles for a General Long-Range Scheme of Location of the Productive Forces of the U.S.S.R.," *Soviet Geography*, V, No. 9 (November 1964), pp. 13–18.

29. Chantal Beaucourt, "Les Methods de la Planification Regionale en U.R.S.S.," *Economies et Societes*, I, No. 3 (March 1967), p. 204.

30. Ibid.

intent of influencing microeconomic decisions of single persons and families to migrate.

Eastern Development

The development of economic activity in the East involved many projects which are grouped here for discussion under the headings of those connected with the opening up of the Virgin Lands, those connected with the development of a third ferrous metallurgy complex, and those connected with the general exploitation of the resources of the East. The eastern or development regions (as the author later denotes them) are indicated on the map displayed in Figure 2.1.

Figure 2.1.
Development Regions of the U.S.S.R.

The Virgin Lands Campaign. Khrushchev, as First Party Secretary, directed the settlement and cultivation of 42 million hectares of land (according to his report in 1963)[31] located in the semiarid eastern steppe of the Soviet Union, north of the deserts of the Soviet Middle East. These lands lay within Kazakhstan (including about 61 percent of the lands) and the R.S.F.S.R. (mainly in the regions of West Siberia, East Siberia, the Volga, and the Urals). Their location is shown in Figure 2.2. Initially they were devoted almost exclusively to the cultivation of grains, but during the period of this study they were put to more varied and less intensive use. Much history of the campaign is not pertinent to the study of migration in the 1959–70 period, but it is desirable to set forth some of the details here. The party, through Khrushchev, initiated the campaign in 1954 and much of what could be claimed to have been finally done in

31. Carl Zoerb, "The Virgin Land Territory: Plans, Performance, Prospects," in Roy D. Laird and Edward L. Crowley (eds.), *Soviet Agriculture: The Permanent Crisis* (New York: Praeger, 1965), p. 29.

bringing land into cultivation had been accomplished by 1956. The undertaking was spectacular and, according to one Western view, "must rank as one of the most significant domestic accomplishments of the Soviet policy during the post-Stalin period."[32]

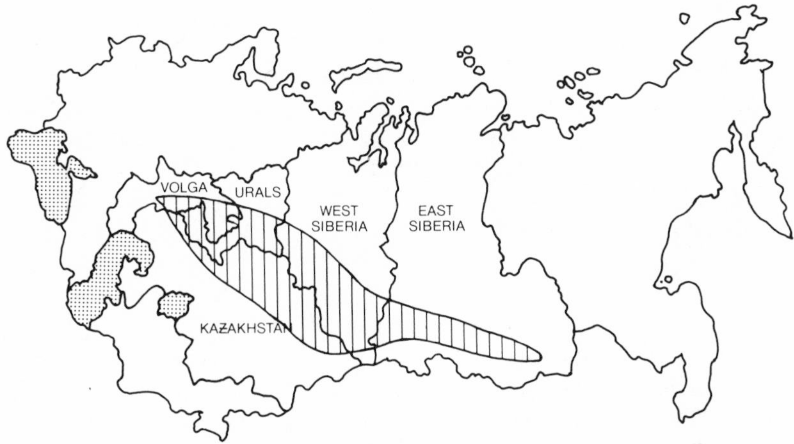

Figure 2.2.
Areas Including Virgin Lands
Virgin land areas indicated by vertical line shading

It is likely that the campaign was conceived as a stop-gap measure to buy time for the implementation of agricultural reform and changes. Agricultural practices such as adequately spaced cropping, stubble-mulching, and leaving land fallow were not used in the first years of cultivation in an apparent attempt to achieve maximal short-run returns. It is therefore possible that these forced-draft methods of the middle and later 1950s may have been followed in the 1960s by mass abandonment of the Virgin Lands. As there were successes in the 1950s (1956 and 1958), so there followed failures and disappointments in the early 1960s (with the exception of 1964). An articulated or tacit admission of failure in the Virgin Lands and consequent, wholesale abandonment of the lands in the early 1960s would obviously have had an important influence on migratory flows within the U.S.S.R.

An admittedly rough and somewhat risky indication of the continued use of the Virgin Lands is given by the annual figures for sown hectares of spring wheat in Kazakhstan, shown in Table 2.3 along with the same figures for the U.S.S.R. and the R.S.F.S.R. There is no indication here of drastic dimunition of efforts to cultivate spring wheat, one of the crops most stressed during the first years of the Virgin Lands campaign. Certainly, there was continued interest in the lands in the early 1960s (1959–62) when a million persons probably

32. Ibid.

migrated in Kazakhstan.[33] After Khrushchev's resignation in 1964, other geographical areas gained attention as underutilized arable land, and greater attention, relative to campaign-style approaches, was paid to scientific, realizable, and modest approaches. Nevertheless, the Virgin Lands were looked to for substantial grain production. In fact, in the opinion of one careful Western student of Soviet agriculture, "the excessive grain-procurement targets . . . fixed for the Virgin Lands in general and Kazakhstan in particular" remained a major obstacle in the attainment of the agricultural goals of 1970,[34] and the "harmful practice of sacrificing long-term agriculture yields for the sake of fulfilling the procurement plan in a given year" was properly characterized [through 1965] as "perennial."[35] On the basis of the above it is concluded that the continued cultivation of the Virgin Lands remained an important concern of the state during the period of this study.

Third ferrous metallurgy base. Policies connected with the development of a third ferrous metallurgy complex is the second subject discussed here in the consideration of the development of economic activity in the eastern parts of the Soviet Union. Setting apart the treatment of ferrous metallurgy from the general policy of exploiting eastern resources is done here because of the historical importance of steel in Soviet planning and in the particular plan associated with the decision to develop a third ferrous metallurgy base. At the time of the announcement in 1956 of the decision to develop the third base, the Soviet Union had ferrous metallurgy bases in the Don-Dnieper area of the Ukraine (based on the Krivoy Rog basin) and in the Urals and Western Siberia expanse (which included the Magnitogorsk and Novokuznetsk centers). The sixth five-year plan had the ferrous metals targets for 1960 shown in Table 2.4. The physical target for pig iron of 53 million tons and the figure of 159 percent imply that the planned increase was about 20 million tons. Plans for the new third base included production of 15 to 20 million tons of pig iron a year, which would have amounted to a substantial contribution from the base to be located in northeastern Kazakhstan, southwestern Siberia and eastern Siberia.[36]

As students of the Soviet economy know, the sixth five-year plan was abandoned during the course of its term; initially it was to be revised, but finally it was replaced by the seven-year plan having the term 1959–65. The objective of creating a third metallurgy base was retained, but apparently its contribution fell short of the initial goal. Since the 1950s two complexes, a West Siberian plant (situated at Novokuznets) and a center located in northeastern Kazakhstan (at Karaganda) have come into operation as the manifestation of the design to

33. V. V. Pokshishevskii, and others, "On Basic Migration Patterns," in G. Demko et al. (eds.), *Population Geography: A Reader* (New York: McGraw-Hill, 1970), p. 322.

34. Keith Bush, "Comment" in Jerzy F. Karcz (ed.), *Soviet and East European Agriculture* (Berkeley: University of California Press, 1970), p. 354.

35. Ibid., pp. 354–55.

36. Alec Nove, *An Economic History of the U.S.S.R.* (London: Penguin Press, 1970), p. 341.

create the third base. Some idea of the quantitative importance of these centers may be gained from the data in Table 2.5. It is obvious from the data that the regional contribution of the areas in which the two new complexes and associated ore reserves are located remained small, although it had grown significantly. The importance of Kazakhstan and Siberia in terms of relative contribution to all-Union totals of iron ore mined, pig iron produced, and steel produced both in 1960 and 1969 is shown in Table 2.6.

Natural resource exploitation. In the consideration of the location of economic activity in the East, national and state interest in exploiting the area's natural resources is the third subject to be examined. This topic received much public attention in the U.S.S.R. during 1959–70.

According to N. Baibakov, Chairman of the U.S.S.R. GOSPLAN, 90 percent of the U.S.S.R.'s fuel resources, large reserves of lumber and ores, and vast hydroelectric potential are located in the eastern regions.[37] According to another account appearing in *Pravda*:

> The USSR has approximately 55 percent of the world reserves of coal, 45 percent of the natural gas, more than 60 percent of the peat. It has significant reserves of petroleum. Of the general world quantity of oil-bearing area, 32 million square kilometers, or 37.1 percent are on the territory of the Soviet Union. Only 8 percent have so far been utilized. The European part of the USSR and the Urals have most of the population of our country. In these areas are located also the chief potentials of the national economy. But 87 percent of the mineral fuel and reserves are located in Siberian, the Far East and the Central Asian republics. In the eastern regions are found the basic reserves of the economic types of fuel: gas, oil and also more than 90 percent of the hydroelectric resources.[38]

In another recent article N. N. Nekrasov pointed out that during the 1966–70 plan significant investment was directed to the eastern regions and that industrial production in all the Central Asian and eastern regions (West Siberia, East Siberia and the Far East) grew by at least 40 percent. The Central Asian and eastern regions produced 30 percent of the Union's natural gas, 18 percent of its oil, 43 percent of its coal, 26 percent of its electrical energy, 21 percent of its cellulose, and 33 to 34 percent of its timber output. Also, readers were told that the creation of industrial complexes in these regions would continue to be one of the most fundamental measures for perfecting the distribution of productive forces.[39]

A rational approach to exploiting the great, general wealth of resources in the East would be to invest in those projects that provide for the greatest relative benefit. Soviet economists and planners have, of course, appreciated

37. N. Baibakov, "Progress sovetskoi ekonomiki," *Pravda,* August 12, 1967, p. 2.
38. N. Mel'nikov, "Milliardy ekonomii," *Pravda,* January 16, 1967, p. 2.
39. N. N. Nekrasov, "Ot Moskvy do samykh do okrain," *Pravda,* December 31, 1970, p. 2.

this, and during 1959–70 investment was channeled to a large extent into projects connected with the generation of energy, thought to be the sector of the East's greatest comparative advantage. The policy was intended to take advantage of the coal reserves (becoming relatively more valuable as the result of depletion of reserves in the European part of the Soviet Union), the hydroelectric potential, and petroleum reserves (oil and natural gas). Theodore Shabad, the Western student and chronicler of Soviet industrial geography and development, identifies the present period of Soviet development beginning in the mid-1950s as being fundamentally different from the preceding period with regard to the exploitation of resources. Basically, the present period evidenced more cost-conscious orientation according to Shabad.[40]

The work of the Council for the Study of Productive Forces exemplifies cost-consciousness. It may be remembered that the Council's *General Scheme for the Location of Industrial Resources* examined various sectors of industry to determine what factors were important in insuring their economical operation, and surveyed the regions of the U.S.S.R. to find out where various commodities could be produced most cheaply. From this had emerged the general desiderata to locate industries related to the generation of energy (generation of hydroelectric power, coal-mining, and extraction of petroleum and natural gas) and the use of energy (refining of light and rare metals and the production of polymers) in the East and to locate industries that are labor intensive and economical with regard to the use of energy in the West.

Aggregative indicators of investment in the non-European parts of the country mark the extent to which the pronouncements in scholarly and popular publications have, in fact, been matched by actual policies. Table 2.7 presents data on the percentage distribution of capital investment over the period 1959–67 of governmental and cooperative enterprises and organizations, excluding collective farms. The data show that investment in the East and Kazakhstan has been carried out to an extent greater than that suggested by allocating investment to regions on the bases of population or gross industrial output.

The 1969 *Narkhoz* provides figures for the Soviet series on the development of the eastern regions. Siberia, East Siberia, the Far East, Central Asia, and Kazakhstan constitute the eastern regions (those east of the Urals) in this series. Those components showing an increase of 5 percentage points or more in relative contribution to the all-Union total in 1969 in comparison to 1960 were the following: kilowatt generating power of electricity generating stations, output (extraction) of crude oil, output of natural gas, output (extraction) of coal, production of tractor seeders, commercial timber felling, production of cellulose, and production of fiberboard.[41] Data on the industries related to generation of energy are shown in some detail in Table 2.8.

40. Theodore Shabad, "Changing Resource Policies in the U.S.S.R.," *Focus*, XIX, No. 6 (February 1969), 7–8.

41. *Narkhoz 69*, pp. 160–64.

In short, evidence of the use of the Virgin Lands, the effort to create a third ferrous metallurgy base, and the exploitation of natural resources, show that Kazakhstan, West Siberia, East Siberia, and the Far East were areas of national economic development. By this it is meant that they enjoyed comparative advantage in the production of materials that were in great national demand and were therefore the object of significant national investment. The U.S.S.R. did not solve its grain production problem, and data on grain sowing fail to indicate any wholesale abandonment of the Virgin Lands as a source of supply during the 1960s. For the same period an increase in the relative shares of iron ore mined and pig iron produced within Kazakhstan and Siberia occurred. The increase in importance of Kazakhstan and the East in energy activities—the extraction of oil and natural gas and the generation of hydroelectric power—was even more significant and was the object of state interest.

Tensions with People's Republic of China

The second issue of concern during the 1959–70 period identified here as possibly having had a major influence on interregional migration was the existence of substantial areas within the Soviet Union which the People's Republic of China claims as its territory. The disputed areas are two immense tracts, one is west of Mongolia (the area of southeastern Kazakhstan and much of Soviet Central Asia) and the other is northeast of Mongolia, north of the Amur River and east of Ussuri River (that part of the Soviet Far East and East Siberia regions that constitute Amurskaia Oblast, Khabarovskii Krai, Primorskii Krai, and Sakhalinskaia Oblast). The areas in question, being approximately 1.5 million square kilometers, were ceded to Russia in the second half of the nineteenth century during the partitioning of China. The People's Republic claims that the treaties of Aigun (1858) and Peking (1860) dealing with what is now the Soviet Far East, the treaty of St. Petersburg (1881), and other treaties dealing with what is now Soviet Central Asia were extracted under "unequal" conditions and thus should not be recognized.

During the 1959–70 period there occurred two major public expressions of concern over China's claims by the Soviet government. The first took place in September 1964 when Japanese Socialists visiting China made public Mao Tse-tung's remarks concerning Chinese claims to territory within the Soviet Union and his charge of a Soviet–American collusion having as its purpose world domination. Since 1954, according to the Soviet view, books and articles have appeared in the People's Republic of China that have claimed parts of Burma, Vietnam, Korea, Thailand, Malaya, Nepal, Butan, and Sikkim as Chinese territory. Territories within the U.S.S.R. claimed by the Chinese were parts of Kirghizia, Tadzhikistan and Kazakhstan and most of the southern Far East. The Soviets had for some years regarded the Chinese as secretly desiring to regain the easternmost areas of the Soviet Union which are so sparsely settled and richly endowed with resources. But the events of September 1964 represented a new development, since the failure of the Chinese government to renounce the public reports emanating from Japan was taken as an explicit, official endorsement of the claims. There resulted an approximately five thousand word editorial in *Pravda* on the "expansionist cold war" being waged by the People's Republic on the Soviet Union.[42]

The second major expression of Soviet concern came following the Ussuri border incident of March 2, 1969, when, according to the Soviet view, about three hundred Chinese troops participated in actions that included the occupation of Soviet territory (Damansky Island in the Ussuri River), the ambush of a Soviet border patrol on the Ussuri River, and combat with larger numbers of the Soviet border patrol. Soviet reaction included editorials in party and state newspapers, a press conference at the Soviet Foreign Ministry, protests to the Chinese government, demonstrations of indignation at the Chinese embassy in Moscow, a front page in *Krasnaia Zvezda* (*Red Star*, the official newspaper of the Ministry of Defense) devoted to admonishing the Chinese adventurers, and published, patriotic letters from the "front."[43]

Whether these developments during the 1960s are properly interpreted as a "great powers" confrontation or an ideological dispute is a question that need not be resolved here. Certainly, the policies of border patrol of the two countries and the issue of disputed territories are suggestive of a "great powers" confrontation. Russian and Soviet experience, notably the "capitalist encirclement" of the early years of the Soviet Union, the two invasions of the country by Germany in this century and the eastern wars with Japan in this century must not be ignored. It seems likely that the Soviets may view their present situation as a confrontation with a potential world power. If the situation during 1959–70 was viewed as a confrontation with a significant possibility of territorial invasion, one would expect that the Soviet Union would have settled more intensively, developed more industrially, and garrisoned to a greater extent the eastern areas. Evidence suggest these things did occur. John Thomas, western student of Sino–Soviet affairs, has identified evidence of contingency plans for war with the People's Republic, of concern to locate more war-related industries and infrastructure in the East nearer potential sites of conflict, and of arguments within the Soviet Union for a preventative strike against China. Thomas also feels that the Soviets are concerned about the possibility of West German and Chinese cooperation in applying pressure on the borders of the Soviet Union.[44] In this regard it is interesting to note the 1969 cartoon in *Izvestiia* showing a prosperous-looking German labeled "provocation in West Berlin" about to shake hands with "provocation on the Ussuri River" represented by an extended blood-covered hand, presumably belonging to a Chinese.[45]

42. *CDSP*, XVI, No. 34 (September 16, 1964), 3.
43. *CDSP*, XXI, No. 10 (March 26, 1969), 1–10.
44. John Thomas, public remarks and private interview at Slavic Studies colloquium (of the University of North Carolina at Chapel Hill and Duke University), Durham, N.C., *circa* March 1971.

Closely related to this question is the general issue of investment in the development regions. To the extent that significant investment occurred there, it is difficult to determine the relative importance of defense and economic considerations in its motivation. Viewing plans for investment or acts of investment, different individuals have reached different conclusions. Harrison Salisbury, the journalist, in 1963 and in 1969 attributed much of the motivation for developing the eastern areas to geopolitical reasons.[46] Surely on the limited question of the development of strictly military capability by the Soviets in the People's Republic of Mongolia and in the East Siberia and Far East regions, Salisbury's accounts must be accepted as evidence of significant arming and fortification of the eastern sections.[47] Outside of Mongolia, Salisbury states the principal concentrations of Soviet forces have developed at Chita (in East Siberia) and Blagoveshschensk (along the Amur River in the Far East) and all along the Ussuri River (in the Far East).[48] In view of Salisbury's accounts it is of interest to note Chou En-lai's recent remark that by 1969 the Soviet Union had prepared for war with China by stationing over a million troops along the northern frontiers of China, even dispatching some of these troops into Mongolia.[49]

There is scant direct evidence of attempts to populate the contested regions. Certainly the miliitary augmentation along the border required some build-up also of civilian population. One bit of evidence of attempt to populate the disputed area was reported in 1969 by *Estonian Events,* an emigre newspaper. Following incidents along the Ussuri River a crash program was supposed to have been initiated for populating Siberia. Calls for emigration were issued on Soviet Estonian Radio (for example on April 26, 1969), but not in easily monitored newspapers. Farmers were to receive free travel and transport with up to two tons of personal belongings, 4,000 rubles credit if desired (repayable over ten years) and compensation for unharvested crops back in Estonia. The paper goes on to note that there have been cases of involuntary transfers of teachers to Estonian colonies in the Far East and that as many as 1,000 people may have left Estonia in March 1969.[50]

POLICIES INTENDED TO INFLUENCE MIGRATION STREAMS

Policies intended to influence migration streams may be grouped under three headings: wage differentials, organized recruitment and resettlement, and moral suasion. The policies falling under these headings are examined in turn to assess the degree to which each was used.

45. *Izvestiia,* March 11, 1969, p. 2.

46. Harrison E. Salisbury, "Russians Going to Area China Claims," *New York Times,* March 22, 1963, p. 8, and *War Between Russia and China* (New York: W. W. Norton, 1969).

47. Salisbury, *War Between Russia and China,* pp. 149–62.

48. Ibid., p. 153.

49. Audrey Topping, "Chou, at Dinner, Describes Birth of Rift with Soviet," *New York Times,* May 21, 1971, p. 10.

50. R. R. Taagepera, "The Impact of the Ussuri Incidents," *Estonian Events* (June 1969), p. 2.

Wage Differentials

The basic features of wage determination have already been outlined; one feature that has only been mentioned in passing, however, is compensation based on normal conditions of work. When conditions of work fell short of those normally specified or expected, the state favored additional compensation. Overtime work, nightwork, and work under disagreeable or dangerous conditions are examples of the kinds of work requiring extra compensation. Of particular interest in this study is work in regions of the Soviet Union that citizens found least attractive. In recognition of this situation, extra remuneration was paid to some workers in some regions.

The state used a system of regional coefficients *(raionnye koeffisienty)* to raise wages in the least attractive regions. The coefficients were simple indices for adjusting upward the basic wages of employees; on January 15, 1959, the following coefficients were in effect for the regions listed:[51]

Islands of the Arctic Ocean	2.0
Other regions of the Extreme North	1.5–1.7
Regions, very similar to the Extreme North	1.3–1.4
Remaining regions of the European North, southern regions of East Siberia, and the Far East	1.2
Urals, southern West Siberia, Kazakhstan and Central Asia	1.15

Application of these regional coefficients on a universal basis (that is, a basis that included all workers in the industrial and service sectors) would have represented a substantial attempt to influence population distribution, but the coefficients were not applied in any such uniform manner.

The coefficients evolved from the post-1956 reform of wages that had had as one of its principal aims elimination of the haphazard aspects of the all-Union policy on wages that had resulted from the uncoordinated (though sanctioned) initiatives of ministries in setting wage levels. Hence, the establishment of all-Union regional coefficients is probably more properly viewed as a codification of the various policies of ministries than as the establishment of new policy to attract great numbers of people to certain regions. With this in mind, one is hardly surprised to learn that generally the coefficients were applied only in certain industrial branches like ferrous metallurgy, coal-mining, chemical industry, machine-building, construction, and geological prospecting. But even within branches of industry, the regional coefficients were not employed uniformly; quite obviously there was some flexiblity with regard to the actual size of the coefficient, and often some firms within a branch were authorized the use of coefficients while others were not. Coefficients were set on the basis of hardships and disadvantages at particular locations.

When they were used in the 1959–70 period, the regional coefficients were applied to the first 300 rubles of monthly pay (exclusive of premiums—*nad-*

51. E. Manevich, *Problemy obshestvennogo truda* (Moscow: Ekonomika, 1966), p. 129.

bavki—for length of service and other special circumstances). In 1965 the average annual money wage for industrial production personnel was probably highest in the coal industry at 2,178 rubles; the all-branch average for industrial workers was reported as 1,240 rubles.[52] These annual figures imply approximate monthly rates of 180 and 100 rubles, respectively, so it appears somewhat unlikely that the 300-ruble base limitation severely limited average payments for location in the forbidding regions.

The trend during the period of this study was towards expanding the classes of workers covered by the regional coefficients. In 1964 persons who constituted the Soviet category of workers "directly involved in providing services to the public" were included.[53] The coefficients for these workers corresponded to the earlier established coefficients for workers in the industrial branches. A much more important change took effect at the beginning of 1968 when the regional wage coefficients were introduced "for workers and employees at enterprises and organizations in light industry and the food industry, education, public health, housing and communal economy, science, culture, and other branches of the Far East and the European North" for which they had not previously been in effect.[54] Prior to this change, Soviet analysts of regional problems and parties interested in the resolution of these problems had criticized the system because it had failed to apply the coefficients to all branches of industry located within the same region. Some Soviet commentators and officials looked upon the 1968 change as having cleared up this problem for once and for all. It is important to note, however, that the situation that existed prior to 1968 in all the regions—the application of the coefficients principally in priority sectors—has not been changed in the regions of East Siberia, West Siberia, the Urals, Central Asia, and Kazakhstan.

In addition to the system of regional coefficients, there existed at the same time a system of premiums *(nadbavki)* to the wages of workers in the Far North. Unlike the regional coefficients system, premiums for work in the Far North applied only to areas that were populated very lightly, since the Far North included most of the sparsely settled Far East and other major political units (and sometimes only parts of them) which are contiguous to the Arctic Ocean. Since their application was more limited geographically, the significance of the premiums for interregional migration flows might have been less than that of the coefficient system, but the author has no figures available to support this speculation. In another sense, however, it should be noted that the significance of the premiums relative to coefficients was enhanced by their uniform application within a particular geographical zone. The premiums were instituted in 1960 when the Presidium of the Supreme Soviet decided "to pay all workers and employees of the state, cooperative and public enterprises, institutions and organizations supplements to their monthly earnings (exclusive

52. Feshbach and Rapawy, "Labor and Wages," p. 83.
53. V. G. Danilevich, *Spravochnik po zarobotnoi plate* (Minsk: Nauka i tekhnika, 1970), pp. 12–15.
54. *CDSP*, XIX, No. 39 (October 18, 1967), 3–4.

of the regional coefficients and length-of-service emoluments).''[55] Thus, it is hard to imagine any significant group of employees excluded from the benefits, while in the case of the regional coefficients, excluded groups constituted a significant portion of regional labor forces.

The terms of the premiums are interesting. The 1960 decree established a schedule that remunerated length of service very handsomely. A worker received no premium until he completed six months, a year or two years (depending upon location) on his job; thereafter, the first 300 rubles of basic wages were augmented by 10 percent during each subsequent six-month, year, or two-year term of work. Length of service counted much, but there were maximum limits set; for the six-month and one-year localities the premium could not exceed 80 percent of the basic wage while in other localities 50 percent was established as the limit.[56] In 1968 the Presidium adjusted the service criteria for the premiums at the same time it expanded the application of the regional coefficients. The length of service increments which came at one- and two-year service points had their intervals reduced to six months and a year, respectively; the maximum premium levels were raised significantly for the workers in the most difficult conditions; and cash bonuses were instituted for persons renewing labor contracts.[57] Throughout the period there were numerous advantages *(l'goty)* afforded to the workers receiving the premiums that included special vacation privileges, additional leave, and payments to cover transportation costs.

The question arises as to how effective these policy measures were. Soviet students of regional problems have generally judged that the coefficients and premiums have only partially offset the disadvantages for which they were often said to be compensating. Thus, early in the public discussion of this period, V. I. Perevedentsev identified the whole complex of living conditions as the proper object of focus.[58] Others working with regional price and wage data have shown throughout the period that the regional cost of living differences were often greater than the regional wage differences.[59] Even after the extensive changes of 1968 (especially important for the Far East) the authors of a monograph on the reproduction of labor resources in the Far East felt that the problems ''still have not been resolved,'' since the measures took insufficient account of the demographic composition of the Far East, the impossibility of earning income on peasant private plots, and the added costs of living in the severe climate.[60]

55. *CDSP*, XII, No. 7 (March 16, 1960), 26–27.
56. Ibid.
57. *CDSP*, XIX, No. 39 (October 18, 1967), 3–4.
58. *CDSP*, XIV, No. 26 (July 25, 1962), 4.
59. D. I. Valentei et al. (eds.), *Narodonaselenie i ekonomika* (Moscow: Ekonomika, 1967), pp. 145–56.
60. L. L. Rybakovskii, *Vosporizvodstvo trudovykh resursov Dal'nego Vostoka* (Moscow: Nauka, 1969), pp. 109–10.

Organized Recruitment and Resettlement

In addition to the use of wage differentials the Soviet Union also used a second set of policies that may be grouped under the heading of labor recruitment. The most important organization involved in this task was Orgnabor, the organized recruitment of labor force *(Organizovannoi Nabor Rabochei Sily)* which has a history extending back many years before the recent period being studied here. Through the 1930s and even into the 1950s Orgnabor channeled rural manpower into urban employment; but in the 1950s Orgnabor's agricultural-industrial channeling became a less important part of its efforts, and it increasingly recruited labor for construction projects in the remote sections of the country. Thus, by the late 1950s typical figures on sectoral destinations of workers were as follows: 18 percent for industrial enterprises, 7 percent for transport enterprises and 70 percent for construction undertakings.[61] By the beginning of the 1960s, Orgnabor was for all practical purposes recruiting only urban workers for nonseasonal construction and industrial work in the least developed parts of the Soviet Union. Its work was regarded as important because of the area requirements for manpower resulting from the changing fuel base, the Khrushchev experiment in education (freeing more young people to join the labor force), and the release of workers in the metal and machine-building sectors.[62]

In the 1960s Orgnabor's main function became the direction of labor into the remotely settled eastern and northern regions, but it continued to recruit seasonal workers for sectors like fishing, peat-bog operations, and lumbering. The State Committees of Labor in the Union and autonomous republics directed Orgnabor's work; below the State Committees were the executive committees of krais and oblasts which supervised field or regional office recruiting.[63] Orgnabor recruits typically signed contracts specifying the period of work they were obligated for, where they were going to have to go, and what the financial arrangements for travel to and return from the site of work were. The typical minimal lengths for contracts were one year, but two years for work in the Far East, and three years for work in the European North. Enterprises usually assumed the responsibility for providing appropriate living space, food services, social and cultural facilities, and normal working conditions.

The question of whether Orgnabor represented voluntary or directed resettlement during the 1959–70 period is an important one, since it has bearing on the general issue of the functioning of the Soviet labor market. Orgnabor's operations had important aspects both voluntary and compulsive, and this fact alone may have had much to do with its atrophy near the end of this period. Soviet sources often claimed that the Orgnabor-effected manpower redistribu-

61. *CDSP*, XII, No. 33 (September 14, 1960), 5–8.
62. Ibid.
63. Aleksandrov, *Trudovoe pravo*, p. 258.

tion was voluntary, but at the same time also claimed that it represented planned redistribution of manpower (in the sense of regional labor balance changes). In the latter sense it cannot be doubted that Orgnabor quotas were obligatory, since plans had to be fulfilled. Use of a voluntary system of resettlement in a planned economic system would have entailed setting of labor prices to effect desired redistribution. (The author presumes the prices reflect not only money wage payments, but also the whole complex of advantages and disadvantages of different employments.) Use of a system of administrative direction would have required selecting individuals to move so as to effect desired redistribution without regard to their preferences.

The interesting case for study here concerns what happens when the state requires plans to be fulfilled, the state sets wages at levels that in many instances do not correspond to the levels necessary for effecting desired migration, and the state allows only mild forms of pressure to be used, like moral suasion (presumed to be a weak policy instrument of direction). Elementary price theory suggests that in this situation price is fixed at a level that results in the persistence of Walrasian excess demand; likely consequences are the persistence of shortages of labor from the buyer's point of view and offering of lower quality labor in the market. One would predict instances of plans of labor recruitment not being fulfilled and instances of poorly qualified laborers being recruited. Some examples follow to indicate the success Orgnabor enjoyed.

The Chairman of the Atka Settlement Executive Committee, Magadan Province (in the Far East region), complained in 1962 to *Izvestiia* that the departments of migration and organized hiring had not, in general, been sending workers with the needed specialties, and in fact had been sending cheaters, drifters, and drunkards.[64] He related the story told by another official: "You know in two years the militia in our district has detected almost 3,000 persons who were hiding from alimony payments. That is why they come to the North. The organized hiring department sent them." One of his own stories is just as revealing: "During the winter this year I myself had occasion to see worthless travelling companions of this sort. . . . A local mining trust was waiting impatiently for new worker reinforcements. And then we met them. They stepped off an airplane and walked across the airfield, and we saw one-half of the newcomers presented not a very pleasant spectacle—they were dead drunk." He felt that the whole truth of the matter was that the representatives of the organized hiring departments enlisted all comers.[65]

There was no evidence that things had changed by 1968 when the Deputy to the Raichikhinsk City Soviet, Amur Province (in the Far East), provided the facts that of the 130 workers who had arrived via Orgnabor in 1967 and had been provided housing and amenities in adequate measure, 9 soon had administrative or criminal proceedings against them, 28 never reported to work, and 9 were fired for systematic violations of labor discipline or for drunkenness.[66]

64. *CDSP*, XIV, No. 37 (October 10, 1962), 18.
65. Ibid.
66. *CDSP*, XX, No. 9 (March 21, 1968), 36.

Figures for the early 1960s indicate that Orgnabor was at that time providing workers for only about 4 percent of the all-Union accessions to industrial work.[67] It is unlikely, given the diminution of Orgnabor's importance, that the figure was ever higher during the 1959–70 period. The figure seems extremely low, but the base on which it is defined, all accessions to jobs throughout the U.S.S.R., must be taken into account. To the extent accessions to jobs in the eastern and northern parts involved migration and could not be filled by direct hiring by employers, Orgnabor played an important part in providing labor.

Another form of resettlement employed throughout the 1959–70 period was the direct assignment of graduates of secondary specialized and higher education institutions for three-year terms to initial jobs, usually in labor-deficient sections of the country. An enterprise was normally forbidden to hire a new graduate not having a certificate of direction sending him to the enterprise. Taking into account the demographic augmentation of labor force in the years following 1960 and the qualitative contribution of newly trained technicians and technocrats, one must conclude that these assignments contributed importantly to the achievement of production plans. Evidence that they did is provided by some of the measures taken to insure that graduates actually went to their assignments. Prior to 1964 the only penalty for not completing one's obligatory initial assignment was forfeiture of the travel allowance that had been advanced to the graduate to get him to the job. Beginning in 1964 a full-time student in higher education was awarded not a diploma upon completion of his curriculum, but a temporary certificate, with the understanding that his diploma would be issued after he finished a year's work at his initial assignment. Later the state authorized enterprises, institutions, and organizations to petition the U.S.S.R. Ministry of Higher and Secondary Specialized Education to revoke the diploma of a graduate leaving his job before the end of his obligation.[68]

The system of obligatory work assignments for *all* school graduates was established in 1928, but by the 1959–70 period the main concern in this regard seems to have been only the graduates from secondary specialized schools and higher education.[69] Graduates from vocational schools were directed to jobs, but concern about whether they reported is not evident. To demonstrate that the directed assignment of specialized secondary and higher education graduates represented a significant control of the entry of skilled workers into the labor force, some reported data and some guesses by the author for 1964–65 and 1964 are listed in Table 2.9.

Moral Suasion

The third category of policies specifically designed to influence microeconomic decisions to migrate was the use of moral suasion, the principal means

67. Feshbach, "Manpower in the U.S.S.R.," p. 725.
68. Ibid., pp. 737–38.
69. Brown, *Soviet Trade Unions*, pp. 24–25.

having been appeals by the Communist party and the state to individuals and groups to migrate to labor-deficient areas; such appeals were based on the notion of every citizen's obligation to contribute to the development of Communism in the Soviet Union. The most spectacular recent example was the Komsomol's call for volunteers to work in the the Virgin Lands in the mid-1950s. The appeals started in 1954 and continued on into the 1960s. During the early years of the seven-year plan (1958–65) about a million youths were sent to Siberia, the North, Far East and Kazakhstan by the Komsomol.[70] Meetings were held in plants, newspapers were filled with reports and appeals, and the Komsomol took special steps to encourage volunteering and to effect transfers.

An indication of the tenor and import of this method of influencing the decision to migrate can be gained from Khrushchev's address in May 1962 to Fourteenth Congress of the Komsomol:

> The Young Communist League has a great deal of experience of participation in the accomplishment of important economic tasks. It may be said that the history of our country has hardly ever known such mass labor heroism as has been displayed by young people in recent years. Some people in the West still cannot understand how millions of young people, at the call of the Party, could leave familiar, built-up areas for the virgin lands, for construction projects in Siberia, the Far East, and the Far North. . . .
>
> We have praised you for this, we are proud, and, I am sure, will always be proud of the deeds of glorious Soviet youth, of the Young Communist League. Much indeed has been done and for this the Country and the Party thank you greatly![71]

Khrushchev, continuing his speech, left no doubt that the Komsomol still had much to do:

> Comrades! I have expressed gratitude to you on behalf of the Central Committee and the government for the good things you have done in the past, but you yourselves know that the appetite comes with the eating. What you have done is good, but does what we have accomplished finish our work? Do not the expanses of Siberia summon us today to new labor accomplishments? Not long ago our fine geologists unearthed rich deposits of high-grade oil in the vicinity of Irkutsk. Well, we have discovered this oil and drilled one well; should we go to sleep now?
>
> Siberia holds countless riches, vast resources of oil, coal, iron and nonferrous ores. Therefore, comrades, let us not cling to the comfortable places we are used to, let us go to areas that are public treasure troves but require hard work. They are undeveloped because there are no people there. When people come, extract the natural wealth and build factories

70. Murray Weitzman, and others, "Employment in the U.S.S.R.: Comparative U.S.S.R.–U.S. Data," in U.S., Congress, Joint Economic Committee, *Dimensions of Soviet Economic Power* (Washington, D.C.: U.S. Government Printing Office, 1962), p. 641.

71. *CDSP*, XIV, No. 16 (May 16, 1962), 13.

> and cities, the new regions will not only become settled and comfortable, they will be great economic and cultural centers of our motherland, of our communist society!
>
> Dear Young Communist comrades and youth, the Central Committee and the Soviet government presumably will call upon you more than once in the future to go to work in new regions. Whom else should we call upon but you? For what and for whose sake are we appealing to you? For the people, for you, for the sake of your happiness and your future![72]

The most noticeable Komsomol achievements in the early 1960s seem to have been at the construction sites in the Far North and Central Asia and, of course, in the Virgin Lands. It was reported during the same Komsomol Congress, that about 3 million young people were working at construction sites under Komsomol auspices and that during the seven-year plan, to date, 8 million Komsomol passes for these purposes had been issued. With regard to the Virgin Lands for the same period it was said that 86,000 young people had gone and taken up permanent residence, while typically about 600,000 Komsomol workers were provided at harvest time each year.[73]

The work of the Komsomol continued in the 1960s especially with regard to the recruitment of workers for construction projects. In fact, the requirements for labor at Irkutsk suggested by Khrushchev in May 1962, did materialize to the extent that in mid-1967 there were eight all-Union Komsomol construction projects ongoing with more than 100,000 young people employed at the site. Eighty percent of the construction workers at the project were 20 to 30 years old, most were said to be Komsomol members. The First Secretary of the Irkutsk Komsomol, after providing these facts, noted high turnover, the sending of poorly trained youth, unrealistic expectations of youth, the failure to provide adequate housing and consumer services, and the arrival of undesirable characters at sites.[74] These problems have already been mentioned here in connection with Orgnabor.

The Komsomol projects remained important in the 1960s, and the same methods for stirring up interest were used by other state and party organizations. Thus, soldiers nearing the end of their active-duty service had their letter to *Krasnaia Zvezda (Red Star)* published under the headline "The Distant Lands Call Us." They wrote:

> At political sessions we are now studying the draft Directives of the 24th C.P.S.U. Congress. Pride wells up in our hearts at the achievements of the Soviet people in building communism and at the vast plans outlined by our own party for the new five-year period.
>
> We want to be in the front ranks of those fighting to bring those plans to life. And we have unanimously decided: After military service we will go to the new construction work in Siberia.

72. Ibid.
73. *CDSP*, XIV, No. 15 (May 9, 1962), 3–7.
74. Ibid.

> At the Siberian construction projects of the new five-year plan we will find work for our strong, skilled hands.
>
> We know that awaiting us is not only the sense of adventure for which the Siberian lands are famed, but also considerable difficulties. . . . But we do not fear difficulties: We are of Army-tempered steel. . . .
>
> We turn with an ardent Young Communist appeal to all soldiers whose terms, like ours, are expiring this spring: follow our example; choose a challenging road in life and join the ranks of the founding builders, explorers and enthusiasts![75]

Soon thereafter appeared a reply from some former servicemen:

> We enthusiastically support their decision to go to work at a new construction project in Siberia after leaving the service. We await you here, dear friends; there is work here for your strong and skilled hands.
>
> Before being transferred to the reserves a few years ago, we did some serious thinking about our life path, as you are doing now; we, too, heard the call of far-off lands. We can now say . . . each of us has found interesting work and loyal comrades here. . . .
>
> None of us can complain about his material status either. Well-appointed apartments for family men and dormitories for single people have become the rule of life here.[76]

A survey of the policies specifically formulated to influence streams of migration reveals that the policies had a consistent objective of providing manpower for those geographical areas which were areas of both significant governmental investment and relatively unattractive living conditions. The wage changes made during this period suggest that the importance of regional differentials as a policy instrument seems to have increased, while all indications are that Orgnabor clearly became less important. The trend of moral suasion techniques is not clear. If these factors only had been affecting migration decisions, it seems reasonable to assert that significant net migration to the areas in question would have taken place. Of course, these were not the only considerations involved in decisions. When everything is taken into account, it is likely that various factors will be seen to have been working at cross purposes. This likelihood is explored in chapter 5.

CONCLUSIONS

Four topics have been examined: the Soviet labor market, Soviet location thought, macrosocietal influences affecting migration, and state policies intended to influence decisions concerning migration. Two principal conclusions emerge. The first is that during 1959–70 state policy afforded sufficient freedom of conduct to workers so that it is not unreasonable to explain the economic behavior of workers (especially their location) on the basis of choice in

75. *CDSP*, XXIII, No. 10 (April 6, 1971), 35.
76. Ibid.

labor markets rationale. The alternative approach would be to explain the job accessions and tenure solely on the basis of governmental actions; this approach is rejected. Its rejection raises the interesting question of identifying the determinants of choice in labor markets and, of course, in no way implies that state measures were unimportant. In this study migration is viewed as the result of choice concerning where to live and work, and the interest is in what factors were important in the location decisions of households. Assessment of the importance of such factors occurs in chapter 5.

The survey of Soviet location thought and location policy in the 1960s showed that the state desired to increase the relative contribution of the eastern regions to all-Union production totals. Among the measures taken towards this end may be numbered the continued cultivation of the Virgin Lands, the expansion of the regional ferrous metallurgy sector, and the investment in the creation of an energy base. The last was particularly important. The continued discovery of large reserves of oil and natural gas in connection with the increasing cost of coal, oil, and gas located in the western regions attracted considerable interest, with the result that the government invested in the East and Kazakhstan to an extent greater than that suggested by allocating investment proportionally on the basis of population or production. Another force acting to interest the state in the development of its eastern regions was the claim of the People's Republic of China to substantial portions of territory lying within the Soviet Union. It seems reasonable to presume that a significant augmentation of military forces occurred in the Soviet East during the 1960s. There is some evidence of efforts to settle people in the disputed areas.

The second principal conclusion is, therefore, that state policy sought in its effort at economic expansion, to motivate workers to migrate to and, to some extent, settle in the regions of West Siberia, East Siberia, the Far East, and Kazakhstan. Specific measures employed were wage differentials for certain regional assignments, the organized recruitment of labor for designated jobs, and calls of state and party officials for volunteers to work in these regions. It was observed that the measures fell short of being sufficiently effective. Regional wage differentials varied among industries and firms of a given region, and the differentials appeared oftentimes to compensate inadequately for the additional costs of living in more severe climates. The recruitment of workers through Orgnabor seems to have diminished during the 1960s, and the quality of workers enlisted, in the presence of relatively low real wage differentials and the absence of coercion, was the subject of seemingly endless complaint. Moral suasion was effective with some, but not with others.

3

"LAWS" OF MIGRATION

Between 1930 and 1964 not a single book was published in the U.S.S.R. on the subject of internal population migration.[1] The dearth of materials on this particular question was not an isolated circumstance. In the late 1920s and early 1930s Stalin tightened his grip on the reins of the Soviet state by, among other things, purging in wholesale fashion specialists serving the government, thereby rendering a chilling effect on the scientific research concerning social phenomena. The statistical apparatus of the state was allowed to deteriorate, so that by the late 1930s the publication of statistical data had ceased completely. The failure to collect social statistics and to conduct social research continued until the late 1950s when party officials instructed the government to end the policy of complete secrecy of state information. In 1957 a meager *National Economy Yearbook* appeared and was followed by more volumes in subsequent years as the Central Statistical Administration almost grudgingly participated in the liberalizing changes that took place in the Soviet state after 1956.

Now more than two decades later the situation has changed. The study of migration within the Soviet Union has been proclaimed an important problem of the national economy and has been the object of significant attention in the Soviet press and in Soviet academic literature. The change in Soviet policy offers the opportunity to compare recent Soviet population movement with generalizations about internal migration phenomena observed for some time now in Western nations. Probably the most famous set of generalizations is E. G. Ravenstein's pioneering "The Laws of Migration" based on the British census of 1881 and subsequent observations concerning the experience of more than 20 countries. Ravenstein concluded that most migrants proceed short distances, that females are numerous in short distance moves, that when migrants do move great distances, they tend to travel to large urban centers, and that the economic motive predominates. In addition he generalized that migration proceeds by stages and that for each stream of migration, a counterstream or reverse flow develops. Ravenstein also surmised that migration occurs more frequently in rural than in urban areas and that the level of population move-

1. V. Perevedentsev, "Sovremennaia migratsiia naseleniia," *Voprosy ekonomiki* (No. 5, 1973), p. 128.

ment increases as an economy becomes more complex.[2] Taking into account much subsequent work, Everett S. Lee restated a set of laws in his 1966 article, "A Theory of Migration,"[3] which summarizes much of what demographers know concerning the volume of migrations, streams and counterstreams, and the characteristics of migrants. It is the purpose of this chapter to determine the degree to which recent Soviet migration can be adequately described by generalizations concerning Western experience.

Rather than adhering to the letter of the "laws" of either Ravenstein or Lee, this survey and comparison proceeds according to an outline based on both works:

I. Volume of Migration in Relation to:
   A. The entire population
   B. Distance
   C. Diversity among areas and peoples
II. Streams and Counterstreams of Migrants
   A. Interregional streams
   B. Rural-urban streams
III. Characteristics of Migrants
   A. The economic motive
   B. Selectivity
      1. Age
      2. Sex
      3. Ethnicity
      4. Skill and education
   C. Migration by Stages

VOLUME OF MIGRATION

Mobility

In recent years it may be estimated that approximately 14 million persons moved each year between population points within the U.S.S.R. The state's internal passport system requires persons arriving in new areas to register with municipal authorities. In urban areas the information from this system is used to compile data about the number of arrivals and areas of origin. In rural regions, however, the population registration systems are generally acknowledged to be ineffective, with the result that the government declines to report the number of rural arrivals. The only information available on the extent of rural migration throughout the Soviet Union is provided by the 1970 census questions on migration. According to the census during 1968–69, 69 percent of all movers arrived in urban areas;[4] thus, an approximate estimate of total

2. E. G. Ravenstein, "The Laws of Migration," *Journal of the Royal Statistical Society*, XLVIII, Pt. 2 (June 1885), 167–227 and LII (June 1889), 241–301.
3. Everett S. Lee, "A Theory of Migration," *Demography*, III, No. 1 (1966), 47–57.
4. *Vestnik statistiki* (No. 2, 1973), p. 86.

moves may be derived by raising the number of reported urban arrivals in recent years[5] by a factor of 1.44 (which equals 1.00 divided by 0.69). By relating the 14 million estimate to total population, it may be calculated that about 5 percent of the population has changed place of residence each year during recent Soviet experience. "Change in residence" denotes the circumstances of a Soviet citizen taking up permanent residence in a new locality or population point. Thus, movements between different cities, towns, urban-type settlements, and rural villages, constitute changes in residence, but movements wholly within them do not. In the U.S. somewhat less than 20 percent of the population moves each year with one-third of that percentage representing migration to new counties of residence.[6]

The ratio of urban arrivals to urban population has been around seven per hundred in recent years, roughly indicating the intensity of arrivals. The ratio of urban arrivals net of departures to urban population has been in excess of one per hundred, revealing that Soviet cities and urban settlements have been growing more than 1 percent a year due to migration. These same ratios for regions may be used to identify divergences from the all-Union pattern. According to the 1967 data,[7] areas of the eastern development regions that contained deposits of oil, coal, and gas—parts of West Siberia, the Far East, and Kazakhstan—exhibited high rates of urban arrival with average or slow rates of urban growth. High arrival rates with high rates of urban growth were experienced in the central regions of the Russian republic, in the Southwest of the Ukraine, and also in Moldavia, Belorussia, and Lithuania. These high-growth areas still had substantial rural populations providing significant numbers of potential migrants. The Transcaucasian republics (Armenia, Azerbaydzhan, and Georgia) had very low arrival rates and low rates of urban growth; the rural inhabitants of Transcaucasian and Central Asian regions did not often migrate to urban localities. In Central Asia, however, urban populations did receive many extraterritorial migrants and thus grew at rates close to the U.S.S.R. average.

Migration and Distance

The general finding that migration between points varies inversely with distance is true for the Soviet case. Most migration occurred within or between bordering major economic regions. From the central regions people migrated to the Northwest and Urals, from the Urals into West Siberia, and from West Siberia into East Siberia, and from there into the Far East. During the early 1960s, more than half of the growth of urban population in the Northwest

5. Vestnik statistiki (No. 10, 1968), p. 89; (No. 3, 1971), p. 74; (No. 11, 1971), pp. 77; and (No. 2, 1973), p. 89.

6. U.S., Department of Commerce, "Mobility of the Population of the United States, March 1970 to March 1971," *Current Population Reports,* Series P–20, No. 235 (April 1972).

7. *Vestnik statistiki* (No. 10, 1968), p. 89.

derived from the out-migration of neighboring central regions. The same was true for urban growth in the Central region containing Moscow; more than half of growth of urban population derived from out-migration of contiguous regions. The figures for urban growth resulting from migration out of adjacent regions were 60 percent for West Siberia, 50 percent for East Siberia, and 70 percent for the Far East.[8] The percentage of urban arrivals from own republic within each of the fifteen republics constituting the Soviet Union, for the most part, varies between 50 and 75 percent; states continuing to have large rural populations are found at the upper end of the spectrum and the Central Asian republics, in particular, are at the lower end.[9]

Recently published data on urban arrivals in the Russian republic during 1966 indicate that the numbers arriving decline exponentially as distances increase.[10] Researchers tabulated a percentage distribution of migrants settling in urban areas according to distance of migration. The "cell width" of the distribution was taken as 250 kilometers or 155 miles. Thus, it was learned that 41 percent of all arrivals came from a distance of 155 miles or less, 9 percent from a distance of 155 to 311 miles, 7 percent from a distance of 311 to 466 miles, and so forth. According to our analysis, the formula $P = 2464 \cdot D^{-0.97}$ where P is the percentage of migrants and D is the distance in miles, describes the entire distribution well ($R^2 = .98$). This fit indicates that a 1 percent increase in distance results in an approximately 1 percent decrease in the number of migrants.[11] Borrowing the notion from physics that attraction varies directly with the masses of objects (let us say objects i and j) and inversely with the *square* of the distance (D_{ij}) between them, gravity models, as applied to migration analysis, suggest (according to $M_{ij} = (P_i \cdot P_j) / D_{ij}^2$) that the exponent for distance might be -2 rather than a number close to -1.[12] But migration studies of the U.S., for example, using regression equations based upon the gravity model analogy typically estimate the exponent of the distance variable to be close to -1.0.[13] Thus, the present finding for the U.S.S.R. of -0.97 is consistent with the usual empirical finding.

8. P. P. Litviakov (ed.), *Demograficheskie problemy zaniatosti* (Moscow: Ekonomika, 1969), p. 170.

9. *Vestnik statistiki* (No. 10, 1968), pp. 90–91.

10. A. G. Volkov (ed.), *Statistika migratsiia naseleniia* (Moscow: Statistika, 1973), p. 43.

11. This follows from an understanding of elasticity, a concept often used in economics to measure the responsiveness of one variable to changes in the level of another.

12. See Walter Isard, *Methods of Regional Analysis: An Introduction to Regional Science* (Cambridge, Mass.: M.I.T. Press, 1960), pp. 493–568.

13. Probably the most famous work finding that the coefficient should be -1, not -2, is that of Zipf. See George K. Zipf, "The P_1P_2/D Hypothesis: On the Intercity Movement of Persons," *American Sociological Review*, XI (October 1946), 677–86. In addition, see Ira S. Lowry, *Migration and Metropolitan Growth: Two Analytical Models* (San Francisco: Chandler Publishing, 1966); Michael J. Greenwood and Patrick J. Gormely, "A Comparison of the Determinants of White and Non-White Interstate Migration," *Demography*, VIII, No. 1 (February 1971), 141–55; Michael J. Greenwood and Douglas Sweetland, "The Determinants of Migration between Standard Metropolitan Statistical Areas," *Demography*,

Data on arrivals at urban points also show the relative importance of shorter-distance migration. In Table 3.1 are listed the percentages of urban arrivals who left points within the same republic. Of course, only a very imperfect picture of the importance of distance is rendered since the geographical areas of the republics vary greatly, the population compositions (with regard to age, sex, and ethnicity) differ, and rural-to-rural migration (surely dependent upon distance) is omitted.

Examining migration into and out of the smaller-sized oblasts[14] reveals the same relationship between migration and distance. The size of an oblast in the Ukraine was approximately 10,000 square miles, an area somewhat smaller than that of Albania or Belgium. In the 1959–63 period, about 33 percent of all urban-to-urban movements involving Ukrainian oblasts occured within a single oblast; of all urban arrivals more than 50 percent departed from points in the same oblast. The corresponding figures for the Ukraine as a single geographical unit of analysis were 67.0 percent (for urban to urban) and 71.9 percent (for all points to urban).[15]

Migration and Diversity

State of progress. According to Ravenstein and Lee, migration increases with the "state of progress" and the "development of industry" within an area.[16] This observation applies to the Soviet case. For example, Northern Kazakhstan, an area of agricultural development during the 1950s, became a region of rapid industrial growth that continued through the 1960s. Industrial transport-supply centers and industrial areas developed so rapidly within the Kustanskii and Pavlodarskii Oblasts that urban populations grew by factors of approximately 3 during 1955–65.[17] The demand for labor in urban areas consistently exceeded supply, and labor turnover was high. Within certain cities, in 1965 alone more than half the persons listed on the labor roles of the various industrial enterprises and construction organizations terminated employment; about three-quarters of all terminations were labor turnover, meaning that they were either worker-initiated separations or dismissals for infractions of work discipline.[18]

IV, No. 4 (November 1972), 665–82; and James D. Traver and R. Douglas McLeod, "A Test and Modification of Zipf's Hypothesis for Predicting Interstate Migration," *Demography*, X, No. 2 (May 1973), 259–76.

14. The reader may wish to consult Appendix A where the nature of Soviet administrative units is briefly described and the relationships among them are indicated. The word "oblast" comes directly from the Russian *oblast'*. The first form, which is now rather standard in Western scholarly discussion of Soviet regional problems, will be used here.

15. P. I. Bagrii et al. (eds.), *Voprosy demografii* (Kiev: Statistika, 1968), pp. 143–44

16. Lee, "A Theory of Migration," p. 54.

17. T. A. Ashimbaev (ed.), *Naselenie i trudovye resursy gorodov Severnogo Kazakhstana* (Alma-Ata: Nauka, 1970), p. 14.

18. Ibid., p. 99.

The employment situation differed in the coal-mining cities of the Urals. Prior to 1959 both employment and population had been growing, but in the 1960s production in the sector declined as new coal resources were developed elsewhere and workers left the cities. Over the 1959–68 period the total number of arrivals and departures from the cities was 1.9 times their population—with, of course, more departures than arrivals.[19] Out-migration was dominant, and much migratory movement was found associated with a high *level* of industrialization and slow *rate* of growth. In general, high levels of industrial development seemed to be associated with high levels of interregional migration. This was observed in the Urals situation where three-fifths of out-migrants from the coal-mining cities left the region, and it was also seen in the Ukraine. In the most developed areas of the Ukraine's Don-Dnieper region, the intraregional component of net migration into the cities was comparatively low, about one-third of the total; while in some western, predominantly agricultural and industrially undeveloped areas with an adequate or more than adequate labor supply for agriculture, the local component was approximately four-fifths of the total.[20]

The 1970 census data allow a comparison between the numbers of internal migrants per thousand population in the various republics[21] and the levels of national income per capita,[22] a measure of industrialization. These sets of figures reveal a positive relationship between the two variables; their linear correlation coefficient is 0.74, a figure which would be 0.81 except for the joint observation on the republic of Kazakhstan. An area of national economic development during the 1950s and 1960s in connection with agricultural, coal-mining, and ferrous metallurgy campaigns, Kazakhstan had a higher than expected level of population mobility, most likely due to the high proportion of prior movers in its population.

Rural-urban movement. The volume of migration within the U.S.S.R. appears to have depended very much on rural-urban differences. Many rural inhabitants were dissatisfied with their circumstances and found attractive the prospect of working in larger population centers. Living conditions on state and collective farms and throughout rural localities lagged behind those of urban areas, despite Soviet efforts to reduce the differences. Before government procurement prices for agricultural products were again raised, before restrictions on private plot production relaxed, and before a minimum level for

19. D. I. Valentei et al. (eds.), *Narodonaselenie i ekonomika* (Moscow: Ekonomika, 1967), p. 102.

20. V. V. Pokshishevskii, "Migration of Population, U.S.S.R," in U.S., Joint Publications Research Service, *Translations on U.S.S.R. Resources*, JPRS 49279 (November 19, 1969), p. 55.

21. Number of persons who changed place of residence within the same republic during 1968–69 [*Vestnik statistiki* (No. 2, 1973), p. 86] divided by thousands of population January 1, 1969 [*Vestnik statistiki* (No. 2, 1971), pp. 85–86].

22. National Income in 1968 [S.S.S.R., TsSU, *Narodnoe khoziaistvo SSR v 1968* (Moscow: Statistika, 1969), p. 580] divided by estimated mid-year population.

the collective farmer's annual wages set (after Party Secretary Khrushchev's resignation in 1964), the remuneration to agricultural workers, especially collective farmers, was low. Although these changes improved the situation somewhat, housing, public health, health services, educational opportunities, transportation services, and trade services usually remained inferior; and retail prices were generally higher in rural areas.

According to Soviet researchers, however, the difficulty lay not so much with the differences in conditions as with people's attitudes towards agricultural work. One survey revealed that secondary school graduates ranked agriculture as least attractive of all occupations, except for work in the service sector.[23] Another attitude survey found that young agricultural workers scored work in the city (in comparison with their work) more favorably on working conditions, length of work day, sanitary-hygienic conditions, requirements for raising skill levels, and arduousness *(tiazhest')*.[24]

Between the two censuses the urban population of the U.S.S.R. increased 36.0 percent while the rural population decreased by 2.8 percent. On a net basis more than 16 million rural inhabitants moved to urban localities. Throughout all regions there was net rural-to-urban migration. Regional differences in rates of natural growth and rural-to-urban migration combined to produce an inverse relationship between levels of economic development and rates of rural population growth. Thus, in Russia slow rates of natural increase and average rates of out-migration in rural areas led to a 12.2 percent decline in rural population while in Uzbekistan, one of the Central Asian republics, high rates of natural increase and low rates of out-migration yielded a 38.1 percent increase.[25]

Rates of rural-to-urban net migration may be defined by:

$$R_j = \frac{M_{.j} - M_{j.}}{P_j} \times 1000$$

where $M_{.j}$ stands for the registered urban arrivals, $M_{j.}$, the registered urban departures, both over the course of a year, and P_j represents the urban population at the beginning of the year; these rates during 1967 for the various Union republics are listed in Table 3.2. Also listed are groupings of regional rates in relation to the all-Union rate.

Six of the seven republics of Transcaucasia and Central Asia are in the low or very low category of part B of Table 3.2. "The problem of the immobility of rural population in certain parts of the U.S.S.R." is the phrase frequently encountered in Soviet discussion of this circumstance which is often linked to

23. V. I. Perevedentsev, *Migratsiia naseleniia i trudovye problemy Sibiri* (Novosibirsk: Nauka, 1966), p. 153.

24. T. I. Zaslavskaia (ed.), *Migratsiia sel'skogo naseleniia* (Moscow: Mysl', 1970), p. 204.

25. V. I. Perevedentsev, "Migratsiia naseleniia i ispol'zovanie trudovykh resursov," *Voprosy ekonomiki* (No. 9, 1973), p. 85.

the significant net interregional migration into Central Asia. Rather low rates of rural-to-urban migration are observed in relatively industrialized and developed areas like Latvia, Estonia, the Northwest, the Center, the Urals, and the Don-Dnieper. In most of these regions the percentage of rural population is rather low and industrial growth has slowed. The opposite situation prevailed in areas like the Moldavian and Belorussian republics and the Southwest and Central Chernozem regions which had high or very high rates of urban growth due to migration.

Somewhat surprisingly, census results show that Ravenstein's generalization—that the natives of towns are less migratory than those of rural parts—appears to apply to recent Soviet experience. They indicate that among movers during the 1968–69 period, the most recent origin was rural for 6.9 million of the total 13.9 million; the remaining 7.0 million had urban origins.[26] When these figures are expressed on an annual basis and are related to rural and urban population numbers for January 1, 1969, they suggest indices of mobility of 33 and 27 movers per thousand population in rural and urban areas, respectively. It may additionally be noted that the moves during 1968–69 were distributed by origin and destination as follows: *rural to rural,* 2.5 million or 18 percent of the total; *rural to urban,* 4.4 million or 32 percent of the total; *urban to rural,* 1.7 million or 12 percent of the total; and *urban to urban,* 5.3 million or 38 percent of the total.[27]

Diversity among peoples. Lee suggests that volume of migration varies with diversity of the people; that is, where there is great uniformity among the people with regard to race, ethnicity, education, or income one may expect less migration than in opposite circumstances.[28] Data provided by the 1970 census allow us to measure ethnic homogeneity in the various republics of the Soviet Union. For example, the 1970 census reports that in Armenia 88.6 percent of the population was of Armenian ethnicity, 5.9 percent Azerbaydzan, 2.7 percent Russian, and so forth. Thus, the republic with 88.6 percent of the population Armenian exhibits a rather high degree of homogeneity. But Kazakhstan with 42.4 percent of the population Russian, 32.6 percent Kazakh, 7.2 percent Ukrainian, and so forth is more diverse and may be said to exhibit low homogeneity.

A measure of homogeneity may be calculated for all republics by using a Gini coefficient, a summary statistic frequently used in economics to characterize the degree of concentration of wealth or income among persons in a population. In the present case ethnic homogeneity is associated with concentration and ethnic diversity with an even distribution. The formula used for the coefficient here was:

26. *Vestnik statistiki* (No. 2, 1973), p. 85.
27. Ibid.
28. Lee, "Theory of Migration," pp. 52–53.

$$G_j = \frac{5000 - X_j}{5000}$$

where: $X_j = 10E_1 + 30E_2 + 50E_3 + 70E_4 + 90\,(100 - E - E_2 - E_3 - E_4)$. E_i is the percentage of the republic population of the ith nationality with i ranging in descending order over the four most numerous nationalities. The E_i values are from the 1970 Census.[29] The coefficients range from 0.72 for homogeneous Armenia to 0.35 for diverse Kazakhstan. Lee's generalization would apparently indicate that areas with high coefficients, indicating ethnic homogeneity, would be areas of low internal migration while regions with low coefficients would have high levels of population movement occurring within their borders. The expected relationship does not appear to hold among the sample of fifteen Union republics. The linear correlation coefficient between ethnic homogeneity and internal migration[30] equals 0.14, whereas the hypothesis suggested a negative coefficient not close to zero. Actually in the case of the U.S.S.R., it appears that the most important statistical relationship between internal migration and ethnic factors is the strong positive relationship between the propensity to migrate and Russian nationality. Adequate attention is paid to this important point in later discussion.

STREAM AND COUNTERSTREAM

According to Lee's generalizations, migration takes place within well-defined streams, following which counterstreams develop. The efficiency of a stream in relation to counterstream depends upon living conditions at the two points. Streams of migration, defined as established routes of point-to-point journey to take up new residence, are thought to develop because migration reduces costs, difficulties, and uncertainty for subsequent movers. The efficiency of stream from a point i to a point j may be defined by M_{ij} / M_{ji} where M_{ij} is the number of migrants going from i to j and M_{ji} is a measure of the reverse stream. The ratio, M_{ij} / M_{ji} is high when: (1) "minus" or negative factors at origin i compel or motivate migration; (2) the ith and jth locations are dissimilar; (3) intervening obstacles, or costs, or difficulties, are great; and (4) times are prosperous.[31]

Interregional Migration Streams

One cannot long study Soviet migration, especially interregional movement, without becoming aware of the existence of streams. During the 1959–70 intercensal period, the state attempted to increase streams from the West to the labor deficient development regions of the East. Prior to this period, well-established streams exhibiting efficiency ratios greater than one, had existed to

29. S.S.S.R., TsSU, *Itogi Vseoiuznoi perepisi naseleniia 1970 goda, IV: Natsional'nyi sostav naseleniia SSSR* (Moscow: Statistika, 1973), pp. 12–15.
30. As defined in note 21.
31. Lee, "Theory of Migration," pp. 55–56.

the Urals, Siberia, the Far East, and Kazakhstan; but during the late 1950s rates of growth due to migration fell in all regions and became negative in the Urals, West Siberia, and perhaps East Siberia. Counterstreams (primarily back to the Ukraine and central Russia) increased and new streams out of the labor-deficient regions (to Central Asia) developed. This latter development became so important that some observers came to regard the developing regions as an "intermediary point" *(perevalochnyi punkt)* through which Russia, the Ukraine, and Moldavia supplied skilled labor to the labor-surplus Central Asian republics. During 1959–65 Russia's four eastern regions, containing 45 percent of its population, accounted for 70 percent of the republic's substantial, net out-migration.[32]

Tables listing the annual number of urban arrivals in various destination regions according to region of origin are probably the richest source of information for determining interregional migration streams. These data, derived from the population registration system mentioned earlier, enable the identification of important interregional migration streams. For the year 1969[33] the information allows the study of migration flows between major economic regions within the U.S.S.R., rather than between Union republics. To examine flows using the former set of units is preferable because they divide the huge Russian republic into geographical units more nearly equal in area and population size. There are 19 major economic regions; thus in theory there are 342 (19 × 18) possible interregional flows. However, in practice the U.S.S.R. has failed to report on those involving movement between region outside Russia and the Ukraine and on movement between regions within them; so that data on only 264 streams are available. Of these one may select flows meeting the criteria:

1. $M_{ij} \geq 15{,}000$
2. $M_{ij} \;/\; 1(P_i \cdot P_j)^{1/2} \geq 1.5$

where M_{ij} is the number of arrivals registered at urban points of region j from region i during 1969 and P_i and P_j are thousands of population in regions i and j on January 1, 1969. The streams thus identified are listed in Table 3.3.

The table reveals several interesting points. First, 23 of the 29 streams are between contiguous areas. While in absolute terms, much of the migration between adjacent major economic regions in the U.S.S.R. undoubtedly involved long distances, in relative terms, this finding supports the earlier generalization about migration and distance. Second, there were important streams into the eastern areas of national economic development. Most of the streams between noncontiguous regions, each of which is marked by asterisk in the table, were either to or from the development regions (West Siberia, East Siberia, the Far East, and Kazakhstan). However, of the twelve streams involving at least one development region, only those from the Urals to West

32. Litviakov, *Demograficheskie problemy*, pp. 168–69.
33. *Vestnik statistiki* (No. 3, 1971), pp. 74–83.

Siberia, the North Caucasus to the Far East, and Central Asia to Kazakhstan would clearly have been considered "rational" by the state in the sense of flowing from labor-surplus to labor-deficient areas. The other streams were either in the wrong direction or were unproductive in the sense of being between pairs of development regions. Third, among the predominantly single direction streams, the region losing population was in several instances a slowly growing industrial region (the Volga-Vyatka or the Urals) or an agricultural region (the Central Chernozem or North Caucasus).

Selecting all streams in which urban arrivals net of departures ($M_{ij} - M_{ji}$) exceeded 10,000 identifies several important interregional streams with high efficiency. These are listed in Table 3.4 along with indices of efficiency (M_{ij} / M_{ji}). Judged principally on the basis of industrial development and climate, in the majority of cases, conditions of life at origin and destination were dissimilar. The Center, Don-Dnieper, and the Urals were industrial centers, and the Central Chernozem, North Caucasus, Southwest, and South were rural areas having low gross industrial output per capita. The South, Southwest, North Caucasus, and perhaps Kazakhstan had relatively attractive climates. Much of the migration out of the Urals must have been related to its slow rate of industrial growth. All of these circumstances are consistent with the high efficiencies predicted by the empirical generalizations of Ravenstein and Lee.

The issue of efficiency of streams to the development regions from interregional migration received special attention. High rates of labor turnover naturally led Soviet analysts to ponder how efficiency ratios could be raised. Much of the discussion focused on the related question of the adaptability of migrants. Studies showed that a given year's out-migrants tended to be the in-migrants of one, two, or three years ago. Representative data for Siberian cities are shown in Table 3.5. In the early 1960s, about 80 percent of the persons leaving the cities of one territory of East Siberia had only arrived within the previous five years. Most of those leaving returned to the regions from which they had come. Ninety percent of those who had arrived from cities returned to cities; 50 percent of those who had arrived from rural localities returned to rural localities.[34]

It appears that persons moving to rural localities in the eastern and Kazakh regions often stayed for a few years and then left. In a particular region of Kazakhstan out-migration rates from certain state farms were as high for residents in their third and fourth years as they were in the first two years. Notorious for leaving were the Ukrainians and Belorussians. Unlike elsewhere, in Kazakhstan most of the interregional migrants who settled originally on farms and then left did not return home, but rather moved to urban areas within Kazakhstan where work was secured in construction and industry. In 1963, of all families leaving places to which they had recently moved, only 7 percent returned to previous places of residence.[35]

34. Perevedenstev, *Migratsiia naseleniia Sibiri*, p. 106.
35. G. Vechkanov, "Raising the Effectiveness of the Territorial Redistribution of Labor Resources," *Problems of Economics*, XII (October 1969), 61–62.

Rural-to-Urban Streams

Intraregional migration streams also existed. Unfortunately, there are no extensive data on them. In the late 1960s, the Siberian Division of the Academy of Science studied in great detail the migration of rural population within the Novosibirsk area of West Siberia. While their study is limited by its regional focus, it nevertheless uncovered much about intraregional migration streams, a greatly neglected subject.

Table 3.6 presents data on migration into and out of the rural areas of Novosibirsk Oblast. Although the table shows the relatively high degree of rural-to-rural migration, it is clear that the most important streams in terms of volume led from rural settlements to medium- and large-sized cities (more than 50,000 and 100,000 persons, respectively). These streams accounted for 90 percent of the population loss owing to net migration from rural settlements.

Indices of efficiency of rural-to-urban streams $M_{.j} / M_{j.}$ throughout the U.S.S.R. during 1967 are displayed in Table 3.7. $M_{.j}$ is the number of urban arrivals in region j from rural localities throughout the U.S.S.R.; $M_{j.}$ is the number of departures from urban areas of republic j for rural destinations throughout the U.S.S.R. It is interesting that central Russian regions where rural-to-urbal movement has long been occurring had relatively high efficiency levels. In these regions it is likely that many migrants had acquaintances and friends in urban places who stood ready to aid them upon arrival, thus making settlement easy. But in general, all the indices seem to be quite high. A somewhat paradoxical reason for this is that rural migrants were sometimes denied permission to settle in cities. For example, in Novosibirsk (undoubtedly the most attractive Siberian city to many enjoying or anticipating the advantage of urban life) in both 1960 and 1965 approximately two-thirds of all rural persons arriving were denied permission to register and settle.[36] Those denied did not necessarily return home; oftentimes they were advised of near or distant urban settlements where they would be welcome. In the light of this, it seems reasonable to presume that the privilege of settling in an urban locality may have been valued dearly by some. In this regard, it is interesting to note that only 10 percent of rural in-migrants from Novosibirsk Oblast into the city in 1960 had left the city by 1969[37]—an extreme, but suggestive example of the valuation of urban tenure.

CHARACTERISTICS OF MIGRANTS

The Economic Motive

According to Ravenstein, streams of migration due to various other causes cannot compare in volume with those which arise "from the desire inherent in most men to better themselves;"[38] Lenin similarly stated that one certain law

36. Zaslavskaia, *Migratsiia sel'skogo naseleniia*, p. 266.
37. Ibid.
38. See Lee, "Theory of Migration," p. 48.

of migration is the "striving of workers to go where things are better."[39] Most observers likewise agree that the economic motive predominated in recent Soviet migration. V. I. Perevedentsev, the leading student, put it this way: "Long experience in the study of the migration allows us to conclude, the economic factors in territorial redistribution are decisive, and that no other measures can lead to rational distribution of labor forces, if economic factors impede this."[40] Workers moved where wages were higher and services greater, housing more plentiful, retail trade more extensive, and climate more attractive.

This propensity to move where things were better was strong not only among industrial workers, as might be imagined, but also among agricultural workers. The observation in one area, that the migration balances of economically strong collective farms were generally positive while those of others were usually negative, in direct proportion to the weakness of the farms, was regarded as typical. On collective farms with high indices of fixed capital per worker, high net profit, high productivity, and high remuneration, there was little out-migration.[41] But many agricultural workers sought a better life by moving to the city, usually to take up industrial work or to study. In the 1960s Soviet planners viewed rural-to-urban migration ambivalently. On the one hand, continuing industrialization and the growth of service sectors required increased labor in the cities. It was also true that agriculture needed additional trained labor, and therefore had to send some of its cadres to urban schools for training. On the other hand, it was perfectly obvious why people went to the city. Workers left to enjoy the higher pay and prestige, greater vacation benefits, less arduous work, and more regular hours of industry; and students went to gain nonagricultural training intending eventually to obtain urban work.

Since workers valued attractive living and working conditions, they left deficient areas which, of course, included the development regions of the East. Although the state used regional coefficients and premiums to raise wage payments, real wages fell short of those being paid elsewhere. The Siberian regions, at least in many localities, also had a relatively small supply of goods for retail trade, poor public transport, and diminished possibilities for private plot and domestic economy. Housing was, of course, also deficient.

Selectivity

During 1959–70 migration was selective, at least according to age, sex, education, and ethnicity, meaning that the frequency of migration changed in relation to these variables. The notion of selectivity emphasizes that migration is nonrandom in the sense that a set of migrants most certainly may not be regarded as a random sample from a population.

39. See D. I. Valentei et al. (eds.), *Problemy migratsiia naseleniia i trudovykh resursov* (Moscow: Statistika, 1970), p. 70.

40. Perevedentsev, "Migratisiia naseleniia," p. 41.

41. L. Bulochnikova, "Sel'skaia migratsiia i puty ee regulirovaniia," *Planovoe khoziaistvo* (No. 8, 1969), p. 72.

Age. Persons of working age constituted a large part of migration streams. In the early 1960s such persons (men aged 15–59 years and women aged 16–54 years) made up about 75 percent of all migrants while only approximately 54 percent of the population. Around 50 percent of all migrants belonged to the subgroup aged 16–30 which represented about 24 percent of the total population.[42]

Data for 1969 show that the percentage of urban arrivals in the working ages was quite uniform throughout the U.S.S.R. regions, around 84 percent except for the Baltic region where there were relatively more arrivals of children and persons over 60 years. On a net arrival basis the percentages of those of working age ranged more widely, being high in relation to the all-Union figure of 73 in Soviet Asia (the three eastern Russian regions, Kazakhstan, Central Asia, and Transcaucasia) and low in several slowly growing industrial regions (Volga-Vyatka, Urals, and Don-Dnieper).[43] High percentages of migrants of working age moving into Asian cities on net account may have been typical throughout the 1960s. According to one source, in various Northern Kazakh cities working-age people comprised from 79 to 85 percent of the numbers migrating, with the subgroup of ages 16–24 making up 41 to 57 percent.[44]

It is interesting to note, concerning the 1969 data, that among persons 60 years or older there were net out-flows from or only nominal in-flows into the cities of Central Asia, Azerbaydzhan and Georgia, East Siberia, and the Far East. Because each of these areas had much of its indigenous population still residing in rural areas, it is possible that what is revealed in these cases was a general tendency of urban inhabitants with ties to the surrounding rural countryside to leave the cities and return to nonnuclear families upon leaving the labor force.

Census data concerning change-of-residence movement of all kinds during 1968–69 indicate much the same kind of age selectivity.[45] The data show that 72.5 percent of all movers were of the working ages, while 64.2 percent of the entire population were of those ages at the time of the 1970 census. The percentages imply an index of percentage working-age movers to percentage of working-age population of 1.34; in the various republics similar indices are found except, again, for the Central Asian republics of Uzbekistan and Turkmenia and for the Azerbaydzhan republic, areas where the indices are considerably higher.

The peak of rural departure among inhabitants aged 15–19, deriving from the life-cycle events of leaving school or continuing training elsewhere, is well known. Some data concerning the subsequent employment of graduates from

42. Litviakov, *Demograficheskie problemy*, p. 159, and J. W. Brackett, "Demographic Trends and Population Policy in the Soviet Union," in U.S., Congress, Joint Economic Committee, *Dimensions of Soviet Economic Power* (Washington: D.C.: U.S. Government Printing Office, 1962), p. 564.

43. *Vestnik statistiki* (No. 3, 1971), p. 76.

44. Ashimbaev, *Naselenie Severnogo Kazakhstana*, p. 95.

45. *Vestnik statistiki* (No. 2, 1973), p. 87.

the rural schools of Novosibirsk Oblast during 1964–66 are shown in Table 3.8. Those finishing incomplete-secondary school were probably about 15 years old and the others completing secondary school, around 17 or 18. During this period more than twice as many graduated from incomplete-secondary school than secondary school.[46] All of the first category going to work in the city and some of the same category receiving additional training at technical and vocational-training institutes left rural areas. Moreover, significant numbers of males who returned to the farm were probably called shortly thereafter for military service. Among the second category (those finishing secondary school), persons obtaining urban employment or receiving further training went to the city and thereby, in the majority of cases, committed themselves at least tentatively to nonagricultural employment and urban residence.[47]

It may be estimated from the data that approximatly a third of each year's graduates went to the city.[48] This high figure cannot be precisely related to the persons aged 15–19 leaving rural areas, but it is consistent with the available evidence. According to Novosibirsk data, the 15–19 age group comprised only 6.2 percent of the population, yet it contributed 16.6 percent of all departures, and according to a more recent survey also taken in West Siberia, this same age group accounted for 23.5 percent of departures of working age population while making up only 16.7 percent of the population.[49] The latter survey states that during 1964–66 the ratio of rural departures of persons aged 15–19 divided by their initial population was .48[50] which, in a stationary population, would imply an approximate annual departure rate of 16 percent of the age group. Of course, people returned from the city in substantial numbers, but the counterstream for 15–19-year-olds was quite weak, being only 47 arrivals per 100 departures in comparison with the overall rate of 70.[51]

A question arises as to whether the West Siberian experience was unique, since the special situation of rapid industrial development in the region may have accounted for the observed pattern of age-selective, rural out-migration. At least in comparison to the European U.S.S.R., it has been emphasized that the Siberian experience was not extreme at all; in fact, the exodus of rural youth was said to have been even more massive in the West. Although undoubtedly measuring the effect of rural out-migration and, unfortunately in

46. Zaslavskaia, *Migratsiia sel'skogo naseleniia,* p. 249.
47. Ibid., pp. 250–51.
48. Assuming that 5.4 percent of incomplete-secondary school graduates went to the city for training (one-tenth of the percentage of those receiving additional training), and then adding the 17.4 percent that acceded to urban work, implies that 22.8 percent of this overall category went to the city. For secondary school graduates, the corresponding figures add to 53.7 percent when it is assumed that all those who received additional training had to go to the city. Weighing the former figure 2.3 times as heavily as the latter (that is, more than 2 times, see text above) yields a combined percentage of 32.2.
49. Zaslavskaia, *Migratsiia sel'skogo naseleniia,* p. 108.
50. Ibid., pp. 108–9.
51. Ibid., p. 108.

addition, the demographic effect of World War II, an observer noted that on certain farms in Belorussia only 10 to 30 percent of the persons born during 1937–47 still worked in the area and that between 1955 and 1965 the average age of rural populations had increased from 36–38 years to 38–46 years.[52]

Sex. Migration was also selective by sex. Among rural-to-urban migrants of working age during 1959–65, men made up 53 percent of the total; at the same time males constituted approximately 47 percent of the rural population of working age. Among 19–22-year-olds women were more numerous in the rural-to-urban streams, due primarily to military service by males and secondarily to movement by females at the time of their marriages. With regard to the latter cause, it may be noted that among those aged 16 to 18 (ages prior to military service by males) the percentages of women and men were nearly equal. Among all rural-to-urban migrants, 50.6 percent were male. Men accounted for larger proportions in Transcaucasia and Central Asia while women were relatively more important among arrivals in Latvia and Estonia, centers of the textile industry employing many women.[53]

According to 1969 data, 55 percent of all urban arrivals and 50 percent of urban arrivals net of departures were male. In the Soviet registration system, the latter flow would be close to the rural-to-urban flow, since the twice recorded urban-to-urban moves would cancel each other out of the total. The 50 percent figure for 1969 may thus be compared with the 50.6 percent figure for 1959–65 as an indication of the stability of age-selectivity. The percentage of men arriving in the cities of Transcaucasia, Tadzhikistan, and Uzbekistan continued to be high. Among all the regions of the European U.S.S.R. (including the Urals) the percentages of women in the arrival streams at urban points were greater than their percentages in the departure streams, indicating that the streams of women into urban settlements were more efficient than those of men; the opposite situation prevailed in most of the non-European regions.[54]

Nationality. Migration was also selective according to nationality. Work done in the early 1960s indicated that Russians were very numerous among arrivals in West Siberia, quite independently of the effect of their population numbers and distances involved. Generally it was found that the percentages of Russians arriving from various origins exceeded by a factor of four to seven their percentages in the population from which they came.[55] Data from the 1970 census are also informative.[56] Relating the approximate number of persons moving per year during 1968–69 to the 1970 population size of each of

52. Ibid., p. 112.

53. Litviakov, *Demograficheskie problemy*, pp. 181–82.

54. *Vestnik statistiki* (No. 2, 1971), p. 75.

55. V. I. Perevedentsev, *Migratsiia naseleniia*, p. 136 and S.S.S.R., TsSU, *Itogi vsesoiuznoi perepisi naseleniia 1970 goda, IV: Natsional'nyi sostav naseleniia SSSR* (Moscow: Statistika, 1973), pp. 12–15.

56. *Vestnik statistiki* (No. 2, 1973), pp. 87–88.

the nationalities in the U.S.S.R. indicates that Russians were the most mobile. The incidence of moving among them was 34 movers per thousand population while the same measure throughout the entire population was 29. Inasmuch as Russians comprised 53 percent of the Soviet Union's population in 1970, the difference between the two figures appears substantial. An unweighted average of mobility among eighteen of the twenty most numerous nationalities equals 17, revealing a level of Russian mobility twice that of other nationalities. The Ukrainians, Belorussians, and Tartars, and the Lithuanians, Latvians, and Estonians also exhibited high levels of mobility. Census data reveal that the number of Russians present in a particular Union republic provides a good partial indication of the level of internal migration. The coefficient of linear correlation between the level of internal mobility[57] and the percentage of population Russian is 0.68. Republics having higher internal mobility than would be expected on the simple basis of the percentage of Russians present were those such as Lithuania and Belorussia where rural-to-urban movement was taking place at a fast pace.

While explanations running in terms of "Russification" or even "colonial exploitation" may be of some value in understanding the predominance of Russians in migration streams, an important consideration is the fact that 14 percent of the ethnic Russian population, about 16.2 million persons, lived outside Russia at the time of the 1959 census. In only three Union republics did Russians constitute less than 10 percent of the population, and since they were most likely concentrated in urban settlements, sizable enclaves of Russian settlement existed throughout the U.S.S.R. Despite Lee's notion that diversity increases the potential for migration, it must be remembered in the case of the U.S.S.R. that different nationalities usually spoke different languages, so that a migrant who went to a place where none of his nationality already lived, faced formidable problems. Thus, even in the absence of a 1959–70 policy to settle Russians outside Russia, the existence of enclaves in various regions made migration for the nationality relatively easy.

Skill and education. Migration was also selective by skill and education. The industrialization of the U.S.S.R. in the 1930s transformed part of an overwhelmingly rural population into an industrial labor force. Over the years the influx of rural inhabitants established a legendary record of peasant ineptitude in the factories. Perhaps having the inexperienced and uneducated countryside workers of the 1930s in mind, Soviet students of labor problems sometimes referred to the migrants of recent years, who were highly qualified and responsive to working and living conditions, as the "new" migrants. Enterprises often knew exactly what kind of labor they wanted. In this connection, in Tashkent, a "Russified" city in the opinion of many, enterprises recruited extraregional (that is, skilled and non–Central Asian) labor so extensively that the appropriate Council of Ministers had to recommend that the practice be

57. As defined in note 21.

stopped since there was an ample supply of labor in Tashkent, and the present author might add, in all of Central Asia.[58]

Among rural-to-urban migrants there were both "new" and "old" types. In the "new" category could be counted secondary school graduates progressing to further training, administrators, and the mechanizers who repaired, maintained, and operated agricultural equipment. In the "old" category were found young, unskilled males (sometimes with families) who remained in demand in the construction sector especially. The classification of urban-bound migrants from rural localities of Novosibirsk Oblast during 1964–66 (see Table 3.9) shows that although public attention focused on the loss of skilled labor from rural localities, other groups left, too.

Migration by Stages

An additional characteristic of migration, besides the importance of the economic motive and the operation of selectivity, is that it occurs in stages. Ravenstein proposed that migration proceeds as an absorption process by which growing towns drew people from their environs and the gaps left by the out-migrants are filled by in-migrants from farther away. Whether this characteristic holds for the period studied in the U.S.S.R. is a moot question. Unfortunately there are not sufficient data to reach a conclusion. On the one hand, the "intermediary-point" role that West Siberia played in the eventual settlement in Central Asia of persons from central Russia has already been noted. Although somewhat different from Ravenstein's idea, due to the distances involved, the phenomenon was nevertheless one of movement in stages. It is also true that the southern regions of Siberia supplied significant numbers of workers to the Far East and Far North and that urban-to-urban out-migration from West Siberia was often interpreted as drawing in migrants from surrounding rural areas.

On the other hand, any notion of isolated rural inhabitants moving to villages, villagers moving to small towns, and town residents moving to small cities, with the process continuing to the large cities, would not seem to fit the facts well. Youths planning to leave villages usually intended to head directly to the big cities, since small urban settlements (places having population less than 50,000) did not have the sought attractions. During the 1960s small- and some medium-sized cities emerged, even in official light, as not having been very appealing places to live, inasmuch as they lacked many of the services of big cities and had labor forces in excess of local needs.

CONCLUSIONS

Despite assertions of fundamental differences between migration in Soviet and market-economy societies, it has become clear that existing generaliza-

58. I. R. Mulliadzhanov, *Narodonaselenie Uzbekskoi SSR* (Tashkent: Uzbekistan, 1967), p. 127.

tions concerning migration processes accurately describe much of recent Soviet experience. The volume of migration within the U.S.S.R. was high; the ratio of "change-of-locality" moves to total population in recent years has been somewhere near .05. People moved more frequently between close than between distant points. The elasticity of movement with respect to distance appears to have been near -1.0. Migration was related to industrial development. Growth of industry attracted workers and caused net in-migration, and high levels of industrial development were associated with high levels of interregional and intraregional migration. The low prestige of agricultural occupations and the attractiveness of urban living and industrial working conditions contributed to high rates of rural-to-urban migration throughout the U.S.S.R. Particularly noteworthy in this regard were the Belorussian, Lithuanian, Moldavian, Kirghiz republics and the Central Chernozem and South regions.

Streams and counterstreams existed. The interregional streams are rather easily identified, the largest usually involved contiguous regions. Streams to the developing regions were inefficient, since counterstreams equalled or exceeded them in volume. This situation did not improve during the 1960s. Intraregional streams into cities tended to be very efficient, especially in instances where the state limited migration into a particular city. Studies showed that, in general, recently settled population was more mobile than long-resident population.

The economic motive underlay most decisions concerning migration in the sense that people sought to settle where living conditions were more attractive. A sufficiently wide segment of the population was responsive enough to living and working conditions so that attempts to explain where people moved on the basis of personal opportunities will be more successful than those on requirements of economic plans. Migration was selective. Persons of working age predominated in migration streams; it appears that about 33 percent more of them are found migrating than would be expected on the basis of their proportion in underlying populations. The life-cycle events of seeking additional training, acceding to first jobs, and marrying explain particularly high mobility among the youngest persons of working age. Men were more mobile than women. Throughout the U.S.S.R. Russians migrate with great frequency. The linear correlation coefficient between the levels of internal migration and of Russian nationality in the various republics is high. According to the 1970 census, it appears that mobility among Russians is about twice that of other nationalities.

4

ESTIMATES

In this chapter migration levels into Union republics and major economic regions are estimated. Residual calculations of net migration for the 1959–70 period and for individual years are presented, and results of a survival technique are also reported. The returns of the 1970 census concerning movement during 1968–69 are briefly noted, and finally the different estimates are discussed. Union republics and major economic regions are the territorial units of analysis.

It is well known that the population of the U.S.S.R. is unevenly distributed. The highest densities occur on the wooded and grass steppes of the Ukraine and central Russia, in Transcaucasia, and on the Baltic-Belorussian plain. The lowest concentrations are found in the arctic expanses and Kazakh and Central Asian deserts. Figures 4.1 and 4.2 indicate the location and the population densities within the units of analysis. It must, of course, be remembered that the units are large and that densities within them are not uniform.

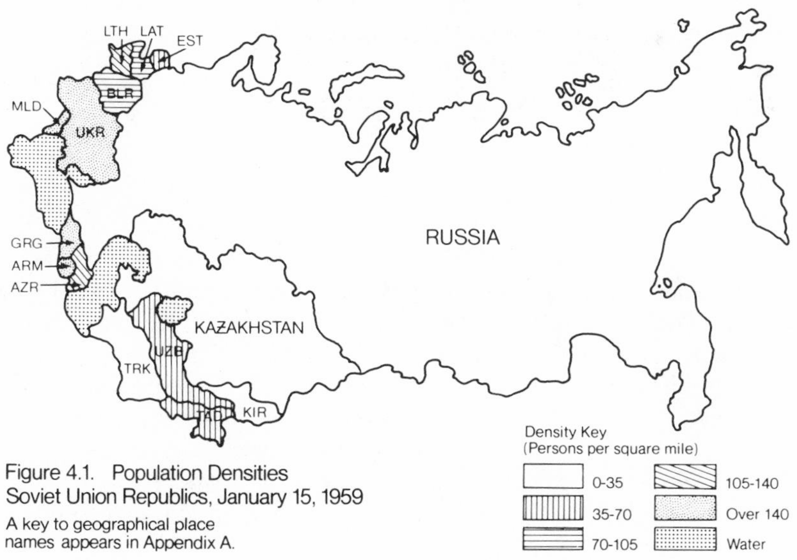

Figure 4.1. Population Densities
Soviet Union Republics, January 15, 1959

A key to geographical place names appears in Appendix A.

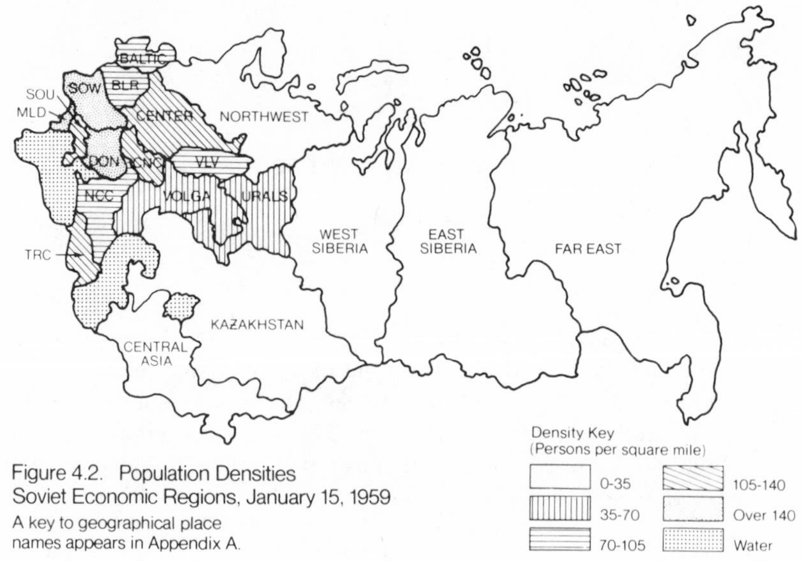

Figure 4.2. Population Densities
Soviet Economic Regions, January 15, 1959
A key to geographical place names appears in Appendix A.

RESIDUAL ESTIMATES

Net migration (in-migration less out-migration) may be estimated by removing the natural increase component (births less deaths) from total population increase, since:

Total Population Increase = (Births − Deaths) + (In-migrants − Out-migrants)

or

Total Population Increase = Natural Increase + Migrants on Net Account[1]

Only data on population increase (implied by periodic population estimates) and on natural increase are required to calculate migration levels by means of this residual technique.

Data

The Central Statistical Administration published crude rates of natural increase for each of the various Union republics for all the years covered by this study, but there are annual gaps in the series for the major economic regions. The rates for constituent Union republics may be summed with appropriate specific weights to obtain rates for the Baltic, Transcaucasian, and Central Asian regions, but no such easy solution is available for the economic regions of Russia and the Ukraine. To obtain plausible guesses for these regions, regressions of time-series trend (with R^2 values greater than .99) were fitted to the reported rates for the two republics. It was then assumed that the pattern of

1. The term "net migrants" is later used to denote the concept of migrants on net account.

natural increase change in each economic region was exactly the same as that of the republic in which it was located. On the basis of this assumption, the pattern for the republic was fitted to the available data for each component region by minimizing the sum of the squared deviations of the reported rates from the time-series pattern. The regional trend lines typically explained more than 95 percent of the variation in the reported regional rates. Although this procedure produced useful estimates, the results did not exhibit perfect consistency with the rates for the inclusive territorial units. To achieve consistency, the regional rates were adjusted very slightly so that when summed, with the appropriate specific weights, they reproduced the rates for Russia and the Ukraine exactly.

The data on population numbers present no problems with regard to availability, but in view of the observations made in chapter 1 about the deviations of the 1970 census enumerations from the numbers expected on the basis of previous annual estimates, there have arisen doubts about the accuracy of these data, especially for major economic regions. For Union republics it seems preferable to use the annual population estimates issued by the Central Statistical Administration in 1971 (rather than those made a short time after the end of each year), since the 1971 figures are free of egregious errors revealed by the census. Unfortunately, revised annual estimates for the major economic regions have not been published, so that one must decide on one's own what, if any, adjustment should be made to the annually published estimates. Again, it is only regions within Russia and the Ukraine that present difficulty since the postcensus population estimates for other regions may be derived by merely adding the appropriate revised estimates for Union republics. The author chose to raise or lower the population figures for the regions in the Russian and Ukrainian republics to the extent that the estimates for the appropriate republic were increased or decreased. This adjustment is certainly questionable and proves, in the end, to be unsatisfactory with the consequence that estimates of annual numbers of net migrants into economic regions of Russia and the Ukraine must be regarded as unreliable.

Estimates for 1959–70

Estimates of net migration in Union republics and major economic regions during 1959–70 are presented in Table 4.1. Since the annual intercensal population figures play no direct part in the calculations leading to the migration estimates, they cannot be the source of any error. The estimates depend only on natural increase data and census counts of population in 1959 and 1970.

The estimates are plausible. V. I. Perevedentsev's regional estimates of net migration for 1959–63[2] and the corresponding estimates of this work for the same period agree to the extent that the Spearman coefficient of rank-order

2. D. I. Valentei et al. (eds.), *Narodonaselenie i ekonomika* (Moscow: Ekonomika, 1967), p. 103.

correlation between the two series is .93. The estimates made for the relative of net migration to total increase may be compared to the estimates of the same relative for the period 1959–65,[3] with the result that the coefficient of rank-order correlation between the two sets of estimates is .93. The work of the present author may also be compared to that of V. V. Pokshishevskii which presented 1959–67 estimates for 16 of the 31 entities for which annual estimates are presented in this study; his 16 were eight areas of highest in-flow and eight areas of greatest out-flow.[4] The rank-order correlation coefficient between Pokshishevskii's estimates and the corresponding numbers estimated here is 1.0.

The results may also be checked by adding the estimates of net migration over the eleven-year period for each of the Union republics. In the absence of rounding errors, errors in the data on natural increase, and net migration into or out of the Soviet Union, this total should be approximately equal to zero since under these conditions the net migration figures would cancel each other out in the summation. The total check figure for the republic estimates presented in Table 4.1 is nearly 800,000 persons which is high, but represents only about 2 percent of the total increase in population that occurred between the two censuses. There may be some upward bias in the estimates due perhaps to incomplete registration of births.

Annual Estimates

Estimates of annual numbers of net migrants for Union republics are presented in Table 4.2.

The drastic change in the pattern of migration in Kazakhstan is the most striking feature of the entries in Table 4.2. The tenth anniversary of the Virgin Lands campaign was triumphantly marked by the Party in March 1962, and the celebration had an air of finality about it, suggesting that dedicated workers could look forward to committing themselves to new tasks of national economic achievement.[5] The estimates of Table 4.2 show that in 1962 Kazakhstan gained 174,000 persons through migration, but that in 1963, the famous crop-failure year, the region lost 25,000 persons. Through 1964–67 substantial in-migration occurred, but it fell far short of the levels attained early in the 1960s. Finally, in 1968 and 1969 modest levels of out-migration are estimated.

Because Kazakhstan received so many migrants on a net basis in the early 1960s, one cannot go too far wrong in presuming that most came either from Russia or the Ukraine. Thus, in 1959 and 1960 individuals from Russia (and to a much lesser extent, individuals from Belorussia) must have been going in

3. P. P. Litviakov (ed.), *Demograficheskie problemy zaniatosti* (Moscow: Ekonomika, 1969), p. 175.

4. V. V. Pokshishevskii, "Migration of Population, U.S.S.R." in U.S., Joint Publications Research Service, *Translations on U.S.S.R. Resources,* JPRS 49279 (November 19, 1969), p. 56.

5. *CDSP,* XIV, No. 16 (May 16, 1962), 12–16.

large numbers to Kazakhstan; in 1961 their numbers dropped, and in Table 4.2 is seen what must have been a substantial contribution from the Ukraine. Because the check figure for 1962 in the table is so high (net immigration for all republics totaling 156,000 rather than a number close to 0), one must be suspicious of that year's figures, but the contrast between the year of 1963 and the years 1960 and 1961 is quite clear. In 1963 there occurred migration into the Ukraine exceeding 100,000, much reduced out-migration from Russia, and net out-migration from Kazakhstan. The last year of large out-migration from Belorussia was 1964, and, probably not coincidentally, the 1965 level of out-migration from Russia rose back towards the levels achieved in the first three years of this period.

Estimates of annual numbers of net migrants for major economic regions are presented in Table 4.3. A check of the estimates for 1969, when cumulative errors are revealed, shows that the estimates for Russian and Ukrainian regions must be regarded as unreliable. Despite this stricture, the estimates are of some interest.

They show where errors in registration of migration probably occurred, and in this regard are consistent with the arguments of chapter 1. The unreasonable 1969 estimate for the Northwest and Center, containing Leningrad and Moscow, in all likelihood resulted from unregistered in-migration. Similarly, the Urals, West Siberia, and the Far East, regions with high departure rates, most likely had much out-migration go unregistered. Perhaps the same phenomenon took place in the Don-Dnieper region too.

If one is willing to assume that biases in registration systems were relatively uniform throughout the period, the estimates reveal that net in-migration into each of the developing regions declined through most of the period. A parallel phenomenon was the decline in net out-migration from the central Russian economic regions.

The estimates also allow some speculation concerning migration in response to the drought of 1963. The harsh winter of 1962–63, which lowered winter wheat output, was followed in the summer by a severe drought in Kazakhstan and West Siberia (as well as parts of Europe), which led to the failure of the spring wheat crop of the eastern areas.[6] How severely grain outputs were reduced may be judged with the aid of Table 4.4 where the drastic drop in output in the areas of the Virgin Lands is evident. During this year of crop failure, out-migration from West Siberia, according to Table 4.3, was 2.8 times the mean of 1962 and 1964, and in-migration into Kazakhstan dropped by a factor of 1.4 in relation to the mean of 1962 and 1964. Despite the unreliable nature of the figures, the difficult year of 1963 appears to have been one of substantial migration from the Virgin Lands. The level of net migration into the Ukraine in 1963, it may be noted according to Table 4.2, was 1.7 times the mean of 1962 and 1964.

6. *CDSP*, XV, No. 45 (November 20, 1963), 18.

CENSUS-SURVIVAL ESTIMATES

The residual estimates presented in Table 4.1 were derived by subtracting natural increase from total population increase. In using this method, inaccuracies in population estimates or instances of incomplete registration of vital events can lead to erroneous conclusions about migration on net account. The discussion on the accuracy of data in chapter 1 raised some questions about the registration of both births and deaths. With regard to the latter, the uncommonly low rates at very old ages raised questions about the completeness of the recording system. For the former, it was established that underregistration was occurring to the extent that 1 to 3 percent of all births probably went unregistered during the 1960s. It is therefore valuable to estimate net migration by a second method, the census-survival technique which, as applied here, requires no information concerning births and thus avoids the use of data which, at least to some extent, have been called into question.

A Proposed Method[7]

If census enumerations are accurate, the national population closed, and mortality experience throughout the country uniform, then the population numbers surviving from a first to a second census in various regions can be easily predicted. A measure of migration on net account can be derived by subtracting actual from expected population numbers. Migration on net account into region i over the time interval t to $t + n$ by persons aged x at time t (designated by $M_{i,x}$) is calculated according to:

$$M_{i,x} = P_{i,x+n,\ t+n} - S_x \cdot P_{i,x,t}$$

where $P_{i,x,t}$ is the population of region i aged x at time t and S_x is a survival probability for persons aged x. Thus, actual population at time $t + n$ ($P_{i,x+n,\ t+n}$) less expected population on the basis of survivorship from time t ($S_x \cdot P_{i,x,t}$) is the estimate of migration. By use of national population figures only, S_x is previously defined as:

$$S_x = \frac{P_{x+n,\ x+t}}{P_{x,t}}$$

where the absence of i subscripts on the P symbols emphasizes that S_x is a national survivorship probability assumed to be representative of mortality experience in the various regions. This exact procedure may, at least in principle, be applied for practically all ages. (An exception occurs when some persons counted in the aggregate $P_{i,n,t+n}$ were born during the interval t to $t + n$, in which case the procedure is modified in an obvious way.)

7. This section deals exclusively with demographic technique. The discussion follows U.N., Department of Economic and Social Affairs, *Manual VI: Methods of Measuring Internal Migration* (New York: United Nations, 1970), chapter 2. The chapter, written by K. C. Zachariah, outlines the census-survival technique concisely and comprehensively.

The extent to which the requirements of accurate enumerations, a closed national population, and uniform mortality are present in the Soviet case must be determined because, if these preconditions are absent, the census-survival technique will likely yield unreliable estimates.

The previous examination of the reliability of the two censuses uncovered no systematic errors in enumeration. It is rarely possible, when applying the census-survival technique, to check directly the accuracy of enumeration; this is especially true for the Soviet case. Indeed, it is difficult to check, even in an indirect fashion, since there has been virtually no public discussion concerning the reliability of the Central Statistical Administration's censuses. It was said here earlier that the increasing importance of censuses in economic planning has motivated the allocation of resources sufficient for achieving a reliable product. Nevertheless, undoubtedly some errors were made. A sufficient condition for an error-free application of the census-survival technique is that the enumerations be accurate or that the errors be uniform in percentage over time and space. The assumption here, in the absence of contrary evidence, is that the errors were small and uniform.

It is widely accepted that the U.S.S.R., among the countries of the world, is relatively closed in terms of absence of substantial flow of change-of-residence migration into and out of the country. International movement is highly restricted; except in extraordinary circumstances, citizens are usually not allowed to emigrate. A general policy of nonemigration was applied in the 1960s. In the analysis below, it appears that there occurred some international migration into the U.S.S.R. of persons of Armenian ethnicity during 1959–60. In relation, however, to the total U.S.S.R. population the numbers were very small.

The third precondition for the correct application of the census-survival technique requires that the level of mortality be the same in each of the territorial units of the country. The survival ratios calculated on the basis of national population numbers must be appropriate for each of the regions. Unfortunately, not much is known about differential mortality within the Soviet Union. The topic receives little attention, probably because officials feel that any documentation of differences in mortality between nationalities might be construed as evidence of an uneven extension of the benefits of socialism. The only regularly published material on differential mortality are crude rates of death (deaths per thousand total population).

Although these rates cannot be conclusive since they reflect the influence of both mortality and, unfortunately in addition, age structure, they do not suggest great variation in mortality. For the year 1965 reported rates of mortality ranged from 5.7 to 10.5 deaths per thousand population, with the average for fifteen Union republics being 7.2. The younger populations like those of Transcaucasia and Central Asia have the lower rates and the older populations of the Baltic states, most notably Latvia and Estonia, have the higher rates. Such a circumstance would likely occur if mortality experience were uniform. A situation of relatively constant mortality could have been effected in part by the widespread extension of effective public health measures and medical services in the period since the Second World War. The record in this regard and also in relation to economic development is frequently proclaimed by the Soviet press. Although public sanitation and medical care in some regards probably leave much to be desired, it cannot be doubted that for some time now the state has succeeded in controlling infectious diseases and in practicing preventive medicine throughout the U.S.S.R.

There are, however, reasons to question a conclusion that mortality experience exhibits little variation. Not much is known about mortality at very young ages. There are no regularly published reports about differential infant mortality. Indeed, the rule of Soviet practice, even in connection with all-Union data, has usually been to publish mortality rates and life table data for the ages 0–4 inclusive rather than for the most customary intervals of 0 and 1–4 years. It is demographic fact that when high and low age-specific mortality schedules are compared, the biggest differences are almost always within the first two years of life.[8] Current Soviet practice in this regard has the unfortunate effect of obfuscating mortality experience at young ages. It is also true that the comparison of different schedules often reveals relatively large differences at ages above 60 years, and this circumstance is likewise relevant in the present instance. As observed in chapter 1, U.S.S.R. crude death rates are low, owing to extraordinary longevity reportedly achieved in some parts of the U.S.S.R. (usually the Transcaucasian republics), and it is possible that mortality levels are much lower in these regions at old ages.

Perhaps errors due to differential mortality can be minimized in the present instance by using the census-survival technique only over intervals lying between very young and old ages. That is, if it is assumed that there is variation in mortality between republics, perhaps one may still apply the technique over ages that contribute relatively little to overall differences. To evaluate the potential of this approach, an experiment was conducted. The 1965 female population of Poland, having an age distribution somewhat similar to that of the corresponding U.S.S.R. population had a crude death rate of 7.0 in 1965.[9] Various schedules of age-sex-specific mortality were applied to the female population and the resulting levels of mortality were noted. The schedules were hypothetical (from *Regional Model Life Tables and Stable Populations*),[10] but representative of different levels of mortality observed in regions of the world. The resulting levels of mortality and the percentages of the change from the original 7.0 attributate to the ages 10 through 59 were calculated. The results were as follows:

8. Ansley J. Coale, *The Growth and Structure of Human Populations* (Princeton: N.J.: Princeton University Press, 1972), p. 14.

9. Nathan Keyfitz and Wilhelm Flieger, *Population: Facts and Methods of Demography* (San Francisco: W. H. Freeman, 1971), p. 459.

10. Ansley J. Coale and Paul Demeny, *Regional Model Life Tables and Stable Populations* (Princeton, N.J.: Princeton University Press, 1966).

Schedule	Resulting Mortality Level	Percentage of Change Attributable to Ages 10–59
East, Level 6	30.6	31
East, Level 15	15.0	32
East, Level 21	13.0	26
East, Level 24	5.0	33
West, Level 6	31.1	39
West, Level 15	15.1	41
West, Level 21	8.3	46
West, Level 24	5.1	30

The percentage increases, ranging from 26 to 46, indicate that between 54 to 74 percent of the hypothetical variation is attributable to the ages 0–9 and 60 and above. Thus, it would appear that applying the census-survival technique over the ages 10–59 only would reduce mortality variation and thereby increase the number of instances in which it could be used. In the present case it is anticipated that restricting attention to the ages of approximately 10–59 would substantially reduce whatever heterogeneity of mortality experience may have existed.

If the census-survival technique, according to the formula

$$M_{i,x} = P_{i,x+n,t+n} - S_x \cdot \mathrm{P}_{\mathrm{i,x,t}}.$$

were applied to estimate net migration into the Union republics during 1959–70, the index i would range over the fifteen republics and t would equal the year 1959; $t + n$, the year 1970; and n would be 11 years. Unfortunately, x cannot take on values equal to single years of age because the Central Statistical Administration published the two censuses giving totals for only five-year age groups and attempts by Western students to gain the more detailed data have failed. Such a circumstance, by itself, would present no problem, since the value of x could be understood to be equal to five-year intervals such as 0–4, 5–9, 10–14 years and so forth. The expected number of persons aged 20–24 years on the date of the 1970 census, for example, could be calculated on the basis of the number of persons aged 9–13 at the time of the 1959 census, eleven years earlier. But since the 1959 census provides only the total numbers aged 5–9 and 10–14, the required figure, persons aged 9–13, is unknown. Because n equals eleven rather than some multiple of five, single-year-of-age data are apparently still required.

An attempt to interpolate the 1959 U.S.S.R. and fifteen Union republic single-year-of-age distributions was made.[11] Because of the highly irregular age distribution of the Soviet Union, reflecting the influences of the revolution and the First World War, the events of the 1930s, and the Second World War, one would expect that interpolation, assuming regular change, would not suc-

11. Using the computer program POLATE as provided by Keyfitz and Flieger, *Population*, pp. 168–86.

ceed in providing good estimates. Fortunately, it is possible to reach a conclusion in this regard. The U.S. Foreign Demographic Analysis Division has been able to piece together a reliable estimate of the 1959 U.S.S.R. age distribution by single year of age.[12] When a comparison is made between the interpolated and U.S.-estimated data, one must conclude that the technique does not produce accurate results. The interpolated series first exceeds and then falls short of the estimated series for a number of years in each instance with the pattern repeating itself several times. Specifically, when the interpolated and estimated results are aggregated into the five-year age groups desired here, the former exceeds the latter, in absolute value, to an unacceptable degree in nearly every instance. Inasmuch as the interpolation worked out so poorly for the U.S.S.R. as a whole, there is no reason to believe that its results provided accurate estimates for the individual republics. Thus, the method, as customarily applied, appears to offer little potential in the present instance.

Although most of the interpolated single-age estimates proved to be inaccurate, it is still true, of course, that the results add to the five-year totals reported in the census. For example, despite interpolation problems, the number of persons aged 10–14 in 1959 is nevertheless still known since it was reported. From one point of view, the ignorance concerning the number of persons aged 9–13 in 1959 stems only from not knowing how many 9-year-olds to add to and how many 14-year-olds to subtract from the reported 10–14-year-old total. Uncertainty about two year-ages, 9 and 14, leads to lack of knowledge about the five-year age group 9–13. Similarly, if the age interval were extended to 9–18, it would be uncertainty about the 9 and 19 year-ages causing the problem concerning the ten-year age groups. Furthermore, if the age interval were vastly extended to 9–48 years, it would likewise be the 9 and 49 year-ages that create difficulty with regard to the 40-year age interval. It is, of course, obvious that the lack of knowledge concerning this last interval is much less than that for a five- or ten-year interval; in fact, the total may be regarded as reasonably accurate because the numbers of 9- and 49-year-olds are relatively small components. It would thus appear to be possible to apply the census-survival technique in a crude fashion to cohorts of persons aged 9–48 in 1959 in each region to gain a reasonably accurate indication of how many persons aged 20–59 would be alive in 1970 in the absence of any migration.[13]

The Results and Comparison

By setting $P_{i,\ 20-59,\ 1970}$ equal to the 1970 population aged 20–59 in republic i and S_{9-48} equal to 0.9672 and $P_{i,\ 9-48,\ 1959}$ equal to the 1959 population aged 9–48 in republic i, the formula:

$$M_{i,x} = P_{i,x+n,\ t+n} - S_x \cdot P_{i,x,t}$$

12. U.S., Department of Commerce, Estimates and Projections of the U.S.S.R., by Age and Sex: 1950 to 2000, International Population Reports, Series P–91, No. 23 (Washington, D.C.: U.S. Government Printing Office, 1973), p. 15.

13. It can be argued that the age interval is much too long. Inasmuch as it is proposed to

produces the $M_{i,9-48}$ estimates of net migration that are listed in Table 4.5. When these estimates are aggregated over all regions, the number of net migrants add up to −4; unlike earlier, this total near zero cannot be regarded as a check on the reasonableness of the estimation procedure. Census-survival estimates of migration must add to 0 when aggregated over all regions; the −4 figure in the present instance is due to cumulative rounding error.

The results of this method are similar to those presented in Table 4.1 in several regards. Previously noted phenomena reappear. There is substantial migration on net account from Russia, and secondarily from Belorussia and then Georgia and Azerbaydzhan, Estonia, Latvia, Armenia, and Kazakhstan seem to have very high rates of net migration per thousand of 1959 census population (aged 9–48).

Since residual estimates were made earlier and census-survival estimates have now been derived, the two sets may be compared to judge their consistency. Although the residual estimates pertain to migration by persons who were either alive in 1959 or born during 1959–70 and the census-survival estimates pertain to migration only among persons aged 9–48 in 1959, the property of consistency between the estimates would nevertheless produce high correlation since the second group of persons is a large component of the first. When the actual data are examined, it is found that the correlation coefficient between the Table 4.1 estimates of thousands of migrants on net account and the Table 4.5 estimates is 0.99, indicating very high correspondence.

Further insight into the results may be gained by comparing rates of migration per thousand population rather than numbers of migrants. These rates, also taken from Tables 4.1 and 4.5, are reprinted in Table 4.6 along with a ratio of

---

calculate a single eleven-year U.S.S.R. survival ratio for persons aged 9–48 and then apply it to the populations of each republic, the age-distribution differences within the 9–48 interval between the various republics and the U.S.S.R. may vitiate the results. It is possible to demonstrate in an approximate sense, the sensitivity of the results to the unorthodox grouping of ages. The U.S.S.R. ratio for persons aged 9–48 in 1959 surviving to ages of 20–59 in 1970 was 0.9672. On the basis of previous discussions, let it be assumed that age-specific mortality experience was approximately uniform during the 1960s in the populations initially aged 9–48 of the various republics and that the age enumerations of 1959 are reasonably accurate. A reasonable pattern of age-specific mortality consistent with the observed level may be chosen after examining U.S.S.R. reports. It is then possible to calculate the expected number of survivors by two methods; first, by applying the 0.9672 ratio to the populations aged 9–48 in 1959 and second, by applying the assumed age-specific schedule to the age-specific populations.

If the results from the first computation depart substantially from those of the second, the proposed method must be evaluated as being too crude. It is anticipated that the simple application of the 0.9672 ratio to the highly aggregated age group will underestimate survivors in young populations, since the 0.9672 ratio overstates mortality and will overestimate survivors in old populations. The expected developments occur, but the percentage deviations of the first figure from second for the various republics are all small, each being in absolute value much less than 0.5 percent. In the young populations of Central Asia and Transcaucasia the deviations range from −0.1 to −0.3 percent, and in the old populations such as those of Latvia and Estonia they lie in the neighborhood of 0.1 percent. It may thus be concluded that the use of this large are group does not prevent reasonably accurate estimation of the surviving population numbers, provided that mortality experience in different republics is uniform and 1959 age distribution figures are accurate.

the residual estimate to the census-survival estimate. If a pair of rates were identical, their ratio would equal 1.00. The actual ratios, shown in column C, most of which are relatively close to 1.00, indicate that in many instances correspondence between estimates is strong. Tadzhikistan is an egregious exception. Because the first estimates refer to entire populations and the second to persons aged 9–48 in 1959, it is likely that the values appearing in column C, rather than being exactly equal to 1.00, should be somewhat less than that figure. This follows from the high propensity to migrate among persons of working ages, a group having greater representation in the population aged 9–48 than in the entire poulation. Accordingly, ratios much greater than 1.00 may indicate an inconsistency between the estimates. By this criterion two more Central Asian republics, Uzbekistan and Kirghizia, must be included along with Tadzhikistan as republics for which the two estimates are probably inconsistent.

Another measure of the overall consistency between the results may be gained by regressing the residual rates (RESID) on the census-survival rates (CSURVI). Ordinary least squares computation results in:

$$\text{RESID} = \underset{(7.01)}{13.72} + \underset{(0.13)}{0.79}\ \text{CSURVI} \qquad R^2 = 0.73 \qquad S.E. = 22.60$$

where standard errors are indicated in parentheses. Sixty percent of the unexplained variation is due to the Tadzhik case. The results of the ratio analysis and this regression suggest that the two methods have produced results that generally agree, with the exception of three Central Asian republics. In these exceptional instances, estimates of rates of migration according to the residual method may be too high. It is possible that in using this method, the birth registration was so incomplete during the 1960s as to cause substantial overestimation of net migration.

1970 CENSUS RETURNS[14]

In the 1970 census, 25 percent of the population were asked how long they had lived continuously in their present population point *(naselennyi punkt)*; for those with less than two years continuous residence, place of previous permanent residence and reason for change of residence were also recorded. The data collected therefore concern migratory experience during only the two years prior to January 15, 1970, a time period which, for convenience's sake, may be referred to as 1968–69. Somewhat less than half of Volume VII of the census is devoted to presenting data deriving from these questions.[15] No information is presented about length of continuous residence, except that all the

14. In some respects these data are probably inaccurate. This question is treated in Appendix C.

15. TsSU, *Itogi vsesoiuznoi perepisi naseleniia 1970 goda,* VII (Moscow: Statistika, 1974).

published data pertain to persons with less than two years tenure in the place of enumeration. Nothing concerning reasons for change of residence is included. There is, however, substantial information about region-to-region streams of migration which are the subject of this section.

The results published in Volume VII have been extrapolated to serve as estimates of migration throughout the U.S.S.R. Its Table 1 is a republic-to-republic stream matrix. There is no region-to-region matrix published in the census, but one may be compiled from data contained in Tables 2–17 of the same volume. The published Table 1 and the compiled table may be used to identify important streams between republics and between regions. If the number of migrants from region i to region j is designated by M_{ij}, then a precise, although somewhat arbitrary definition of "important" can be given. Let the definition embody the criteria that:

1. The stream be quantitatively significant, that is, $M_{ij} \geq 10{,}000$;
2. The excess of arrivals over departures be large, that is, $(M_{ij} - M_{ji}) \geq 5{,}000$;
3. The efficiency of the stream be great, that is, $M_{ij} / M_{ji} \geq 1.5$; and,
4. The stream and counterstream be large in relation to the populations of origin and destination, that is, $(M_{ij} + M_{ji}) \cdot 1000 / (P_i \cdot P_j)^{1/2} \geq 2.0$ where the P's designate 1970 census populations.

Using these standards, the republics and regions listed in Table 4.7 emerge as points of origin and destination of important streams. The arithmetic averages pertain to the 210 (15×14) interrepublic and the 342 (19×18) interregional streams, respectively.

These data are especially interesting in that, unlike the other estimates of this chapter, they provide information about point-to-point streams. Important streams from the Volga-Vyatka and Central Chernozem of central Russia, the Urals and West Siberia, the southwest area of the Ukraine, Central Asia, and Kazakhstan are reported. Several streams into the Center, Don-Dnieper, North Caucasus, and the Far East are obvious. The appearance of Central Asia in the first list of areas losing population is somewhat surprising.

An indication of the importance of interregional migration in relation to underlying populations may be gained from the rates presented in Table 4.8. These measures are unorthodox in that the entries of columns A and B refer to the experience of 1968–69, but are expressed here at annual rates. Column C of the table provides a measure of movement both into and out of areas and column D provides a measure of migration on net account. Among the republics, it is surprising to learn that the census returns indicate population gain due to migration in Russia. Among the regions, the high sums of in- and out-migration combined in the regions of eastern Russia, in the South, and in Kazakhstan are notable. Extraordinary population gain due to migration is observed in the Far East and South, with less extreme loss in the Volga-Vyatka, Central Chernozem, the Urals, West Siberia, and Central Asia.

DISCUSSION

Much that is familiar to students of interregional migration appears in the results of the previous sections. Often Soviet analysts approached the problem from the perspective of where the supply of labor necessary for the economic development of the eastern regions was to be obtained. Viewing it this way, observers frequently pointed out the obvious, that the two republics with the largest populations, Russia and the Ukraine, both of which had achieved high levels of economic development, were logical sources of labor supply. Typically, the observers also noted that the Ukraine had a positive rate of net migration which it would not have if it had been contributing substantially to national economic development by supplying labor to the eastern regions.[16] The data presented here are consistent with this frequently made observation, and, in general, the tables show the extent of net migration into those republics often described as labor-surplus areas: the Ukraine, Moldavia, and the Central Asian republics.[17] Noteworthy, but not surprising, are the high rates of net migration into Latvia and Estonia, republics having the highest standards of living in the U.S.S.R. (at least to the extent that crude measures like national income and trade per capita may be said to measure standard of living).

Another frequently noted phenomenon, obvious in the estimates presented here, is the large-scale out-migration from the Central Chernozem and Volga-Vyatka regions, that are often regarded, along with the Center region, as the principal source of labor supply for the developing regions. The Central Chernozem, Volga-Vyatka, and Center regions experienced high rates of rural out-migration during the 1960s, the decrease in rural population over the eleven-year period in these regions being 15, 22, and 24 percent, respectively. That the estimate of net migration into the Center region shown in Table 4.1 is actually positive, raises the question of whether the Center region may properly be considered part of this area of labor supply. The presence of Moscow Oblast and City (with suburbs) within the region provides the answer to the question, since the intercensal increase in population in these two territorial entities comprises practically all of the increase in population in the entire Center region.[18] The other oblasts of the region fit the eleven-year pattern observed in several of the large political units of the Central Chernozem and Volga-Vyatka regions, a pattern of loss of population or nominal increase in population.

Also familiar is the situation suggested by this study's estimates of net migration for the Urals, West Siberia, East Siberia, and the Far East, presented in Table 4.1 and restated in the same manner (net migrants per thousand 1959

16. For example: V. V. Pokshishevskii et al., "On Basic Migration Patterns" in George J. Demko et al. (eds.), *Population Geography: A Reader* (New York: McGraw-Hill, 1970), p. 322; Pokshiskevskii, "Migration of Population, U.S.S.R." p. 61; and V. I. Perevedentsev, "Migratsiia naseleniia i ispol'zovanie trudovykh resursov," *Voprosy ekonomiki* (No. 9, 1970), pp. 40–41.

17. Tables 4.1, 4.5, and 4.8 are not wholly consistent with regard to Central Asia. This issue is treated later in this section.

18. Theodore Shabad, "News Notes," *Soviet Geography* (September 1970), p. 589.

population) here: Urals, −61.4; West Siberia, −63.4; East Siberia, −16.1; and the Far East, 30.9. Since the two Siberian regions and the Far East and Kazakh regions received capital investment in excess of the amounts suggested by allocating investment among regions proportionately on the basis of population or gross industrial population, it was decided in chapter 2 that they might be termed regions of national economic development or development regions. Yet throughout the period students of economic geography and population migration and Soviet labor planners documented and grappled with the persistent problem of labor shortages in these areas. It may be inferred that the relaxation of controls on labor during the 1950s, the disinclination to invest on a scale sufficient to raise living conditions, and the policy of substantial, but seemingly insufficient, regional differentiation of wages led to the labor experience of the 1960s in which choices of work locations by workers differed from the choices desired by planners.

An examination of the population streams between these regions is instructive. Census data on movement during 1968–69 are available. Table 4.9 shows the magnitude of streams on net account according to the census returns. At first glance, the predominance of positive figures above the main diagonal of Part A of the table would suggest that perhaps the most noteworthy aspect of population exchange within the regions is that there seemed to be a network of streams that on balance sent population into the Far East. The data suggest that on net account the Urals region supplied population to all the other regions, that West Siberia gave up migrants to each of the other development regions, that Kazakhstan yielded population numbers to East Siberia and the Far East, and that East Siberia itself provided migrants to the Far East. Thus, relatively well-developed regions would appear to have been sending population to the less-developed, perhaps more forbidding and remote locations. In this regard, it would appear that the out-migration streams from West Siberia to East Siberia were especially significant in relation to underlying populations of potential resettlers.

But further consideration of the data suggest that while the Urals, West Siberia, and Kazakhstan sent migrants eastward on net account, they at the same time gave up much more to the totality of all the other regions located to the west or south. This last circumstance is the one that press commentary indicates state planners and party leaders regretted. In their opinion, it may be guessed, the figures in the "All Other Regions" column of Part B of Table 4.8 should all have been much less than 1.00 as they were for the Far East and East Siberia. On the basis of the familiar classification of regions as having either a labor deficit or surplus, the census data suggest that many Soviet officials would judge that too many people left West Siberia and Kazakhstan for the Center, North Caucasus, and Don-Dnieper regions. Furthermore, with regard to population increase in the Far East, the gain from western and southern regions was more than from the eastern regions. Movement within the eastern regions, therefore, has provided only modest increases in the Far East's labor supply. In view of this circumstance and the fact that the eastern regions themselves are regarded as labor-deficient areas, even the great gain in the Far East from very distant regions is in all likelihood regarded as too low.

The distinctive status of the Far East region with its positive net migration estimate for 1959–70 and, according to the census, with a population gain during 1968–69, probably owed much to a special state interest in providing work force in the region. Regional coefficients were applied extensively and were of greater significance in raising wage payments in the Far East. In those territorial regions not lying within the Extreme North, regional wage coefficients were higher for the Far East than the coefficients for the East Siberia, West Siberia, Urals, and Kazakh regions. Certainly the 26 September 1967 Central Committee and Council of Ministers Resolution[19] extending the use of the regional coefficients to workers in the nonproductive sectors throughout the Far East and Chita Oblast (of East Siberia) is a concrete example of special state interest in this region. It has been estimated that during 1959–65, through agricultural settlement, Orgnabor, and penal assignment, 300,000 individuals were directed to the Far East and that about half of the arrivals of new workers in the Far East in the early 1960s were channeled there through organized resettlement.[20]

The extraordinarily high rate of in-migration to Armenia, especially in its relation to the rates of neighboring Georgia and Azerbaydzhan is surprising. Figures in Tables 1.5 and 1.7 have shown that errors were made in the registration of births, deaths, or migration in Armenia. It is relevant to note that during the 1960s reported crude rates of birth and natural increase fell drastically in Armenia from 40.3 and 33.5, respectively, in 1960 to 22.8 and 17.6, respectively, in 1969. No other non–European Union republic experienced a decline of this order during the 1960s. One logical possibility with regard to the high estimate of migration into Armenia is that it is too high simply because natural increase did not fall as much as was reported; nevertheless, other information indicates that the estimate perhaps should be as high as it is.

Between 1959 and 1970 in no Union republic, except for Armenia, did the percentage of ethnic Armenians increase substantially. In 1959, 88.0 percent of the population of Armenia was declared to be of Armenian ethnicity and in 1970, 88.6 percent. The only republics besides Armenia in which substantial numbers of the nationality lived were Russia, Georgia, and Azerbaydzhan. The increase of ethnic Armenians over the eleven-year period in these republics may be decomposed into average annual rates of Armenian increase: Russia, 1.4 percent; Georgia, 0.2 percent; and Azerbaydzhan, 0.9 percent. First, it may be noted that these rates are far below the rates of natural increase that one might associate with individuals of Armenian extraction. Second, it may be seen that the rates of Armenian increase in Georgia and Azerbaydzhan (0.2

19. *CDSP*, XIX, No. 39 (October 18, 1967), 3.

20. L. L. Rybakovskii (ed.), *Vosproizvodstvo trudovykh resursov Dal'nego Vostoka* (Moscow: Nauka, 1969), pp. 22–23.

percent and 0.9 percent) were certainly far below the rates of total population increase in the republics over the eleven-year period (1.4 and 3.0 percent, respectively). Third, it has been reported that substantial movement from Azerbaydzhan rural to Armenian urban points took place during 1959–70.[21] Finally, it may be remembered that Table 1.5 showed both Georgia and Azerbaydzhan with census enumerations falling short of the numbers expected on the basis of previous annual estimates. These circumstances, although certainly not sufficient to establish the validity of the hypothesis that considerable unregistered in-migration of Armenians into the Armenian republic occurred during 1959–70, are all consistent with such a hypothesis.

V. V. Pokshishevskii recently (1969) and very briefly addressed himself to the phenomenon of migration into Armenia, but seemed more impressed by its "peculiar nature" than its scale, noting that the population of the republic was very homogeneous, that Armenians in other republics were attracted to Armenia, and that some Armenians were being repatriated from abroad.[22] All this is consistent with the view expressed above, but it is unfortunate that the extent of repatriation, perhaps the key to the whole problem, was not specified precisely. According to Pokshishevskii, up to 100,000 Armenians had migrated from abroad during the postwar years alone.[23]

The extent of net migration into Central Asia remains somewhat unclear since the available evidence is not wholly consistent. The residual estimates of the first section imply high levels of increase due to migration on net basis in Kirghizia, Tadzhikistan, and Uzbekistan. These results agree with the usual observations found in the Soviet literature of the 1960s on the regional aspects of labor supply. Commentators frequently noted the unfortunate circumstance of both a labor surplus in the area and continued arrival on net account of persons to the area from outside.[24] However, the census-survival estimation of the second section of this chapter yielded somewhat lower rates for Kirghizia and Uzbekistan and a much lower rate for Tadzhikistan. In this last case, the survival technique showed no population gain due to migration. In the analysis conducted above, it was concluded that the residual estimates probably were too high due to the failure to register all births in these areas.

The 1970 census surprised students of Soviet migration with its data that implied Kirghizia, Tadzhikistan, and Uzbekistan ranked fifth, third, and second, respectively, among the 15 republics in terms of population *loss* due to migration (see Table 4.8). The residual estimates (Table 4.1) imply ranks of third, fifth, and seventh for these republics in terms of population *gain*, and the survival estimates (Table 4.5) yield ranks of fifth, eleventh, and seventh in *gain*. It is true that the census data pertain to only 1968–69 and that other

21. Litviakov, *Demograficheskie problemy*, p. 188.
22. Pokshishevskii, "Migration of Population, U.S.S.R.," p. 57.
23. Ibid.
24. I. R. Mulliadzhanov, *Narodonaselenie Uzbekskoi SSR* (Tashkent: Uzbekistan, 1967), p. 127; Litviakov, *Demograficheskie problemy*, p. 158; and, A.G. Volkov, *Statistika migratsiia naseleniia* (Moscow: Statistika, 1973), p. 230.

estimates pertain to 1959–70, but this does not resolve the gross discrepancy, since the residual estimates for 1968–69 listed in Table 4.2 while showing a decrease in the numbers of persons arriving on a net basis during the last two years of the intercensal period, do not reveal population loss on net account.

Appendix C analyzes the problem in some detail. The main conclusion reached there is that responses to the census questions concerning migration were inaccurate. Persons failed to recall or to inform enumerators of their arrival within the two years prior to the census in regions in which the state did not want population gain due to migration. In Appendix C two comparisons are made. Census estimates of net migration are checked against residual estimates for 1968–69, and census estimates of net arrival at urban points are examined in relation to population-registration estimates of net arrival at urban points in 1969. In both instances it is seen that census estimates of net migration into Kirghizia and Uzbekistan are extraordinarily low and that perhaps estimates for Russia and Kazakhstan are high. It is therefore concluded that net migration into Central Asia was positive. It also seems true, however, that the residual estimates of Table 4.1 have an upward bias due to incomplete birth registration, so that the survival estimates of Table 4.5 may provide the best point estimates of rates of net migration rates during 1959–70.

CONCLUSIONS

By subtracting components of natural increase from total population increase, estimates of net migration into Union republics and major economic regions for the entire 1959–70 period and for individual years were derived. A particular problem in applying a residual method in this instance is that estimates of the annual numbers of migrants on net account depend crucially on the annual estimates of births and deaths. In view of the positive check figures for net migrants over all regions, it would appear that data on natural increase are somewhat low imparting an upward bias to the residual estimates. This circumstance may have been especially prevalent in the cases of Kirghizia, Tadzhikistan and Uzbekistan, and perhaps Armenia.

By applying a single U.S.S.R. survival proportion to the populations aged 9–48 in 1959 in the various republics, expected survivors aged 20–59 in 1970 were estimated. The differences between the enumerated and expected numbers were taken as estimates of net migration. The correlation coefficient between these estimates and the corresponding residual estimates was 0.99. Further analysis indicated, however, that there was inconsistency in perhaps three instances, certainly for Tadzhikistan, and for Kirghizia and Uzbekistan. The high degree of correspondence between the residual and survival estimates was taken as evidence that the relative weakness of birth registration data did not vitiate the residual results, an important conclusion since the residual estimates are more extensive than the census-survival results.

Data from the 1970 census on change of residence during 1968–69 were examined. Their great value lies in their information about point-to-point movement instead of merely population growth due to migration. The state inquired as to place of previous permanent residence of persons moving during 1968–69. The usefulness of the data for the present study is restricted by the apparent presence of respondent bias and the short time interval that the questions covered. The first consideration is studied in Appendix C where it is concluded the net movement into Kirghizia and Uzbekistan is understated in the census returns and overstated perhaps for Kazakhstan and Russia.

Although Soviet commentators frequently noted the low levels of out-migration from the Ukraine to the development regions, the work of this chapter shows that substantial migration on net account into the Ukraine occurred, with a fair amount into the Don-Dnieper region and a high, although in absolute numbers quantitatively less important, level into the South. The out-migration on net account from West Siberia and the Urals was large—about 6 percent of 1959 population. Out-migration is also estimated for East Siberia but not the Far East where population increased by about 3 percent due to migration. Traditional sources of labor-supply for interregional migration, the Volga-Vyatka, Central Chernozem, and Center regions, had rather high rates of out-migration, around 10 and 6 percent for the first two, with the rate for the Center region having been lowered by the high levels of in-migration to Moscow Oblast located outside the capital.

Among the somewhat less familiar observations are the substantial levels of migration into Latvia and Estonia, Armenia, the North Caucasus, and Uzbekistan, Kirghizia, and Tadzhikistan. Over half of the population growth during 1959–70 in the two Baltic republics may be directly attributed to a positive balance of migration. The situation in Armenia remains only partly understood. According to estimates of this chapter, the intercensal change in the republic's population due to migration was 8.7 percent. Possible causes are errors in vital events registration, repatriation of Armenians from outside the U.S.S.R., and out-migration of ethnic Armenians from neighboring Georgia and Azerbaydzhan; certainly the last factor was operative. The population of the North Caucasus grew by nearly 8 percent due to migration between 1959 and 1970; arrivals in rural areas were especially important in the total. The attractive climate of the region, the presence of new settlers in neighboring Virgin Lands areas, and the Virgin Lands campaign itself were contributory. In contrast, in those Central Asian republics mentioned above, although undergoing population increases of perhaps up to 5 to 8 percent due to migration, most of the gain occurred in cities. In these republics the presence of high natural increase tended to dominate the economic-demographic situation. The extent of net in-migration into these republics is somewhat uncertain. Failure to register all births may have erroneously raised the residual estimates.

The most striking feature of the annual estimates of migration is the pattern of development in connection with the Kazakhstan and the settlement of the Virgin Lands. During 1959–62, the last years of the Virgin Lands campaign, Kazakhstan gained about 180,000 persons a year due to migration. For 1963, the year the spring wheat crop failed because of severe drought, it is estimated 25,000 more persons migrated from than to Kazakhstan. In the same year the level of net out-migration from West Siberia was approximately two-and-a-half times that of 1962 or 1964, and net in-migration for the Ukraine was almost twice that occuring in 1962 or 1964. During the early 1960s Russia (especially the Central Chernozem, Volga-Vyatka and Center regions), the Ukraine and Belorussia were important sources of labor supply for the Virgin Lands; by the mid-1960s Belorussia appears to have been no longer significant in this respect, and at the end of the period it appears Kazakhstan was no longer gaining population due to migration.

5

DETERMINANTS

In chapter 3 it was found that despite assertions of fundamental differences between migration in Soviet and other societies, existing generalizations concerning Western countries describe much of recent Soviet experience rather well. The volume of migration within the U.S.S.R. was high, with people moving most frequently between close points. Growth of industry attracted migrants, and migratory mobility was associated with high levels of industrialization. Streams and counterstreams clearly existed, with the largest involving contiguous regions. Intraregional streams to cities tended to be very efficient. The economic motive underlay many decisions concerning migration. Selectivity of migration evidenced itself in the proportion of people in school and young working ages who migrated, the higher propensity of men to move and preponderance of Russians in the streams.

The present chapter examines the apparent determinants of streams of migration between republics and major economic regions during 1959–70. First, three views or theories of the migration process are examined; then, their observational implications for the analysis of streams are specified; finally, the competing theories are tested and a conclusion reached about their relative explanatory power.

VIEWS OF THE MIGRATION PROCESS

In this section views of the migration process that may be termed a contemporary ideological view, a Soviet social science view and a Western view are examined.

A Contemporary Ideological View

One view articulated in the U.S.S.R. derives from Karl Marx's analysis of capitalism and V. I. Lenin's studies concerning migration in Russia. Fundamental to it is the notion that capitalism and socialism are entirely different economic systems. Marx thought general statements concerning economic and social phenomena to be impossible, rather each economic system possessed its own laws concerning its operation. Following this line of thought, some Soviet spokesmen discuss population issues in relation to their perceptions of the capitalist and socialist laws of population. The first is based upon Marx's "law of relative surplus population" which is an integral part of the economic theory of the capitalist dynamic leading to the immiseration of the working class. The worker sells his or her labor, the source of all value, as a commodity at a price that just covers the cost of reproducing it. By means of this process, surplus value is generated and is expropriated by the capitalist who, as a profit-seeker, invests in additional capital that typically is labor-saving. Thus, the workers, who are the source of all value, contribute in production to their redundancy, or relative surplus.

Lenin extended the Marxian view to cover the phenomenon of migration. He asserted that the economist who wanted to understand the development of capitalism in Russia ought first to ask what exactly had resulted from population redistribution there. He maintained that decisions to migrate were based upon evaluations of social conditions at point of departure and point of prospective settlement and that people moved where they thought conditions were better. In connection with the study of the development of capitalism in Russia, Lenin even identified what has been termed the "law of population mobility" which is said to be part of the capitalist law of population. The concept holds that capitalism once developed, as may be identified by the emergence of large-scale, capital-intensive industry, calls forth population mobility. As areas produce for more extensive markets and trading relations are expanded, increased population mobility is required. The demand for labor grows, but unevenly through time, accelerating during periods of frenetic expansion and falling during crises. These circumstances according to Lenin require workers to transfer continually to new work locations in an attempt to keep employed.[1]

It is this last notion that seems to be used to distinguish between migration in capitalist and socialist societies, and it is at this juncture that the paradigm sometimes appears to be dogmatic. Under capitalism, migration is said usually to be spontaneous *(stikhiinaia)* while under socalism it is deliberate *(soznatel' naia)*.[2] From a social viewpoint, the first notion seems to suggest that migration is unplanned, perhaps irrational and wasteful while the second seems to suggest the opposite. In connection with this distinction, the "socialist law of population," which appears to be a wholly Soviet creation, is raised. Its contents have been disputed. Certainly, the law suggests that under socialism, as distinguished from capitalism, there is no unemployment of workers. Prior to 1960 it was generally interpreted to mean additionally that in a socialist society full and rational employment would be achieved, making for the material and moral advancement of the population, along with population growth. With the slowing of population increase in the U.S.S.R., the last

1. D. I. Valentei and E. Iu. Burnasheva, *Voprosy teorii i politiki narodonaseleniia* (Moscow: Moskovskii Universitet, 1970), pp. 6–7.

2. E.g., see Smulevich, "O sovremennom Mal'tuzianstve," p. 39 or A. G. Volkov, *Statistika migratsiia naseleniia*, p. 300.

element appears to have fallen by the wayside with the result that the law is now interpreted as implying full and rational employment, making for advances in the welfare of the working population. A stronger view holds that the essence of the law is that full employment is achieved with the worker contributing to production on the basis of a new work ethic.[3]

In this last regard it is sometimes maintained that as socialism proceeds toward full communism a new orientation of the worker will develop along with a change in the concerns of the worker. Abolition of the fear of unemployment and recognition of the important task of communist construction is said to lead to a new worker who is more productive and satisfied. This person has been characterized as possessing better health, heightened political and social consciousness, a more internationalist ideology along with goals in life more focused on social service and development than private gain.[4]

On these bases it is deduced that there can be few migration problems in comparison with those found under capitalism. It is maintained that migration flows within the U.S.S.R. are determined by the planned areal distribution of investment in productive and population-serving facilities, by the planned differentiation of living conditions, by calls from the Party and government for resettlement and by the assignment of graduates from institutions of secondary-specialized and higher learning to directed first assignments.[5]

A Soviet Social Science View

Soviet academicians such as V. I. Perevendenstev (Institute of the International Workers Movement), L. L. Rybakovskii (Central Scientific Research Laboratory for Labor Resources), T. I. Zaslavskaia (Institute of Economics and Organization of Industrial Production, Siberia), and V. D. Zaitsev (affiliation unknown) who are further removed from government administration have developed a second, more complex view in the last ten to fifteen years.

Concerning the individual decision to migrate the consensus view appears to be that a rather complex model is appropriate. It is thought that people weigh the benefits and costs of moving in a rational manner. Specifically, whether a move is evaluated as gainful or not depends upon the difference in the vectors of living conditions at the present and alternative locations, weighted according to whether the decision-makers have information about the variables comprising the difference vector and by the importance of each of the components to the decision-making unit. A scalar measure of potential benefit results. Then costs are taken into account where again there is a vector, with its elements weighted also by information and importance measures yielding a scalar quan-

3. L. A. Arutiunian, *Sotsialisticheskii zakon narodonaseleniia* (Moscow: Nauka, 1975), pp. 22–26.
4. S. M. Kovalev, *Formirovanie novogo o cheloveka* (Moscow: Mysl', 1971), pp. 28–29.
5. Smulevich, "O sovremennom Mal'tuzianstve," p. 39.

tity. Whether a move takes place or not depends upon whether the measure of benefits less costs and less a threshold measure is positive or not.[6]

Apart from particular questions about how the model operates, two general concerns arise. One is whether the U.S.S.R. institutional setting allows such an approach. The consensus among students within and outside the U.S.S.R. is that is does. For the 1959–70 period the state allowed sufficient freedom of movement so that a de facto labor market operated. To be sure, directed first assignment of state-trained graduates, organized programs of resettlement and social calls for mobilization existed, but these mechanisms did not account for the bulk of population and labor mobility. The second concern is whether the model is operational. It appears to have been used only as a conceptual framework of the variables that ought to be considered. If such is the case, it is understandable. The model is complex. It would require measurement of various aspects of living conditions, the importance which people attach to them, and the degree to which people are informed about them. Further, it would require similar measures for costs. In addition, the notion of threshold value above which the net benefits must lie seems problematic. If this last variable cannot be measured, the theory would be in danger of becoming tautological, since whether a unit moved or not could be supposed to have resulted from whether it had a low or high threshold.

A second line of research, deriving from the concern of researchers in the eastern regions in the early 1960s over the deleterious effects of out-migration, has concentrated on the determinants underlying streams of migration. It was frequently observed there that interregional migration streams into the area were exceeded by counterstreams. Since there was an explicit interest in lowering the rate of out-migration, the question of determinants became important. Those most commonly set forth have been: economic, ethnic, natural-climatic, geographic, and social-psychological.

The term "economic factor" most frequently is used to denote the concept of the entire complex of material living conditions. Ideally, Soviet researchers would like to have a single measure characterizing the economic quality of life, but they admit that such measurement is not presently possible. Objective indicators, to use the Soviet term, of aspects of living conditions are wages per capita, housing space per capita, retail trade turnover per capita, personal assessment of housing adequacy, assortment and supply of consumer goods, institutions of child-care per child, communal and cultural workers per capita, hospital beds per capita and doctors per capita.

The ethnic factor takes into account the fact that the U.S.S.R. is a multinational state. Russians make up about half the population, with Ukranians, Uzbeks, and Belorussians making up an additional quarter. To complete the population about a hundred more nationalities must be included. If one sets aside the Russian, Ukrainian, and Belorussian nationalities, about a third of the

6. Zaslavskaia, *Migratsiia sel'skogo naseleniia*, pp. 37–42.

remaining population has mastered Russian as a second language according to the 1970 census.[7] Studies have repeatedly found the Russians to be the most mobile nationality.

The natural-climatic factor refers primarily to variations in climate. Other things being equal, people avoid harsher climates. When located in such places they will require additional food, clothing, and shelter. The probability of adaptation has been found to be inversely related to the dissimilarity between the conditions at previous and present settlements. The geographic factor takes account of the fact the rates of population exchange between places have been found to be an inverse function of distance. The social-psychological factor is a catchall category to include the facts that people are responsive to some degree to state and Party calls for migration and that social attitudes in localities suggest certain decisions concerning migration are or are not appropriate.

In connection with the study of determinants, researchers recognize that if they want to reach conclusions about the importance of single factors in dealing with multiple factor explanations, they will have to find some way to hold other variables constant. One method for accomplishing this in the present context is to seek out from the totality of cases those point-to-point streams which appear to have extraneous factors held constant. Thus, a researcher investigating the effect of climate studied movement from places of varying climate into three cities with different climates in West Siberia. In addition, he controlled to keep distances constant, to keep occupational profiles between origin and destination constant and to keep ethnicity from varying too much. In the end the effect of coldness of climate in stimulating return migration to warmer places was revealed.[8] This general approach of reaching conclusions by selective comparisons is the methodological trademark of much Soviet literature on migration.

An alternative strategy is to take all the cases, obtain measurements on all the variables, and use multivariate statistical techniques to reveal separate influences. The promise of this approach is, of course, that it may be possible to gain quantitative measurement of the relationship. Its frequent failing, however, is that relationships among the data cannot be ferreted out and the variances on the estimates of responsiveness are so high that one's understanding is imprecise in the extreme.

Although this latter approach has been infrequent in Soviet work, it is likely to be used more often. An example will suffice to indicate the way in which multiple regression has been used. V. D. Zaitsev undertook a single equation explanation of net migration into the approximately 80 regions that make up the R.S.F.S.R.[9] He posited that the rates of net migration depended upon the development and distribution of productive forces, industrial development,

7. TsSu, *Itogi vsesoiuznoi perepisi 1970*, p 20.

8. V. I. Perevedentsev, *Metody izucheniia migratsii naseleniia* (Moscow: Statistika, 1975), pp. 117–19.

9. A. Z. Maikov (ed.), *Migratsiia naseleniia RSFSR* (Moscow: Statistika, 1973), pp. 3–32.

relative wages, growth of housing space, medical services, educational institutions, trade and household services, average January temperature, and length of annual frost-free period. The single equation explained 67 percent of the variation in the dependent variable and had most of its coefficients of the correct sign. Those for the development of and distribution of productive forces, relative wage and growth of housing space tested clearly as significant and of the correct sign. Zaitsev even calculated elasticities for them of 1.80, 11.70, and 4.39, respectively. The two coefficients for climate appear to be significant, but the one for January temperature seems to be of the wrong sign.

Western Views

For the regression analysis of streams of migration two theoretical lines concerning the experience in Western institutional setting seem relevant: the investment in human capital approach developed by economists and the general push-pull approach used by demographers, regional scientists, and economists. The investment in human capital approach speculates that persons move because the present value of the whole of benefits and costs of living elsewhere exceed those of remaining where they are by a margin greater than the cost of moving. M.P. Todaro in applying a variant of this approach to rural-urban migration in a Third World context proposed a modification that is of general applicability. His idea may be stated in the following manner. If for a decision-maker the value of remaining at present location is the sum of the discounted present value of the benefits there, then perhaps the corresponding measure for the potential destination ought to be adjusted by a measure of probability when the realization of the benefits is uncertain.[10]

Setting matters out more formally, the present value of remaining at origin (PV_i) is evaluated by:

$$PV_i = \int e^{rt} i Y_i(t) dt$$

where r is a rate of discount, t is time in the future, i is a unit vector, and $Y_i(t)$ is a vector of monetized valuations of factors at origin i at time t. The present value of benefits at j at time t is defined by:

$$PV_j = \int e^{rt} P_j(t) Y_j(t) dt$$

where most of the variables are defined analogously and $P_j(t)$ is a vector of probabilistic expectations for realizing the benefits of j at time t. Movement is said to occur when: $(PV_j - PV_i) > C_{ij}$ where C_{ij} is the cost of moving. If the expressions $(PV_j - PV_i - C_{ij})$ are added over all decision-makers and then divided by population size at i, an average value results. One might presume that the aggregate out-migration rate from i to j would be some function of the

10. M. P. Todaro, "A Model of Labor Migration and Urban Unemployment," *American Economic Review*, LXIX (March 1973), pp. 183–93.

average value. Then perhaps the net migration rate could be predicted according to $M_{ij} / P_i = f(PV_j - PV_i - C_{ij})$ where M_{ij} is the number of migrants moving from i to j and P_i is the population size at i.

The composition of the average sum that is the argument for the last function is complicated. The elements that go into the determination of C_{ij} vary across individuals. The value of PV_i depends mainly upon the values of $Y_i(t)$ which vary over time, individuals and constituent elements. The value of PV depends upon $P_j(t)$ as well as $Y_j(t)$ which both vary in a similar fashion. To go from this theoretical construct to directly observable magnitudes in explaining migration streams requires a host of simplifying assumptions. The problem of variation through time is often avoided by a presumption that the current values of variables are proportional in a uniform manner to their future values so that the current magnitudes may be taken as accurate proxies for discounted present values. The problem of variation across individuals is assumed away by adopting the convention that whatever variations there are can be ignored at the cost of getting approximate, but still valuable results. Even after these two heroic assumptions, one still must measure the elements making up $Y_i(0)$, $Y_j(0)$ and $P_j(0)$.

If it is assumed that the only benefit of location at j that is uncertain is the wage from work, then a probabilistic assessment is necessary only for that one factor. When dealing with aggregated data, it would appear that measuring such a probability would be nearly impossible, but perhaps one could presume that the probabilities are a positive function of the rate at which employment is growing less the rate at which the labor force is being augmented owing to natural increase, that is, the aging of cohorts of the local population and into and out of the labor force. Thus, it may be useful to include employment growth less labor force growth among the determinants of streams of migration. Reasoning in a similar fashion, some researchers have used unemployment rates as a converse measure of excess demand.

To specify the elements comprising $Y_i(0)$ and $Y_j(0)$, the factors at origin and destination, the literature of push-pull studies is helpful. This approach, of course, views migration streams as being determined in part by levels of corresponding factors at origin and destination. Very frequently measures of wages, unemployment and amenities at origin and destination have been used. When point-to-point streams have been examined, the notion of a gravity model has often been incorporated into the push-pull framework.[11] The gravity model states that the interaction between two entities is proportional to the potential between them and inversely related to distance. In migration, the potential has been measured by the product of population sizes at origin and

11. See Michael J. Greenwood, "Research on Internal Migration in the United States: A Survey" *The Journal of Economic Literature,* XIII, No. 2 (June 19750, pp. 397–433; R. Paul Shaw, *Migration Theory and Fact: A Review and Bibliography of Current Literature* (Philadelphia: Regional Science Research Institute, 1975); and Kenneth G. Willis, *Problems in Migration Analysis* (Lexington, Mass.: D. C. Heath and Co., 1974).

destination and the distance, by travel mileage between the two. Thus, a typical regression might appear as:

$$\begin{aligned} \ln M_{ij} = {} & \ln a + b_{li} \ln W_i + b_{lj} \ln W_j + b_{2i} \ln U_i + b_{2j} \ln U_j \\ & + b_{3i} \ln A_i + b_{3j} \ln A_j + b_{4i} \ln P_i + b_{4j} \ln P_j \\ & + b_5 \ln D_{ij} + e \end{aligned}$$

where "ln" in each instance denotes "logarithm of"; *i* and *j* stand for origin destination points, respectively; and, the variables are: migrants (M_{ij}), wages *(W)*, unemployment levels *(U)*, amenity levels *(A)*, population levels *(P)* and distance *(D_{ij})*.

IMPLICATIONS

To test the three explanations it is first necessary to draw out their implications for the available data which are: net migration rates into the fifteen Union republics for 1959–70 as a single time period, the same kind of rates for the nineteen major economic regions for the same time period, republic-to-republic arrival rates at cities for 1967 and 1969. The first two sets of data resulted from residual calculations of chapter 4. The units of analyses, Union republics and major economic regions, both separately partition the geographic space of the U.S.S.R. The republics are important in government, but are unequal in size; the regions, being more similar in size, are better units for regional analysis. The last two data sets are officially published materials deriving from the system of obligatory population registration in urban areas.[12]

Test 1A

The ideological view of the migration process seems to have both strong and weak versions. The strong asserts that given the socialist law of population and the record of socialist and communist construction in the U.S.S.R., there can be few migration problems. Workers move where the state and Party judge they are needed. Thus, if some regions are declared to be labor-surplus and others, labor-deficient, the Party should be able to effect redistribution simply by stating that workers are needed in the deficient regions. Net migration should occur into those regions declared labor-deficient. Specifically, all the regions could be classified as labor-surplus, labor-deficient, or neither, and the migration rates for the three classes compared. This comparison between the migration levels and the labor statuses of the regions will be referred to as Test 1A.

Test 1B

The weak version of the ideological view states that the movement of labor force about the U.S.S.R. is determined by the spatial pattern of investment.

12. *Vestnik statistiki* (No. 10, 1968) and (No. 3, 1971).

Presumably, where investment proceeds at a pace much faster than the growth of local labor force, excess demand for labor is generated and in-migration occurs. Where investment proceeds at a pace slower than labor force growth, excess supply of labor is generated and out-migration occurs. According to this view, labor redistributes itself to eliminate the excess demands and supplies. A simple model seems to be suggested. If there is a technological capital-labor ratio across regions of the economy, $k = K/L$, where k is constant and K is capital and L is labor, then in a full-employment economy the change in labor employment (ΔL) is: $\Delta L = (1/k)I$ and the need for migrants (ΔL_m) caused by investment (I) is: $\Delta L_m = (1/k)I - \Delta L_1$ where ΔL_1 is change in already located labor supply. Further assuming that migrant labor is some constant fraction of migrant population, that is $L_m = fP_m$, the last result could be rewritten:

$$\Delta P_m = \frac{1}{kf} I - \frac{1}{f} \Delta L_1$$

In principle, this is a reduced form expression that states that an increase in investment should raise migration on net account and an accleration in the increase in local labor force should lower it. If the theory is correct, a regression of net migrants during 1959–70 on investment and labor force change owing to increase and aging of long-resident population should produce a good fit. The theory suggests that $1/f$ is positive and $1/kf$ is positive.

Test IIA

The Soviet social science thinking on migration is incompletely developed in at least two regards. The decision to migrate approach does not appear to have been used in any comprehensive empirical work and may even be nonoperational, and the factors of migration view has not been used much in comprehensive multivariate analysis. The few statistical studies that have been done curiously fail to include all the variables that the selective comparison work suggests are relevant: living conditions, ethnic considerations, natural-climatic conditions, the geographic factor and the social-psychological factor. Ethnic, geographic, and social-psychological considerations have usually been neglected.

The factors of migration literature can be elaborated for application in a regression test. Specifically, for a study of levels of net migration into various regions, the dependent variable (arrivals on net account per thousand population) can be said to be a function of:

1. Economic living conditions as measured by levels of wages and retail trade per capita,
2. Ethnic considerations as measured by the proportion of the population of the republic or region that was Russian in 1959,
3. The natural-climatic factor as measured by mean January temperature, and

4. A social-psychological factor as measured by a dummy variable taking on the value of 1.0 for regions that the state was actively seeking to settle.

In addition, the Soviet literature repeatedly points out that a necessary condition for population movement is job availability. A nonbinary measure of the extent of excess demand present could be employment growth less labor supply growth stemming from long-resident population. The last would be a fifth factor to be included. This specification will be referred to as Test IIA.

Test IIB

For a study of republic-to-republic urban arrival streams the Soviet factors of migration literature could be interpreted to mean that the dependent variable (arrivals at the cities of republic *j* from republic *i* per number of inhabitants at *i* times number of urban inhabitants at *j*) is a function of:

1. Economic living conditions as measured by wages and retail trade per capita at both origin and destination,
2. Ethnic considerations as represented by a measure of ethnic affinity (prior ethnic exchange),
3. Distance as measured by air distances between capitals,
4. The natural-climatic factor as measured by mean January temperature at both origin and destination,
5. Social-psychological factor as measured by a dummy variable taking on the value of 1.0 for regions that the state was actively seeking to settle,
6. A measure of excess demand at destination for employment, calculated by employment growth less labor supply growth owing to the increase and aging of local population and to rural-to-urban migration within the same republic.

This specification will be referred to as Test IIB.

A Third Test?

The Western view relevant for the present study consisted of two components, the human capital and the push-pull approaches. The former, as far as this study of determinants is concerned, led to the latter which suggested that economic conditions, amenity conditions, and perhaps unemployment rates would be relevant determinants. For explaining net migration rates, the specification would likely have some measure of economic living conditions, amenity conditions, the most important certainly being climate, and unemployment rates. A theme of the push-pull literature is that there is not a rigid list of determinants relevant for all situations; researchers have felt free to adapt the list and definition of variables to fit particular empirical situations being studied. If the present study continues in this tradition, the approach should be modified to include the ethnic variable that Soviet studies have shown to be important, and the social-psychological factor, the importance of which is an open question.

A problem arises now in that the specifications for the Soviet social science and the Western views are nearly identical. Four of the five factors mentioned in connection with Test IIA have been listed again here. The one difference concerns the use of labor demand growth indicator in the Soviet social science view and an unemployment rate here. These two variables, however, really measure the same thing, the degree of excess demand in the market. When the excess demand is high, that is, the rate of employment growth is exceeding the rate of labor supply growth owing to local population growth and aging, the first measure will be high and the second, low. In contrary circumstances, the opposite will prevail. Based upon theoretical arguments[13] and the unavailability of measures of umemployment for the U.S.S.R., the former measure is the one that must be used, even in the testing of the Western view, and this last change reduces the Soviet social science and Western views to approaches having the same observational implications.

The same is true for any test developed to study the republic-to-republic urban arrivals. Most of the variables in the two factor lists are the same, the one exception being again the measure of excess demand. The discussion above applies and makes the two approaches observationally equivalent. Thus, if the Tests IIA and IIB provide good explanations, the results will have to be regarded as consistent with both approaches. This is disappointing, but cannot come as too great a surprise, since the approaches appeared similar to begin with.

FINDINGS

The data and their sources are described in Table 5.1. In instances where eleven-year migration rates are used in comparisons involving Union republics, the case of Tadzhikistan is omitted because its estimate did not pass plausibility tests.[14] In Tests 1A, 1B and IIA the results for regions should be given more attention because the regions, being geographically more homogeneous and more nearly equal in size, are better units for analysis.

Test 1A consists of a comparison of net migration rates (MR) for an eleven-year period in Union republics and economic regions based upon a classification of the various areas as labor-surplus, neutral, or labor-deficient. The Central Asian and Transcaucasian republics were taken to be labor-surplus along with the Ukraine, Belorussia, and Moldavia; the Baltic republics were judged to be neutral; Kazakhstan and Russia were taken to be labor-deficient. Among the regions, Central Asia, Transcaucasia, the Southwest, the South, Belorussia, Moldavia, Volga-Vyatka, Central Chernozem, and North Causcasus were regarded as labor-surplus; the Northwest, the Center, Volga, Urals, Don-Dnieper and Baltic regions were classified as neutral; West Siberia, East Siberia, the Far East, and Kazakahstan were taken as labor deficient. The

13. R. A. Hart, "Interregional Economic Migration. Some Theoretical Considerations," *Journal of Regional Science*, XV (No. 2–3, 1975), pp. 134–35.
14. See p. 76ff.

results are displayed in Table 5.2. In the Average Values section are listed the numbers of net migrants during 1959-70 per thousand population on January 15, 1959. The data should show a decline from top to bottom if population had moved from labor-surplus to labor deficient regions. But they do not. The regional data, for practical purposes, show that the migration rates were the same for the three classes. A formal analysis of variance suggests the same thing, that it is reasonable to presume that the rates were the same. Thus, there is no support here for the strong version of the ideological view that labor simply moves to where it is needed.

Test IB consists of regressing levels of net migration (MIG) on levels of investment (I) and changes in domestic labor supplies (LS). The first variable is the number of migrants on net account during 1959–70, the second is an estimate of total investment during the period, and the third is an estimate of net increase in labor force during the interval due to members of the 1959 population. According to the view that migrants are attracted to where investment is taking place, the regression fits should be close. But those reported in Table 5.3 are not. Because of the great variance in the geographic size of the republics, it was presumed that the standard deviation of the error term of the model was proportional to population size; this consideration suggested a simple generalized least squares (GLS) approach. Ordinary least squares (OLS) sufficed for the regional analysis. Both equations, however, produce poor fits. In the case of the republics the actual and predicted values are negatively correlated and in the case of the regions the positive correlation is very weak. The belief that migrants simply move in direct relation to investment is not supported by these findings.

Test IIA consists of regressions of eleven-year migration rates (MR) on trade per capital levels (TRADE), average wage levels (WAGE), the number of Russians per thousand population in 1959 (ETHNIC1), employment growth (EMPLOY), average annual temperature (TEMP) and a dummy variable for state calls to settle (EXHORT). The OLS results for both republics and regions cannot be trusted because of collinearity among the independent variables. There are four zero-order correlations exceeding 0.50 in absolute value in the republic data and five having the same property in the regional data. Accordingly, principal component estimation[15] based upon four components and ridge regression[16] were used in the hope of reducing substantially the variance of the estimators at a cost of introducing some bias. The results are reported in Table 5.4. The numbers there are Beta coefficients which attempt to eliminate the influence of disparate units of measurement. Their interpretation is that an increase in one standard deviation of an independent variable yields the indicated standard deviation change in the dependent variable. In the case of the

15. B. T. McCallum, "Artificial Orthogonalization in Regression Analysis," *The Review of Economics and Statistics*, LII, No. 1 (February 1970), 110–13.

16. Arthur E. Hoerl and Robert W. Kennard, "Ridge Regression: Biased Estimation for Non-Orthogonal Problems," *Technometrics*, XII, No. 1 (February 1970), 55–82.

regional results all the variables have the expected sign except for the EXHORT variable, for which there was no anticipation. The ethnic and employment growth variables seem to be the most important. Temperature has a positive effect, too. The influence of the economic factors seems to be secondary. The synthesized Soviet-social-science and Western view as developed here receives some support.

Test IIB examines point-to-point urban arrivals in relation to populations at origin and destination (MIGR) as a function of differential trade per capital levels (TRADE-), wage levels (WAGE-), average temperature levels (TEMP-) along with ethnic affinity (ETHNIC2), distance (DIST), employment growth at *j* (EMPLOYJ), and calls to settle (EXHORT). Complete descriptions of the variables are given in Table 5.1. Separate estimates of the parameters are made for 1967 and 1969 and are presented in Table 5.5. The coefficients for the trade, wage, ethnic, and distance variables may be interpreted as estimates of elasticities. The OLS estimates are disappointing in that for both years the values for TRADEJ, WAGEI and TEMPJ have the incorrect sign and are statistically significant. The fits are, however, reasonably good and the coefficients for TRADEI, WAGEJ, ETHNIC and DIST are of the correct sign. Despite the fact that each of the regressions has 210 observations, there is still evidence of collinearity. A linear combination of all the independent variables except for WAGEJ, for example, is able to explain about 75 percent of the variation in WAGEJ, indicating that there is substantial linear dependence among the regressors. The biased techniques for estimation yield the results listed under PC-4 and RIDGE. These results are somewhat difficult to interpret. They do indicate that the ethnic and distance factors have substantial influence. The TRADE- variables seem to have little. The WAGEJ effect appears to be somewhere between 0.5 and 1.0, that of WAGEI is ambiguous. The influence of TEMP- is slight. These results seem to be consistent with the synthesized views of Soviet and Western social scientists.

CONCLUSIONS

The quantitative work of this chapter suggests that there is no support for the ideological views of the migration process. People did not move and settle according to the government's desires for additional labor. The migration rates into labor-surplus areas were for practical purposes the same as those for labor-deficient areas. Nor did a simple explanation based upon the areal distribution of investment and conditions of local labor supply explain much of the process. Multivariate approaches, based upon Soviet and Western thinking, proved more successful. The work for net migration levels over 1959–70 shows the employment growth factor and ethnic considerations were important. The temperature and trade per capita factor also emerge as important determinants for the more noteworthy regional analysis.

For the annual point-to-point streams, the ethnic and distance factors explain much of the variation. Wage at destination appears to have a significant effect too. It appears to have to have a much stronger effect in the one-year gross migration explanations than in the eleven-year net migration explanation. Perhaps this results from the propensity of young people to go off to the remote areas for the short term to earn and save the high wages paid there and then return to their earlier locations. Several other variables in the explanations do not have the anticipated effects. This is somewhat disappointing. Our analysis for urban arrival streams is perhaps greatly affected by the large and disparate units of analysis (Union republics), the collinearity of the regressors and the inadequacies in the data. Appreciating this last possibility, it may at least be concluded that simple ideological views do not advance our understanding of the 1959–70 migration processes. The more elaborate explanations based upon people's desires to enjoy economic, natural, and social amenities are much more helpful.

6

ECONOMIC EFFECTS

The economic effects of interregional migration include effects on the compositions of populations and labor force, requirements for social capital, and levels of production. It is impossible to conduct a complete study of all these effects on an extensive basis, since the phenomena are regional and the requisite data on employment, wages, and production are not generally available. Necessarily, one relies to a large extent on isolated observations and limited research to identify the existence and magnitude of these effects.

POPULATION AND LABOR FORCE

Effects on Summary Demographic Measures

Migration changes population compositions at origin and destination and may alter the characteristics of migrants and members of losing and gaining populations. Through compositional changes, which are relatively easy to identify and which receive attention here almost exclusively, interregional migration in the U.S.S.R. almost certainly affected summary measures of fertility, population sex ratios, the areal distribution of labor and human capital, and regional levels of employment.

As the crude rate of birth dropped during the 1960s, due to a changing age distribution and, especially in later years, to a decrease in age-specific fertility rates at all ages, the question of whether the Soviet Union would be adequately populated in the future received increasing attention. Knowing that under present circumstances future labor supply depends almost completely on present levels of child-bearing, some Soviet observers became concerned with the effects of migration on summary measures of fertility in various regions.

Migration generally increased crude rates of birth in regions gaining population and decreased them in losing regions. For one thing, a good deal of all migration involved rural-to-urban movement. In the Soviet Union, as elsewhere, crude rates of birth in rural areas generally exceed those in urban areas. An example of this mechanism at work is provided by northern Kazakhstan where, during the early 1960s, nearly 80 percent of the urban arrivals came from rural localities. Over the 1959–64 period the crude rate of births for all of Kazakhstan fell by 30 percent, but in northern Kazakh cities growing quickly on account of net migration, rates fell on the order of 20 to 25 percent while in cities growing slowly or losing population, they fell by as much as 45 percent.[1] Again in connection with rural-to-urban migration, some Soviet demographers, noting that the age-sex structure of rural populations had become distorted by selective migration, expressed concern over the viability of these populations. In this regard it is interesting to note that in 1968 within the Ukraine, the crude rates of birth in rural and urban localities were practically equal and that in a number of oblasts, rural rates actually fell below urban rates.[2] Thus, to the extent that interregional migration was composed of rural-to-urban moves it lowered crude rates of birth in areas of exodus and raised them in areas of arrival. Another factor having the same effect would appear to have been the dominance of persons of working age in migration streams, particularly those aged 16–30, who were, of course, also of child-bearing age.

Perhaps there were instances in which crude rates were reduced by interregional migration. According to Table 4.1 the 1959–70 population increase owing to net migration in Central Asia was 5 percent. Inasmuch as this region had the highest crude rates of birth in the U.S.S.R., the addition of almost any outside national group would have worked, other things being equal, to reduce crude birth rates in the Central Asia republics. This is not an inconsequential consideration since, according to 1958–59 data, completed female fertility among Central Asian nationalities was near six births and among Russians was between two and three births.[3]

Very little is known about the more interesting question of what happened to the fertility of migrants (rather than what happened to crude birth rates). In the absence of adequate census data, only a very few surveys seem to exist. In Yerevan, the capital of Armenia, the fertility rate of married female migrants aged 25–29 and arriving during this stage of life was reported as 45 percent higher than the corresponding rate for nonmigrants. Subsequently, the specific rates of migrants fell, so that at around age 34 there was no difference between migrants and long-resident population.[4] In Latvia, however, it appears that the completed family size of migrants was no greater than that of nonmigrants, and consequently, despite their relatively great numbers, migrants had no special effect on the overall measures of Latvian fertility.[5] The finding is not particularly surprising in that rural-to-urban movement was relatively unimportant in Latvian in-migration and the neighboring areas, from which population arrived, were demographically similar to Latvia.

1. P. I. Bagrii et al. (eds.), *Voprosy demografii* (Kiev: Statistika, 1968), p. 180.
2. D. L. Broner and I. G. Venetskii (eds.), *Problemy demografii* (Moscow: Statistika, 1971), p. 121.
3. A. G. Volkov et al. (eds.), *Voprosy demografii* (Moscow: Statistika, 1970), pp. 164–65.
4. D. I. Valentei et al. (eds.), *Problemy migratisii naseleniia i trudovykh resursov* (Moscow: Statistika, 1970), p. 99.
5. Broner and Venetskii, *Problemy demografii*, p. 233.

Since men predominated among migrants, an obvious effect was produced on the sex ratios in gaining and losing populations. The effect in conjunction with the loss of males during World War II, was sometimes important. At the time of the 1959 census the U.S.S.R. ratio of females to males was 1.220. Since it has already been noted that in Russia this ratio was generally higher in rural localities, it is not surprising that much of the attention this problem received came again in connection with the urban-to-rural migration problem. In the case of the Ukraine, the 1970 census showed female-to-male ratios of 1.160 in the cities, 1.273 in rural areas, and 1.354 on collective farms.[6] Throughout the period, of course, natural processes worked to lower the ratio in areas where it was formerly high. In Latvia and Estonia, however, migration was clearly important in the very substantial decrease in the ratio between 1959 and 1970, since males were very numerous among in-migrants and migration was a very important part of total population increase.

Labor Force Compositions

Net migration also affected the quantitative and qualitative compositions of labor forces at origin and destination in the same ways that populations were changed.

A population's dependency ratio may be calculated by dividing the number of persons too young and too old to work by the number of those within the working ages. Obviously, over a short period of time an excess of births over deaths (positive natural increase) works to raise the ratio while net in-migration, given a predominance of working-age persons entering the population, acts to lower it. Stated in other terms, under typical circumstances an increase in the component of population increase due to in-migration initially lowers the dependency ratio. The ratios of migration change to total population increase were calculated for various regions and are displayed in Table 6.1. Since all the areas had an excess of births over deaths, it follows that 1.000 is an upper bound for the index. Areas with high indices, most notably Latvia, Estonia, and the South region of the Ukraine, but also Kazakhstan, Kirghizia, and Armenia, may have experienced a decrease in the dependency ratio.

Quite apart from whatever changes occurred in dependency ratios which, after all, were influenced not only by migration, but also by initial age distributions and the regimens of birth and death, it is, of course, true that any area having a positive migration balance did have its potential labor force augmented. It is possible to guess the extent to which this occurred for various Union republics by first assuming that three-quarters of all migrants on net account were within the working-age intervals at the end of the period and then relating their numbers to the populations of working age on January 15, 1959. In Table 6.2 may be seen the large contributions migration made to the labor forces of Uzbekistan, Kirghizia, and Tadzhikistan (where 1959 dependency ratios were highest at around 1.0), Kazakhstan and Armenia, and Latvia and

6. Ibid., p. 121.

Estonia (where populations were relatively old).[7] Inasmuch as Russia had at the time of the 1959 census approximately 56 percent of the total U.S.S.R. working-age population and among the republics losing population on balance due to migration, had nearly 90 percent of the persons of working age,[8] its role in supplying labor would appear to have been overwhelming.

Since skilled persons constituted an important part of migration streams, it is almost certain that interregional movements altered their areal distribution. In this regard it is interesting to study the distribution among Union republics of one category of highly skilled manpower: the graduates of secondary-specialized schools and of institutions of higher education. Despite some occasional bits of evidence to the contrary, it appears that there was not significant unemployment among these workers. As a result, it may be assumed that the numbers wanting to work and actually employed were approximately equal. Accordingly, regional data on the growth of employment of these workers would indicate how much their supply, or more precisely, quantity supplied increased. The 1969–65 percentage increases of employment of workers trained at some time in specialized secondary schools and higher education institutions are shown in Table 6.3. The U.S.S.R. increase of 46 percent represented 4.1 million persons; during the same period about 5.5. million graduates were added to the supply.[9]

Of course, supplies of highly skilled labor grew both as the result of migration and local training. A rough adjustment may be made to isolate the effect of migration. The number of graduates during 1961–65 may be approximately estimated by the formula:

$$N = \frac{(R_{60} \times P_{60}) + (R_{65} \times P_{65})}{2} \times 0.1 \times 5.94$$

where:

N is the number of graduates,

R_i is the number of graduates during the ith year per 10,000 population in the 1960s,

P_i is the population (thousands) on the first day of the ith year during the 1960s,

.1 is necessary to give an estimate in thousands, and 5.94 is the interval in years—with the data sources indicated below:

R_i—*Narkhoz 65*, p. 700.

P_{60}—*Vestnik statistiki* (No. 2, 1967), p. 94.

P_{65}—*Narkhoz 64*, p. 12.

The resulting values for N may be divided by increases in employment to develop indices of production of new graduates to increased utilization of all

7. A. I. Goluzov and M. G. Grigor'iants, *Narodonaselenie SSSR* (Moscow: Statistika, 1969), p. 72.

8. Ibid., p. 8.

9. TsSU, *Trud v SSSR* (Moscow: Statistika, 1968), p. 25.

graduates. Regions with indices below the all-Union index would likely be receiving highly skilled labor resources from other regions while those below would be supplying them.[10] These indices are displayed in Table 6.4 where it may be seen that the only republic with an index higher than the all-Union one is Russia.

The Spearman rank-order correlation coefficient between number of points below the all-Union index and population percentage change due to migration is .59. The linear correlation is quite high among the subset of observations that excludes Belorussia, Moldavia, and Lithuania. In these republics the number of points below the all-Union index is much greater in relation to level of net migration. This may be explained in part by their special place in interregional migration balances. Of the European republics these three had the highest percentages of rural population and were thus viewed as labor-surplus regions able to provide workers to the agricultural and construction sectors of other regions. Yet at the same time industrial production and urban population were growing quickly within these republics, establishing a strong demand for skilled workers in cities. Intrarepublican urban-to-urban flows were almost certainly very high,[11] but it is doubtful that native populations were able to provide all the highly skilled labor that was required. It appears, then, that these three republics provided relatively unskilled labor to other regions while receiving skilled manpower.

Flexible-Price and Fixed-Price Explanations

In the discussion of interregional movement of highly skilled persons, changes in regional quantities of labor supplied were assumed to be identical to changes in employment. Particularly with regard to other classes of workers, it seems prudent to investigate other theoretical possibilities in which changes in quantity supplied might not have been equal to changes in employment, and in which wage rates might have changed.

The neoclassical economic (flexible-price) theory of wages suggests that, other things being equal, migration eliminates regional differences in wages. But since it is necessary to take account of all the advantages and disadvantages of various regional employments, the neoclassical proposition must be reformulated to say that migration works to eliminate differences in overall attractiveness of various geographical locations. Among the factors on which the attractiveness of an area may depend, some like climate are unaffected by migration, others like housing supply appear somewhat affected, and still others like wage levels probably are very responsive to migration. It is likely that regional wage levels assume an important role in bringing about equilibrium, and since some other factors change only a little or not at all, equilibrium regional wages will differ to compensate for the totality of differences in other

10. The argument assumes a uniform rate of attrition from the population of graduates working.
11. See Table 3.3.

factors. Under most imaginable circumstances and with unchanging demands for labor, the process of adjustment towards equilibrium requires the relative decrease of wages in attrative areas.

It is possible to outline (with unchanging regional demands for labor) a fixed-price theory, differing from the neoclassical view primarily in the fact that wage levels do not change. Starting again with a disequilibrium situation of geographical settlement and assuming an arbitrary set of regional wage levels, one still expects workers to move according to relative advantage. But the achievement of a settlement equilibrium may be problematical. If wage levels do not change, only factors like housing supply, public services, or employment opportunities are left to effect equilibrium. Perhaps the most powerful equilibrating mechanism in this situation would be employment opportunities, as measured by excess demand or excess supply (unemployment). One may envision unemployed workers leaving areas of general unemployment for job-plentiful areas. Yet what role is left for this mechanism in an economy where labor is in short supply in the totality of all economic regions? It seems probable that the movement of people from less to more attractive areas would continue for a very long period, all the time increasing excess demands in former regions and reducing them in the latter ones. If a settlement equilibrium were ever achieved, it would be characterized, in general, by nonzero regional excess demands for labor, meaning that in both disequilibrium and equilibrium, regions of labor-deficit would persist.

The dynamic [12] predictions of the two models are the interesting ones. According to the neoclassical view, in a growing economy (that is, one in which the demand for labor is increasing) and with other likely circumstances, employment would increase more and wage levels less in relatively attractive regions. Excess demands for labor would not be observed. According to the fixed-price approach under most likely circumstances, excess demand would be observed and would increase in unattractive regions while decreasing in the attractive areas. The fixed-price theory predicts that employment would decrease and wage levels would not rise in unattractive regions. It appears, then, that the course of events in unattractive areas may decide which, if either, approach is correct. The former theory predicts large increases in wage levels and relatively low increases in employment; the latter predicts no increases in wage levels, decreases in employment, and the persistence of excess demands.

Surrogate measures of employment and wage-level changes within Union republics are available. For the former the percentage increase growth of employment of blue- and white-collar workers *(rabochie i sluzhashchie)* over the 1960–69 period may be used.[13] Since regional wage data are not generally available,[14] a proxy, the percentage increase in trade per worker, is used.[15]

12. Or comparative static in the case of the first model.
13. *Narkhoz 69*, p. 533.
14. Gertrude E. Schroeder, "An Appraisal of Soviet Wage and Income Statistics," in Vladimir G. Treml and John P. Hardt (eds.), *Soviet Economic Statistics* (Durham, N.C.: Duke University Press, 1972), p. 291.
15. *Narkhoz 69*, pp. 533, 603.

The variables are interpreted as measures of the increase in employment and in wage level, respectively; their values along with correlations between the series are listed in Table 6.5.

Neither theory appears to predict accurately the developments in unattractive regions (taken as Russia, Belorussia, Georgia, and Azerbaydzan where migration diminished total population). The fixed-price approach predicted no increase in wages, yet large increases appear to have occurred in Russia and Belorussia. The presence of the increases in the proxy for wages unambiguously contradicts the fixed-price hypothesis, at least to the extent that it has been developed here. With regard to neoclassical view, it was predicted that high wage increases and moderate employment increases would be observed in the unattractive regions, but in this latter instance the cases of Georgia and Azerbaydzhan exibited contrary developments. So the flexible-price approach seems to be inadequate, too. But Georgia and Azerbaydzhan have long been areas of high natural increase, implying that during the 1960–69 period their populations of working-age were substantially increased by the aging process. It would appear, therefore, that in testing the model and important determinant of the supply of labor (and hence of the employment level) had been neglected. To determine the effect of interregional migration on employment and wage levels, it will apparently be necessary to take into account the effect of varying birth rates some years prior to approximately 1955.

The effects of increased labor supply through both migration and natural processes may be explicitly taken into account by a modification of the following deterministic, static model of demand and supply:

$$\begin{array}{ll} \text{demand} & Q_d = aP + b + F \\ \text{supply} & Q_s = \beta + \phi \end{array}$$

where Q and P are quantity and price: a, b, and β are parameters; and, F and ϕ represent the potential effect of shift factors. Supply is taken as exogenous.[16] The model may be made dynamic:

$$\begin{array}{ll} \Delta Q_d = a \, \Delta P + \Delta F & \text{demand} \\ \Delta Q_s = \Delta \Phi & \text{supply} \end{array}$$

An important component of ΔF is growth in the demand for labor over time; other components may be taken as stochastic. Important elements of $\Delta\Phi$ may be labor supply increases due to migration and to wholly internal population growth. This model may then be taken, for present purposes, as:

$$\Delta EMP = a \cdot \Delta WAG + CON + e$$

$$\Delta EMP = \gamma \cdot MIG + \delta YOU + CON + \epsilon$$

where:

ΔEMP = employment change, column A, Table 6.5

ΔWAG = wage level change, column B, Table 6.5

16. This structural form yields a relatively good fit with acceptable parameter values.

CON = trend constant
MIG = population change due to migration, column C, Table 6.5
YOU = percentage of 1959 population aged 0–15 years[17]

Consistent estimates of these relationships are:

demand change	$\Delta EMP = -3.33\,\Delta WAG + 151.10$	$R^2 = 44$[18]
	F value	(9.99)
supply change	$\Delta EMP = 0.57\,MIG + 2.04\,YOU - 9.29$	$R^2 = .36$
	t and F values (0.55) (2.48)	(3.44)

The model, formulated to isolate the effect of migration on employment and wages, shows it to have been unimportant. Although the estimated coefficient for migration in the supply change equation is positive (the anticipated sign), it is not statistically significant and contributes almost nothing to the explanatory value of the equation.

This finding, while of some consequence, does not allow the general conclusion that migration had no influence on regional changes in wage and employment levels. First, the equations explain very low percentages of the total variation. The author's version of the neoclassical model, assuming equality of changes in quatities supplied and demanded, may be incorrect. One cannot be sure that the model has captured the essence of the process. Most likely the truth concerning wage change lies a good distance from the polar extremes of the neoclassical and fixed-price approaches. Second, since the units of analysis were Union republics, migration between major economic regions within Russia and the Ukraine is ignored, thereby making the sample a somewhat special one and reducing its total variation. Third, the aggregation over sectors of the economy and classes of workers, which could not be any greater, is probably much too great. Undoubtedly, within specific sectors and classes, the effects of migration are more obvious, a circumstance already observed for the class of highly skilled workers.

The evidence of this section does not advance matters very far. While it has been seen that net in-migration raised crude birth rates, its effects on fertility, independent of the compositional mechanism, is uncertain. Although it has been learned that dependency ratios and labor supplies were affected, the quantitative dimensions cannot be precisely fixed. Regional trends in the growth of employment and labor supply of highly skilled workers have been examined and it emerges that migration contributed importantly to employment growth, increasing the stock of these workers in areas of in-migration. But when growth of employment and net in-migration in Union republics for a broad class of workers are examined, there seems to be little relation. A modified neoclassical view incorporating the likely effects of migration does

17. Goluzov and Grigor'iants, *Narodonaselenie*, p. 72.
18. Estimated as: $\Delta WAG = -0.30\,\Delta EMP + 45.43$ $R^2 = .44$
t and F values (-3.16) (9.99)

not explain the observed variation well and does not reveal migration to have been very significant in employment and wage-level determinations.

REQUIREMENTS FOR SOCIAL CAPITAL

Changes in population composition owing to migration almost certainly altered the requirements for social capital. In this regard likely consequences and instances of effects are noted briefly in the absence of extensive data.

Much of the discussion about the capital costs of population growth has been concerned with the problem in underdeveloped countries. A simple version of the argument runs as follows: Suppose a society produces income *(Y)* in fixed relation to is capital stock stock *(K)*:

$$Y = \alpha K$$

Additionally, it is assumed that well-being may be approximated by income per member of total population *(P)*. It follows that population growth diminishes welfare, since:

$$\frac{Y}{P} = \frac{\alpha K}{P}$$

may be written as:

$$\ln \frac{Y}{P} = \ln \alpha + \ln K - \ln P$$

which, upon differentiation, yields:

$$g_{Y/P} = g_K - g_P$$

where g denotes a growth rate. Obviously,

$$g_{Y/P} > 0 \text{ requires } g_K > g_P$$

and in this sense population growth mandates capital growth to maintain per capita standards of living.

The situation is not so simple when population growth is due to migration and the marginal product of labor is positive. If a neoclassical production function with capital and labor *(L)* arguments is assumed then:

$$g_{Y/P} > 0 \text{ only requires } g_K > \frac{Y}{f_K K} [g_p - g_{Y.L}]$$

where f_K is marginal product of capital and $g_{Y.L}$ is the growth rate of income strictly due to changes in labor. Either a high marginal product of labor or a sharp increase in the quantity of labor can make the expression in square brackets negative. This being the case, migration in which laborers predominate does not necessarily require an increase in capital services to sustain per capita income levels.

Once the assumption of the homogeneity of capital is dropped and its stock is regarded as a collection of different goods, it becomes clear that migration, while not increasing the demand for some measure of aggregate capital, may nevertheless change requirements for particular goods. The costs that a society incurs to provide facilities and human skills to dispense over time—social services like housing, medical care, and education—to a population with a changing composition may be called demographic investments. Both underdeveloped and economically advanced countries have experienced these costs in connection with high rates of natural increase in population during this century. With regard to growth due to migration, it appears that economic demographers have judged the costs to be insignificant. Perhaps the fact that the costs do exist is obscured by the circumstance that many migrants, being of working age, are from a community's viewpoint, able to offset social capital requirements by economically productive activity. If a person is regarded as a capital asset, having a stream of costs and returns, his maximum present value is probably reached during his early working years after child-rearing and long before old age. But this neglects one cost that is likely to be rather high for migrants and is pertinent to the Soviet case, the cost of housing.

A real-world society interested in continuously maximizing its growth rate does not miss its mark by much if it always allocates investment to sectors where marginal output-capital ratios are highest. A variant of this rule, used in connection with the description of Soviet practice, is that investment has usually been concentrated where greatest potential cost reductions existed.[19] According to this approach, steel, fuel, machinery, and electric power received investment; housing with its low output-capital ratio, received very little.

The quantitative and qualitative deficiencies of the Soviet housing stock, if not legendary, are certainly well known. Although the situation improved somewhat during 1959–70, housing remained scarce and overcrowded. Urban housing space *(obshchaia poleznaia ploshchad')* per capita rose from 8.9 square meters per inhabitant at the end of 1960 to 10.0 at the end of 1965 and 10.9 at the end of 1969.[20] Despite interest in improving the housing situation, especially during the seventh five-year plan, the state did not effect any drastic reorientation of investment towards housing construction; in fact, the percentage of total capital investment by all economic entities allocated to housing declined slightly during the 1960s.[21] And it continued to be easy for regular readers of the Soviet press to compile strings of stories about shoddy construction, disrepair of facilities, and lack of amenities in housing.

19. Rush V. Greenslade, "The Soviet Economic System in Transition" in the U.S., Congress, Joint Economic Committee, *New Directions in the Soviet Economy* (Washington, D.C.: U.S. Government Printing Office, 1966), p. 6.

20. *Narkhoz 69*, p. 569 and *Vestnik statistiki* (No. 2, 1971), p. 85. These figures include living and nonliving space (that is, halls, kitchens, closets, and pantries). Living space is generally figured to be two-thirds of total space *(obshchaia poleznaia ploshchad')*. See T. Sosnovy, "The Soviet City," in U.S., Congress, Joint Economic Committee, *Dimensions of Soviet Economic Power* (Washington, D.C.: U.S. Government Printing Office, 1962), p. 330. The figures also include privately owned housing, the construction of which slowed during the 1960s. At the end of 1969 such housing represented about 30 percent of total space.

21. *Narkhoz 69*, pp. 504–5.

In view of these circumstances, the increase in demand for housing due to in-migration must generally have been unwanted. While it is at least conceivable that the addition of a child to a family may have been in certain instances relatively inexpensive in terms of housing requirements, this certainly was not true for migrants. Enterprises acted accordingly. An observer dealing with rural out-migration noted that industrial, transport, and construction enterprises always requested that state labor committees send from the collective farms single persons rather than workers with families. The reason for this "narrowly departmental" outlook, according to the observer, was the desire to minimize concerns and costs connected with the provision of adequate living conditions for workers.[22]

The capital costs of population growth due to in-migration have been an important consideration in the long-standing Soviet desire to control migration into large cities. At least since the 1930s when the Central Committee prohibited the construction of new enterprises in several of the largest western cities, the party has tried to restrict the growth of its biggest cities. Over the years, a program of curtailing investment and population growth (through migration) in many large cities has developed. These policies were reaffirmed at the Twenty-Second and Twenty-Third Party Congresses during the 1960s, and the majority view seems to have become that the additional costs of housing, mass transit, sanitation, air pollution, and congestion resulting from additional urban growth were simply too high in most large cities. Enterprises and ministries did not usually agree, since the advantages of skilled labor supply and developed infrastructure of education, communication, and transportation were still available in the large cities and the costs of locating there could sometimes be ignored because they were external to the firm or could other times be minimized by hiring a certain kind of labor.

Housing was scarce in the developing regions. Russian Central Statistical Administration work documented the extent to which the eastern regions lagged behind the Russian average in housing per capita and percentages of housing equipped with running water, central heating, and sewers.[23] The situation was no better in Kazakhstan after the experience of the 1950s when some "Virgin Landers" had lived in tents. The government planned to improve the housing situation there, but plans were never realized. During the mid-1960s housing plans were fulfilled to the following extents in Kazakhstan: 1963, 34 percent; 1964, 41 percent; 1965, 52 percent; and 1966, 26 percent. In 1966 state and collective farms in northern Kazakhstan brought into use only 19 percent of the planned housing for new settlers. Although settlers throughout the period were advanced direct, long-term credits, they often could not be used to the fullest extent possible due in part to the short supply of building materials.[24]

22. Broner and Venetskii, *Problemy demografii*, p. 125.

23. V. V. Pokshishevskii et al. "On Basic Migration Patterns," in George Demko et al. (eds.), *Population Geography: A Reader* (New York: McGraw-Hill, 1970), p. 329.

24. G. Vechkanov, "Raising the Effectiveness of the Territorial Redistribution of

PRODUCTION

In this section are examined the economic effects of population redistribution on production, the effects of labor surpluses and shortages, and the problem of rural-urban balance in production.

Economic Approaches

To maximize national product, marginal analysis suggests that labor be distributed to make its marginal product the same in each of the various regions of an economy. Assuming that there are costs of transporting product to some central point of consumption and that there are regional differences in the cost of sustaining labor does not complicate things greatly. The only requirement is that the marginal products of labor in distant and costly places be raised to offset the additional costs. By using MPL_D and MPL_C to represent the marginal products of labor at a distant point and at the central point, respectively; T_D to denote the unit product transport costs from a distant point to the central point; and, C_D to stand for the cost of sustaining a unit of labor at a distant point in relation to the central point, the rule would typically require:

$$MPL_D(1 - T_D) - C_D = MPL_C$$

If it is assumed that there are diminishing returns to labor everywhere, then the marginal product of labor in a region is raised by applying relatively less labor there. Thus, maximization requires the application of less labor in a distant region if C_D or T_D is high.

On the other hand, if MPL_D is thought to be very high, T_D is moderately low, and C_D not too high, then the distant areas receive much labor. Chapter 2 has shown that the resource-rich eastern regions were regarded as yielding very high returns to the employment of additional labor. Transport costs were felt to be fairly low, since developmental efforts were concentrated on products like gas, oil, and electric power which could be transported rather inexpensively. It is possible, however, that the costs of maintaining labor in the distant regions were systematically underestimated, leading to excessive employment of labor there.

What it cost to maintain labor in these regions appears to have been known only very approximately. In the opinion of some observers, all that could be said was that actual expenditures were insufficient since labor left these areas throughout the period. Others pointed out that planners did not even have accurate information on family expenditures necessary to maintain the same standard of living in the various regions. Nevertheless, some estimates were made. According to one, it cost 16,000 rubles for capital and current outlays to transport, house, and provide services for one industrial-production worker in

---

Labor," *Problems of Economics* (October 1969), p. 63.

the northern parts of the East.[25] According to another, for the eastern regions in general, around 1000 rubles in outlays for resettlement and around 9000 rubles in capital infrastructure were required per worker, the latter figure being about five times the requirement in the western U.S.S.R.[26] It is doubtful that these costs encompassed the notion of premium living conditions to compensate for unattractive natural conditions; they did not directly reflect higher wage costs associated with regional coefficients and premiums.

Another way of looking at the problem of distributing population for maximum economic benefit is Ye. I. Ruzavina's linear-programming formulation.[27] The author's objective is to redistribute population to maximize increase in net product. Regions of the economy that have excess labor are designated by $i = 1, \ldots, m$; the number of excess laborers in the ith such region is designated by A_i. Regions that can use more labor are designated by $j = 1, \ldots, n$; and the amount of labor that is transferred from the ith to the jth region is designated by x_{ij}. The k_{ij} values represent the cost of transferring labor from i to j; the total expenditure amount available is K. In the objective function, c_j is the quantity of net product gained for each worker transferred to the jth region. With the symbols the problem may be stated as:

$$(1)\ \text{maximize} \quad \Delta Y = \sum_{i=1}^{m} \sum_{j=1}^{n} c_j \, x_{ij}$$

$$(2)\ \text{subject to:} \quad \sum_{j=1}^{n} K_{ij} \leq A_i \quad i = 1, \ldots, m$$

$$(3) \quad \sum_{i=1}^{m} \sum_{j=1}^{n} K_{ij} \leq K$$

$$(4) \quad x_{ij} \geq 0 \quad i = 1, \ldots, m; \quad j = 1, \ldots, n$$

Thus, the addition to net product is maximized by relocating laborers, subject to the constraints that the numbers moved do not exceed the numbers available and that the limit on expenditures is not surpassed.

This formulation reflects the way Soviet planners approached the problem. For one thing, it avoids what might be called "explicit marginalism," the use of marginal analysis formally identical to often deprecated work in the West. This, in itself, is hardly important in this context, but it is interesting to note

25. V. Yanovskiy, "Men in the North," U.S., Joint Publications Research Service, *Translations on U.S.S.R. Labor*, JPRS 46794 (November 4, 1968), p. 10.

26. E. S. Rusanov, *Raspredelenie i ispol'zovanie trudovykh resursov SSSR* (Moscow: Ekonomika, 1971), p. 165.

27. D. I. Valentei et al. (eds), *Narodonaselenie i ekonomika* (Moscow: Ekonomika, 1967), pp. 159–62.

that the Ruzavina *c* coefficients encompass several notions. Certainly, the extra output produced is their most important component, but it would appear that they ought also to reflect transportation costs and additional costs of maintaining labor associated with some regions. Undoubtedly they do, but all this is left to the reader's imagination since the author only identifies the coefficients as "the increases in net product per worker."[28] Finally only labor in so-called labor-surplus regions is subject to transfer, whereas in the neoclassical formulation all labor may be moved. This aspect probably derives from the tendency in public discussion to relegate regions into either a "labor deficient" or "labor-surplus" category. In principle, it is better to regard all workers as available for transfer.

Labor Surpluses and Shortages

Ruzavina's approach may be used to survey the economic effects of migration. The effects of labor-surpluses in some regions, shortages in others, and the costs of labor turnover are examined in turn.

The increasing scarcity of industrial labor stemming from the exhaustion of the two traditional sources for raising overall labor force participation rates, the rural population and the female population, was an important problem for the Soviet economy. Two parts of the U.S.S.R., however, were regarded as being particularly capable of supplying labor in the developing regions through the mechanism of migration and their failure to do so led to problems in maintaining full employment.

In the rural areas of non-European republics, natural rates of increase generally exceeded 2 percent a year; during 1959–70 the rural population of the republics of Central Asia, Transcaucasia, and Kazakhstan all increased substantially in contrast to the decline in all-Union rural population. One efficient-redistribution-of-labor scenario anticipated that increasing number of rural inhabitants in Transcaucasia and Central Asia, in conjunction with more efficient agricultural production, would allow the large-scale transfer of labor into industrial or construction work in other regions. But the low mobility of these populations frustrated whatever designs of this sort existed. Thus, in Uzbekistan, of 100 able-bodied collective farmers released from agricultural production, only a few more than 10 moved into other types of employment, the vast majority choosing to settle on their private subsidiary plots.[29] In the collective farm sector it is interesting to note that the following land-to-labor (hectares of collective-farm land in production divided by number of collective farm households) ratios prevailed in 1969[30]: All-Union, 6.8; Russia, 11.1; Ukraine, 4.7; Transcaucasia, 1.8; and Central Asia, 2.7. While production may be less capital-intensive in Transcaucasia and Central Asia, it nevertheless

28. Ibid., p. 160.

29. L. Bulochnikova, "Sel'skaia migratsiia i puti ee regulirovaniia," *Planovoe khoziaistov* (No. 8, 1969), p. 62.

30. *Narkhoz 69*, pp. 404–5.

remains likely that these data indicate more labor in collective farming than was necessary, especially when the large families in these regions are taken into account. Generally in these circumstances, the ratio of labor-days worked in relation to labor-days available was low, indicating to planners that reserves of labor were available and to others that underemployment of labor existed.

In the small- and medium-sized cities of the western U.S.S.R., there were still reserves of labor, too. A 1965 Central Statistical Administration survey of participation rates in 416 small- and medium-size cities found that 45 percent of the nonworking, able-bodied population could have joined the labor force without adverse consequence for the domestic economies of their households. The majority of the individuals constituting the 45 percent were female.[31] Keeping in mind the problems experienced in deciding who is and who is not in the labor force when calculating unemployment rates, one may venture to interpret statements like "[there exist] considerable reserves of labor in small towns, especially in the western regions of the Ukraine, Belorussia, a number of areas of Transcaucasia, and also in central regions of the R.S.F.S.R."[32] as euphemistic admissions of problems in attaining full-employment.

While underemployment and perhaps unemployment existed in some areas, labor shortages persisted in the developing regions, most notably West Siberia.[33] In 1970 it was reported that there were one million unfilled jobs in the R.S.F.S.R. alone, most of them being in the East.[34]

In industry, the general shortage of workers caused attractive employment sectors to be close to fully manned and unattractive ones to be drastically understaffed. In the early 1960s, construction, urban transport, and community services were particularly short-handed in the Siberian regions.[35] The same situation prevailed in 1970, at least in the construction and transport sectors.[36] In the Far East during most of the 1960s, the regional coefficients made industry, transport, and construction particularly attractive, and it was the service sectors that were short of labor. In 1965 the premium of industrial wages over education and health services were 11 and 29 percent, respectively, throughout the R.S.F.S.R., but in the southern regions of the Far East they were 39 and 56 percent.[37] In general, industrial enterprises at urban localities in the East did not lack relatively unskilled labor.

31. P. P. Litviakov (ed.), *Demograficheskie problemy zaniatosti* (Moscow: Ekonomika, 1969), pp. 200–10.

32. A. N. Kosygin, "Ob ulushenii upravleniia promyshlennost'iu sovershenstvovanii planirovaniia i ucilenii ekonomicheskogo stimulirovaniia promyshlennogo proizvodstva" (Moscow: Politizdat, 1965), p. 16.

33. V. I. Perevedentsev's *Migratsiia naseleniia i trudovye problemy Sibiri* (Novosibirsk: Nauka, 1966) is the pioneering work in this field and provides much of the material that follows.

34. Radio Free Europe, "Migration Against Plan" (September 1, 1970), p. 2.

35. V. I. Perevedentsev, *Migratsiia naseleniia*, p. 53.

36. Radio Free Europe, "Migration Against Plan," p. 2.

37. L. L. Rybakovskii (ed.), *Vosproizvodstvo trudovykh resursov Dal'nego Vostoka* (Moscow: Nauka, 1969), p. 57.

Skilled labor, however, was in short supply. Again as might be expected, it was the attractive employment situations that were more adequately manned. In 1961, among the largest enterprises of Novosibirsk, the electro-terminal equipment and turbine-generator plants had 65 and 60 percent, respectively, of the qualified workers they desired, while the housing construction *combinat* had 40 percent of its requirements. Generally, the employment of qualified workers in the East was limited by their short supply. In the machine-building sector the percentages of workers falling in the lowest two skill levels were 56.6 for West Siberia, 58.0 for East Siberia, and 45.5 for the European parts of Russia; the corresponding percentages for the two highest skill levels were 6.0, 4.3, and 9.8, respectively.[38]

The shortages sometimes left capital unused in production. At one point a third of all idle equipment in machine-building plants in Novosibirsk could not be used because of the absence of trained operators. At other times enterprise directors compensated for shortages of skilled manpower by hiring greater numbers of unskilled, with the result that total work force norms were exceeded. The shortages contributed to lower levels of labor productivity in comparison to levels in other regions.[39]

In the agricultural sector of the East some observers concluded that manpower shortages severely curtailed production. As might be expected, land-labor ratios in eastern regions were above average as may be seen for 1969 in Table 6.6. Man-days worked on the collective farms of Siberia in relation to elsewhere were high. In 1969 the number of man-days worked per able-bodied collective farmer was approximately 80 percent of the Siberian level in the Ukraine, North Caucasus, and Central Chernozem, 70 percent in Belorussia, and 60 percent in Georgia.[40] In view of the shorter growing seasons, less favorable natural conditions, and occasional requirements for quick work, manpower shortages led to low levels of product per unit of land. According to one speculation, to have provided the agricultural units of West Siberia with labor on a scale comparable to the whole R.S.F.S.R., approximately 700,000 persons would have to have been relocated.[41] Despite this statement, the problem, as might be expected, lay more with qualitative than quantitative requirements for labor. A survey of rural councils in West Siberia revealed that 61 percent of the vacancies in agricultural enterprises and on collective and state farms required persons with high professional training; 14 percent, persons with incomplete secondary school training; and only 25 percent, unskilled persons.[42]

Since high rates of labor turnover and low rates of efficiency in migration were found in areas where labor was in short supply, these related phenomena

38. Perevedentsev, *Migratsiia naseleniia*, pp. 53–54.
39. Ibid., pp. 54–55.
40. *CDSP*, XIV, No. 26 (July 25, 1962), 3.
41. T. I. Zaslavskaia (ed.), *Migratsiia sel'skogo naseleniia* (Moscow: Mysl', 1970), p. 91.
42. Ibid., p. 89.

raised costs of production, too. During 1960–64 the following annual flows (thousands of persons) occurred in labor-deficient, northern Kazakhstan cities:[43] arrivals, 149.3; departures, 111.7; net arrivals, 37.6. According to one view, the last figure shows the benefit of migration (the increase in regional labor supply) and first two figures indicate the costs of migration (the number of people that were moved to realize the benefit). By assuming that labor productivities of individuals are the same in various sectoral employments, it can be said that the sum of the first two figures minus the last indicates, in a very rough fashion, that 223,000 persons a year moved without benefit to the national economy.[44] A direct cost of this movement was calculated by assuming that 75 percent of all migrants were of working age, that 60 percent of the persons of working age participated in social economy and that each move caused a loss of 20 work-days; thousands of work-days lost were therefore:

$$223 \times .75 \times .60 \times 20 = 2007$$

This was the equivalent to 7,500 full-time, annual workers who, according to average labor productivity levels, could have produced 28 million rubles of national income. Since the assumption of uniform labor productivities is certainly questionable, it is difficult to believe that the crude calculation tells the whole story of costs and benefits. In this regard it should also be pointed out that transport costs are ignored.

Labor turnover was high in the Far East. Data covering 1960–67 showed that annually between 27 to 31 percent of the labor force of industrial enterprises left for reasons that officials interpreted as falling within the labor turnover category. Survey investigation established that average interruption of work lasted 23 to 25 days, which implies an equivalent loss of 11,000 to 12,000 workers per year. In addition to costs of interruption at work, it was found that even when they were fully qualified for vacant positions, new workers took 3 to 5 months after starting a job to achieve output norms. During this period their performance was some 20 to 25 percent below that of experienced workers. These costs translated into an equivalent loss of 9,000 to 12,000 workers per year. In addition, government-financed moving costs had to be taken into account in appropriate instances. By including all these costs, the annual loss due to labor turnover in Yakutia and Magadan Oblast alone[45] was calculated to be between 75 and 80 million rubles.[46]

In the particularly severe conditions of the northern regions of the Far East and the Far North, turnover costs were especially high. The majority of workers did not settle permanently, but left after one to three years of work or sometimes after only a few months service. Due to the capital-intensive methods of

43. T. A. Ashimbaev (ed.), *Naselenie i trudovye resursy gorodov Severnogo Kazakhstana* (Alma-Ata: Nauka, 1970), p. 36.
44. Ibid., pp. 248–49.
45. These two areas are rich in nonferrous ores and are important nationally in this regard.
46. Rybakovskii, *Vosproizvodstvo trudovykh resursov Dalnego Vostoka*, pp. 59–60.

production, idle-equipment opportunity costs in mining, an important sector there, were very large. In addition, even the best qualified workers from other regions had to master the particular techniques that the extreme conditions of the North required, so that learning periods on jobs tended to be prolonged. As might be expected, additional problems in maintaining production discipline, quality output, and good use of equipment were encountered at some enterprises since it was not unusual for over 50 percent of an enterprise's staff to be replaced over the course of a year.[47]

Employment Mix

The rural-to-urban migration that occurred during 1959–70 drew attention to the question of agricultural-industrial employment balance. While most rural-to-urban migration proceeded wholly within major economic regions, the interregional component was significant and merits attention here. During the early years of this period, the industrial urban labor force was augmented only slightly by the natural growth of working-age population, but it did receive substantial contribution from rural-to-urban migration. During 1959–65 the diminution of the U.S.S.R. rural population (due to both migration and territorial reclassification) exceeded its natural increase. But this did not prevail uniformly, since the all-Union decrease resulted primarily from declines in Russia and the Ukraine which offset increases in the rural populations of Central Asia, Transcaucasia, Kazakhstan, and Moldavia.[48] Thus, the concern over the viability of agriculture was limited mainly to the situations in the first two republics.

To discuss the problem in terms of total population is, of course, to miss much of its nature, since those leaving the rural areas were the young and the skilled who, both in terms of quantitative and qualitative input of labor, offered the best prospects for increasing agricultural production. It has already been seen in chapter 3 that persons aged 15–29 in many instances probably made up more than 50 percent of persons leaving rural localities. Among the agricultural workers the propensity to migrate increased with education. On certain West Siberia farms in the 1960s, if the intensity of migration among all workers is taken as 100, the intensity among persons who finished 0–3 grades is 40, and among persons who completed 4–10 grades, 120.[49]

Although agriculture continues to be regarded as a neglected sector, capital investment was substantial during 1959–70. According to one careful Western estimate, labor input (employment) in agriculture between 1959 and 1964 decreased slightly (by 8 percent), the use of land and productive livestock increased slightly (by 6 and 10 percent, respectively) and the use of variable and fixed capital increased significantly (by 44 and 67 percent, respectively).[50]

47. Yanovskiy, "Men in the North," pp. 3–4.
48. Litviakov, *Demograficheskie problemy zaniatosti*, pp. 175–77.
49. Zaslavskaia, *Migratsiia sel'skogo naseleniia*, p. 177.
50. Douglas B. Diamond, "Trends in Output, Inputs, and Factor Productivity in Soviet

According to official data, between 1960 and 1969 the fixed-capital stock *(osnovnye fondy)* employed in agriculture doubled.[51] To the extent that investment involved the introduction of complex agricultural machinery, the requirement for skilled labor grew.

Important in this regard were mechanizers, persons who operated, maintained, or repaired agricultural equipment and who have become notorious in the literature of agricultural labor problems. Mechanizers always seemed to be in short supply. In West Siberia at the beginning of 1967, about 40 percent of all vacancies in agricultural enterprises (including collective farms) were in the mechanizer job category. Enterprises were staffed in this category at about 85 percent of state requirements, with the worst shortages concentrated in the repairman specialty on collective farms and tractor-machinist speciality on state farms.[52] The state tried to eliminate the shortages, but since the training mechanizers received often made them well qualified for industrial employment, the state's efforts produced meager results. During the mid-1960s newly trained mechanizers in West Siberia did no more than replace losses due to natural causes (mostly retirements) and labor turnover (this latter class comprising 83 percent of the total loss).[53] In the Ukraine in 1967–68 the situation was somewhat better. The number of mechanizers increased by 2.3 percent, but the relative of attrition from work force to increase due to training was .76.[54] In other words about four mechanizers a year had to be trained to increase the labor force by one person.

While not agreeing with the great importance that some Soviet officials attach to labor productivity indices as measures of efficiency, one can nevertheless appreciate that the shortage and labor turnover of mechanizers did lower labor productivity. That they did so is frequently asserted in Soviet publications without much evidence concerning the magnitude of the effect. It is reasonable to presume that shortages of labor kept some equipment idle and that turnover increased training costs.

CONCLUSIONS

Interregional migration raised crude rates of birth and lowered female-to-male ratios in most regions of net arrival. It increased labor supplies on the order of 10 percent in Latvia and Estonia, in Kazakhstan and the Central Asia republics (except for Turkmenia), and in Armenia. The important source for the increases was Russia. (Georgia, Azerbaydzhan, and Belorussia also lost labor supply through migration.) Examination of the growth of employment of

Agriculture," in U.S., Congress, Joint Economic Committee, *New Directions in the Soviet Economy* (Washington, D.C.: U.S. Government Printing Office, 1966), p. 348.

51. *Narkhoz 69,* p. 301. All estimates of capital in this paragraph refer to undepreciated capital stock.

52. Zaslavskaia, *Migratsiia sel'skogo naseleniia,* pp. 178, 209.

53. Ibid., p. 209.

54. Broner and Venetskii, *Problemy demografii,* p. 130.

highly skilled workers and annual additions to their numbers from institutions of training indicates that Russia was an extremely important source of these workers. A simple neoclassical model designed to show the effect of migration in markets for labor of all kinds provided a poor explanation of observed variation. The alternative posed by the author, a fixed-price model, was contradicted by the facts. The models appear to have been too simple and the data too aggregative.

Migration increased the demand for social capital in gaining regions. State government and individual enterprise in connection with migration acted to minimize costly investment in housing.

Social costs of production at various sites appear to have been known only imperfectly. Rough estimates of investment requirements for locating a worker in the East at around 10,000 rubles was quite high. Workers left labor-deficit areas for labor-surplus ones. As a consequence, underemployment and unemployment or "employment problems" existed in surplus areas while labor shortages persisted in areas where the state sought to develop production at above-average rates. The shortages and labor turnover in the presence of sometimes difficult natural conditions and relatively abundant capital availability lowered labor productivity.

7

CONCLUSION

In 1972 the Soviet Union celebrated the fiftieth anniversary of its formation. Despite Soviet press accounts suggesting that economic progress had occurred smoothly and evenly over the Soviet period, the achievement was, of course, not realized in any such fashion. Much of Soviet development has been explosive, fitful, and erratic. Perhaps the last event of extraordinary order, however, was Stalin's death in 1953. Since then there have been more gradual changes, constituting what has come to be known as de-Stalinization. In this respect the year 1956 was important. In that year Khrushchev denounced Stalin in secret session before the Twentieth Party Congress, the Central Statistical Administration resumed publication of several statistical abstracts, and the state formally removed the war-related imposition of military discipline on the labor force. Shortly thereafter in 1959 the second reliable Soviet population censuses was conducted, followed eleven years later by the third population count. The conduct of two censuses over a relatively short time allows the residual estimation of net migration, and the changes in Soviet society make plausible the analytical approaches used in this work.

State policy is always important for migration, though its evidence varies with particular situations. Because the U.S.S.R's experiences with forced labor, collectivization, rural-to-urban transfer of population, and the evacuation of the West during World War II are so impressive, one can hardly neglect state policy in the study of Soviet interregional migration, even if the period is recent.

Two principal conclusions emerge from this study's concern with the 1959–70 period. The first is the state allowed workers sufficient freedom of movement so that it is not unreasonable to maintain that a Union-wide labor market operated. In 1956, removal of criminal-law penalties for leaving work on one's own volition transformed the labor-turnover problem from a legal in to an administrative national-economic problem. Thereafter much literature on the causes of labor turnover in various situations began to appear regularly. By 1965 the Central Statistical Administration was reporting nearly two-thirds of all separations in industry were classified as labor turnover; arguments appeared elsewhere claiming that even these figures understated the extent of voluntary quitting.

Workers were surveyed as to why they were quitting. Evasive replies such as "leaving the region" or "changing place of inhabitance" were the most frequent ones; however, these reasons were closely followed in relative frequency by such material considerations as working conditions, living conditions (most importantly, housing), and wages. To an important extent relative wages determined the distribution of workers among sectors and regions. Evidence of this was provided by the course of events in the 1950s. As de facto controls on labor became less important in the decade following World War II, the existing thicket of irrational wage differentials began increasingly to cause allocational problems. The state, motivated also by considerations of equity, finally decided to attend to these problems in 1955 when it began eliminating irrational differentials, a job which continued well into the 1960s.

Besides the literature on labor turnover, discussion that appeared in the Soviet press suggests the use of a labor market model to interpret Soviet interregional migration. State leaders during 1959–70 spoke of the importance of working out the distribution of labor solely on the basis of voluntary means by paying close attention to material incentives. Another indication of a market model is the criticisms of the process of labor allocation appearing in the press; correspondents often complained that workers did not have enough information about opportunities, that the allocation process was haphazard, or that workers should not have been allowed as much freedom as they enjoyed. In addition, practically all agreed the dominant motive in decisions concerning moves was personal valuation of material conditions of life and work.

The second principal conclusion is the state sought to develop the three eastern regions of Russia and northern Kazakhstan. During the 1950s the remarkable Virgin Lands campaign was conducted; and despite the tribulations of the early 1960s, the area continued to be looked to for substantial agricultural output. Plans were formulated in the late 1950s for the development of a third ferrous metallurgy base in the expanse of northeastern Kazakhstan and southern Siberia. During the 1959–70 period the East received attention as an area of great energy potential having vast reserves of coal, gas, oil, and hydroelectric energy. Each of these sectors showed an increase of at least 5 percentage points in terms of regional contribution to all-Union output between 1960 and 1969. During the subperiod 1959–67 these development regions received about 24 percent of all investment (except that undertaken by collective farms) while, in 1965 for instance, producing about 13 percent of gross industrial output and having about 15 percent of the U.S.S.R. population.

Additional evidence is provided by policies designed to influence workers to relocate in the development regions. These included wage differentials, Orgnabor recruitment, appeals to the citizenry, and directed first assignment of school graduates. With the exception of the Far East and Extreme North, it is doubtful, however, the wage premiums in development regions compensated for the extra living costs. Nevertheless, they were in effect only for the development regions. Orgnabor supplied labor for construction and industry in the same regions. This organization, but certainly not its function, appears to have lapsed near the end of the period with the rise of the State Committees for the Utilization of Labor Resources. Orgnabor's spotty record in providing the kind of workers enterprises wanted is partially attributable to its being charged with filling vacancies in the least attractive job assignments (in terms of wages and prestige).

A problem raised at the outset was determining the nature of differences in population distribution and migration between societies. A more limited and manageable question, addressed in chapter 3, is how well do existing generalizations about migration (taken as the well-known statements of E. G. Ravenstein and Everett S. Lee) describe the 1959–70 Soviet experience. Although data deficiencies limit the survey, it is concluded that the generalizations are rather accurate for the Soviet case.

In 1967 the number of registered moves per thousand population within the U.S.S.R. probably approached the number of intercounty moves per thousand population in recent years in the U.S. Since one may roughly equate U.S. counties with Soviet *raiony* and since Soviet "registered moves" between population points include intra-*raion* changes in residence, one may guess that the data reflect lower population mobility in the U.S.S.R. On firmer ground, one may certainly conclude people moved more frequently between near points than between distant points. Within practically all geographical units of analysis, most movement occurred completely within the region. Growth of employment opportunities attracted workers and caused net immigration; high levels of industrial development were usually found associated with high levels of interregional migration. Where industry was a relatively small but growing part of regional economic activity, rural-to-urban migration was likely to have been high in relation to regional population and interregional movement. The low prestige of agricultural occupations and the attractiveness of living and working conditions in the city combined to produce high rates of rural-to-urban migration throughout the U.S.S.R.

Migration took place within well-defined streams and counterstreams. Important long-distance streams were movements within the development regions, and movement from these regions to Central Asia. Throughout the period the largest interregional streams involved contiguous areas. Among numerically significant interregional streams in 1969, those involving areas dissimilar in agricultural-industrial mix or climate, as a rule, exhibited high efficiency indices. Specifically, with regard to differences in economic activity, movement occurred from the Central Chernozem and North Caucasus to Don-Dnieper and from the Central Chernozem to the Center; and with regard to differences in climate, there were departures to the South and North Caucasus regions on the Black Sea. The slow rate of industrial growth in the Urals, resulting in relatively unattractive employment prospects, was reflected in efficient out-migration to the Don-Dnieper, Volga, and North Caucasus. Intra-regional streams into cities tended to be very efficient; in some instances this was due to the rapid growth of attractive urban employment opportunities and in other instances to controls on in-migration in the largest cities that made residents reluctant to leave for fear of being unable to return.

Migration was selective by age, sex, ethnicity, and education. Typically, persons aged 16–30 years made up about half of all urban arrivals on net account while being roughly a quarter of total population. Those of working ages (which included the 16–30 year-olds) comprised about three-quarters of urban arrivals net of departures. In these net arrival figures urban-to-urban moves counting once as an arrival and once as a departure are netted out so the data reflect the selectivity of rural-to-urban migration. When only urban arrivals were tabulated, working ages usually constituted about 85 percent of the total. In rural populations persons finishing school, by and large those aged 15–19 years, very likely had extremely high propensities to migrate to the city, perhaps on the order of annual probability of .15.

Much of the attention that selectivity received came in connection with the issue of rural-to-urban migration. During the 1959–70 interval the rural population of the U.S.S.R. decreased by nearly 3 percent, due primarily to out-migration and secondarily to administrative reclassification of settlements. As a rule, it was the young, educated male who left the rural area. The process has continued for so long that Soviet discussions relate barely credible instances of the average age of some farm populations being fifty years, the near-total absence of men of marrying age, and the drastic deterioration of the productivity of the labor force. Particularly noteworthy in this last respect was the perennial shortage of mechanizers. The state was barely able to train individuals to operate and repair agricultural machinery as fast as industry could hire them—or the persons they replaced.

It became obvious during the 1960s that population was moving out of labor-deficient to labor-surplus regions. By the end of the decade it was realized that this development had amplified existing regional differences in fertility to produce the very high rates of population growth observed in southern regions so much in contrast to those reported within the Russian republic. Estimates here confirm these Soviet observations and present some quantitative measures of effects.

By far the biggest loser of population was Russia, giving up approximately 1.5 million persons on net account over the eleven-year period. Of course, since its population was so large, the loss in relation to its 1959 population was only slightly more than 1 percent. Within Russia extraordinary regional losses occurred in the Central Chernozem and Volga-Vyatka, and Urals and West Siberia regions. Population decreased due to migration by about 6 percent in the Central Chernozem and 10 percent in the Volga-Vyatka region. These, along with the Center, were frequently regarded as principal sources of manpower for the development regions. But by 1969 West Siberia, for example, had on urban-to-urban account a positive in-flow of population in relation to only the Volga-Vyatka region (and the contiguous Urals and East Siberia regions). It appears the streams from Central Russia to the development regions decreased and at the end of the period may have been exceeded in volume by counterstreams. The losses of population on account of migration from the Urals and West Siberia were both on the order of 6 percent. This loss in the Urals was due in part to the decrease in the region's importance in coal mining and ferrous metallurgy. Inasmuch as the same sectors were expanding in the development regions, workers migrating from the Urals could have found employment there but for the most part moved to western industrial areas.

Since living and working conditions in West Siberia were not particularly rigorous compared with those in the other development regions, it is somewhat surprising to find out-migration was greatest in this region. Part of the explanation lies in its special "intermediary-point" role. For migrants arriving in West Siberia there were several options. Obviously, one was to stay and settle. If the new life proved disagreable, a second option was a quick return to the West which, while certainly no minor undertaking, was a good deal easier than the same sort of exit from East Siberia or the Far East. If, on the other hand, life in Siberia proved to be manageable and rewarding, the migrant could move on to the east or north where regional coefficients were substantially higher. The willingness to migrate hundreds or even thousands of miles to a hard life is not uniformly and abundantly distributed in various populations. Despite labor shortages in the region, West Siberia, of course, had a relatively high incidence of this characteristic in its population. This fact was not lost on enterprises in East Siberia and the Far East, with the result that West Siberia was an important source of labor for these regions. Finally, for those who decided attractive living conditions were more important than extra compensation, employment opportunities in Central Asia and Kazakhstan were available.

The situation in the development regions had deleterious economic effects. High rates of labor turnover meant the less productive efforts of new employees took up significant portions of total labor time. In addition, due to the general shortage of labor, enterprises were often unable to fill vacancies immediately with the result that the departure of an employee caused loss of production time. In West Siberia rural-to-urban migration served to hold down labor turnover to a level relatively near that of the whole U.S.S.R., but this gain for industry was, of course, won at the expense of agriculture. In the development regions, the enterprises which fared better in fulfilling labor requirements were those which were located in attrative sectors or were authorized the most substantial regional coefficients. A relatively short supply of skilled labor meant production was often executed in ways that economized on this scarce factor.

Belorussia and the Southwest lost about 3 percent of their populations due to migration, and Georgia and Azerbaydzhan lost between 1 and 2 percent each. Departures on net account from Belorussia occurred during the first years of this period when the state remained interested in providing additional labor for agriculture and construction in Kazakhstan; despite its small size Belorussia was quite important in this regard. After 1964, however, departures from and arrivals in the republic were approximately equal. Although less clear, it is likely that similar developments occurred in the Southwest, another labor-surplus region. The course of events in the Transcaucasus, experiencing modest losses in Georgia and Azerbaydzhan and the startling 8 percent increase in Armenia, remains unclear. The available evidence indicates substantial numbers of ethnic Armenians left Georgia and Azerbaydzhan for their native republic during 1959–70. The extent to which repatriation of Armenians from outside the U.S.S.R. contributed to the Armenian increase is undeterminable. Employment grew slowly in both Georgia and Azerbaydzhan, explicably in the latter case because of a relative decrease in the importance of its petroleum industry.

Modest increases in population took place in several industrial regions (the Northwest, Center, and Don-Dnieper) and in regions where industrial production was growing rapidly (Lithuania and Moldavia). The populations of the industrial regions undoubtedly would have grown faster had not the U.S.S.R. tried to limit drastically in-migration into its largest cities. It may be guessed that the government thought it was doing a better job in this respect than it did; for when the 1970 population counts were taken, many more people were enumerated in the Northwest and Center regions than could be expected on the basis of population estimates published annually during the last years of the 1960s. Highly skilled workers constituted an important part of migrants leaving Russia for Lithuania and Moldavia. During the 1960–65 period, employment of persons holding degrees from institutions of higher education and secondary school appear to have been very great in relation to the regional production of graduates, indicating in-migration may have made possible the employment increases.

Large increases in population due to migration occurred in the Baltic, Central Asian, and Kazakh regions.

The populations of Latvia and Estonia, which in terms of per-capita-income-type measures led the other regions of the U.S.S.R., increased by about 7 or 8 percent. Taking rough account of initial age distribution and the age selectivity of migration, it appears their labor forces were augmented on the order of 10 percent. Because each was growing so slowly from the small excess of births over deaths, the increase in numbers due to migration accounted for more than half of the total increase in population between 1959 and 1970. In addition, since the crude rate of natural increase among migrants was probably higher than the same rate in the total population, an obvious effect was rendered.

Among the regions termed labor-surplus by planners and commentators, the Central Asian republics stood first. Yet, enough persons migrated to Uzbekistan, Tadzhikistan, and Kirghizia, so that labor forces may have increased due to migration on the order of 8, 11, and 12 percent, respectively. At the same time substantial numbers of new workers were added to the labor forces each year since these populations had long been growing at rapid rates.

Had interregional streams into these republics been limited, enterprises would have been forced to fulfill growing requirements for labor by drawing more of the rural population into the urban labor force. No such limitation was, however, in effect so that Central Asian enterprises recruited labor from outside the region, thereby avoiding substantial training costs and perpetuating a surplus of rural population. Attempts to induce the rural inhabitants of Central Asia to work in agriculture in other regions did not succeed to any important extent.

Substantial numbers of population migrated to Kazakhstan. It appears almost three-quarters of a million persons may have gone there on *net* account during 1959–62, the last years of the Virgin Lands campaign. The rapid growth of the agricultural sector and the exploitation of natural resources, called for additions to the labor forces of construction and industry. Agricultural settlers arriving one to three years previously in the Virgin Lands often obtained urban employment. Their departure from farms created vacancies that had to be filled by additional interregional migration from Russia, the Ukraine, and Belorussia. These processes were interrupted by the severe drought and crop failure of 1963. After gaining approximately 180,000 persons a year as the result of migration in prior years, it is estimated Kazakhstan lost 19,000 persons during 1963. (Out-migration from West Siberia, containing part of the Virgin Lands, also increased sharply in the same year.) The level of net migration into the Ukraine was 2.5 times that of 1962 and 1964. Thereafter, data indicate the old pattern may have been reestablished; but it soon became unimportant so that by the end of the 1960s, Kazakhstan may actually have had a negative migration balance.

Explanations of why people moved that are based on personal opportunities seem to do a relatively good job of identifying important influences. With regard to net interregional migration, it is found that rates of inflow were high in areas where the complex of living conditions was attractive, the climate was moderate, employment opportunities were growing, and rural-to-urban migration was proceeding relatively slowly. With regard to 1967 and 1969 point-to-point urban arrivals, it was additionally discovered that ethnic affinity between regions increased migration and distance decreased it.

The "total complex of living conditions" in a particular region remains a somewhat ambiguous but valuable concept representing things like the quantity and quality of housing, the availability of services, food, and retail trade goods, and the accessibility of child-care institutions and schools. It is possible, from a statistical point of view, to speak of a single measure because the various components, when expressed in per capita terms, are highly correlated. Further, it is argued that trade per capita, the component chosen as a proxy for all by virtue of planners' efforts to balance wage payments with consumption expenditures, is also likely to be correlated with wage payments per capita, surely an important consideration for migrants, but one on which accurate data could not be obtained. This being the case, it appears the proxy used accurately captures many of the differences in material living conditions between regions.

It was this notion of the complex of living conditions to which Soviet migration students outside the planning apparatus paid so much attention. It is clear that citizens were allowed substantial freedom to choose regional location, and they demonstrated their preferences by moving to the southern, non-Russian regions with attractive climates and to those western regions offering the best living conditions. But the state preferred workers leave labor-surplus regions (central Russia and the southern regions) for the labor-deficit development regions. As long as the government largely forswore administrative measures to resettle persons, its alternative was to use material incentives to a substantial degree. This would have required better living conditions in the development regions, implying at least some of the following: higher regional coefficients and their more extensive use, an expanded housing stock, better recreation facilities, more schools and child-care institutions, and lower prices for goods and services. The capital cost of locating a single worker in the East was somewhere near 10,000 rubles, this figure taking no account of the notion of providing premium living conditions to compensate for remote and harsh location.

The Soviet Union is a vast country, and the problem of distributing productive resources spatially is important. In chapter 2 the curious mix of administrative measures and material incentives used to effect redistribution of population to the labor-deficit regions was documented. In chapter 4 it became clear that a good deal of population movement involved exodus from the very areas in which the state desired additional concentration of population. In chapter 5 it is observed that variables purporting to measure the attractiveness of living conditions (such as trade per capita, climate, and employment opportunities) explained the observed variation rather well.

The government proved unwilling to use either administrative measures or material incentives sufficiently to influence the location decisions of individuals; as a result the labor distribution desired by the state was not achieved. At the same time that the state was seeking to move labor to the resource-rich, labor-deficient regions, it was also locating industry in labor-surplus regions to preserve its claim that the Party long ago and permanently abolished unemployment. This is likely to continue as long as the state is unwilling to set policy instruments at levels necessary to effect the desired regional distribution. It would seem, however, that the situation may eventually be disturbed by the increasing value of energy resources located in the eastern U.S.S.R. Developing these resources has long been based on an appreciation of the high costs of additional use of depleted or poor-quality resources in the western regions. As costs in the West continue to increase, the state will probably be willing to use the required material incentives to a greater extent.

TABLES

TABLE 1.1. AVAILABILITY OF DATA BY REGIONS.

Data	U.S.S.R.	Union republics	Major economic regions	Large political units	Cities
Annual population estimates	yes; 3,2, 5,4	yes; 5(No.2,1971), 2,4,3	yes; 2,5,4,3	yes; 2,4,3	yes; 2,4,3
Annual crude rates of natural increase	yes; 3,2,5	yes; 3,2,5	1960, 1963-67; 2,5,3	1960, 1963-67; 2,5,3	no
Annual age-specific rates of natural increase	yes; 2,5	no	no	no	no
Migration data	yes; 3,5,1	yes; 3,5,1	yes; 1	no	yes; 5

Sources: 1. *Itogi vsesoiuznoi perepisi naseleniia 1970 goda*, VII (Returns of the 1970 All-Union Population Census, vol. VII); 2. *Narodnoe khoziaistvo* (The National Economy, Narkhoz)--the annual statistical yearbook of the Central Statistical Administration; 3. *Naselenie SSSR 1973: Statisticheskii sbornik* (U.S.S.R Population 1973: Collected Statistics); 4. *SSSR Administrativno-Territorial'noe delenie soiuznykh respublik* (U.S.S.R Administrative and Territorial Divisions of Union Republics)--a listing of major political units and their populations and constituent entities: issued quasi-annually; 5. *Vestnik statistiki* (The Statistical Herald)--the monthly journal of the Central Statistical Administration.

TABLE 1.2. CALCULATION OF POPULATION ESTIMATE FOR IVANOV REGION ON 1 JANUARY 1971.

	Total population	Urban	Rural
1. Population estimate, 1 January 1970	55,400	20,753	34,647
2. Changes during 1970:			
a. natural growth (number of births minus number of deaths)	1,281	415	866
b. mechanical growth (the number of arrivals minus departures)	-195	625	-820
c. administrative-territorial changes:			
1. assignment of two *sel'sovety* to Vasil'ev	-1,200		-1,200
2. transformation of villages into settlements of urban-type		3,000	-3,000
3. Population estimate, 1 January 1971	55,286	24,793	30,493

Note: Example taken from Soviet source.

Sources: TsSU, *Posobie po statistike dlia raionnykh i gorodskikh inspekturov gosudarstvennoi statistiki* (Manual of Statistics for Regional and Municipal Inspectors of Statistics) (Moscow: Statistika, 1970), p. 349.

TABLE 1.3. COMPARISON OF AGE-SPECIFIC DEATH RATES OF TOTAL POPULATIONS (Deaths Per Thousand Person-Years).

Ages	Sweden 1965	U.S.S.R. 1966-67	U. S. 1965
0	13.5	6.9	5.3
1-4	0.7		
5-9	0.4	0.8	0.4
10-14	0.3	0.6	0.4
15-19	0.7	1.0	1.0
20-24	0.8	1.5	1.3
25-29	0.8	2.0	1.3
30-34	1.1	2.6	1.7
35-39	1.6	3.4	2.4
40-44	2.2	4.1	3.7
45-49	3.2	5.3	5.8
50-54	5.5	7.9	9.1
55-59	8.4	11.3	13.9
60-64	14.2	17.4	20.6
65-69	23.8	25.9	31.7
70-74	40.8	40.5[a]	45.5
75-79	70.0	62.0[a]	68.1
80-84	118.0	90.7[a]	106.8
85+	215.2	160.9[a]	202.0

a. Calculated by author by means described in text.

Sources: U. N., Department of Economic and Social Affairs, *Demographic Yearbook*, 1966 (New York: United Nations, 1967), pp. 436, 471; *Narkhoz 67*, pp. 38-39.

TABLE 1.4. COMPONENTS OF POPULATION CHANGE, 1967.

	Highest regional rate	Lowest regional rate	All-Union average rate
Births per 1000	35.6 (Turkmenia)	12.0 (Center region)	17.3
Deaths per 1000	10.6 (Latvia)	5.7 (Kazakhstan)	7.6
Arrivals at urban settlements per 1000 urban inhabitants	103.7 (Far East region)	26.0 (Georgia)	66.3
Departures from urban settlements per 1000 urban inhabitants	91.6 (Far East region)	20.5 (Georgia)	57.3

Note: Data taken directly from Soviet sources.

Sources: *Vestnik statistiki* (No. 10, 1968), p. 89; *Narkhoz 67*, p.41.

TABLE 1.5. PERCENTAGE DEVIATIONS OF CENSUS ENUMERATIONS FROM EXPECTED NUMBERS OF POPULATION ON JANUARY 15, 1970 IN UNION REPUBLICS AND REGIONS.

Area	Percentage deviation	Area	Percentage deviation
Russia	0.7	Lithuania	-0.5
Northwest	1.4	Latvia	0.6
Center	2.9	Estonia	2.1
Volga-Vyatka	0.7	Transcaucasia	-0.6
Central Chernozem	1.1	Georgia	-1.6
Volga	0.5	Azerbaydzhan	-1.1
North Caucasus	0.1	Armenia	2.9
Urals	-0.8	Central Asia	-1.2
West Siberia	-0.8	Uzbekistan	-1.2
East Siberia	0.8	Kirghizia	-3.0
Far East	-3.0	Tadzhikistan	-0.6
Ukraine	-0.0	Turkmenia	0.7
Don-Dnieper	-0.8	Kazakhstan	-1.8
Southwest	0.2	Belorussia	0.3
South	1.5	Moldavia	-0.3
Baltic	0.9		

TABLE 1.6. EFFECTS OF ERRORS IN REGISTRATION ON THE RELATION BETWEEN ENUMERATIONS AND ESTIMATES OF POPULATION.

Births	Deaths	In-migration	Out-migration	Result
Over-registration	Under-registration	Over-registration	Under-registration	Census < estimate
Under-registration	Over-registration	Under-registration	Over-registration	Census > estimate

TABLE 1.7. PERCENTAGE REVISIONS OF PREVIOUS ESTIMATES OF ANNUAL POPULATION FOR SELECTED UNION REPUBLICS.

	LAT	EST	GRG	ARM	UZB	KIR	TAD	KAZ
1959	0.0	0.0	0.0	0.0	0.0	0.0	0.0	0.0
1960	0.0	0.0	-0.0	0.3	2.0	-0.4	0.4	-2.4
1961	0.1	0.1	-0.2	0.6	2.3	-0.5	0.8	-2.9
1962	0.2	0.1	-0.3	1.1	2.6	-0.9	1.1	-3.3
1963	0.5	0.5	-0.4	1.2	0.7	-0.4	1.5	-2.0
1964	0.5	0.6	-0.6	1.4	0.8	-1.4	1.6	-1.9
1965	0.6	0.9	-0.7	1.7	0.9	-1.4	-0.5	-2.0
1966	0.8	0.9	-0.9	2.1	-0.2	-1.4	-0.7	-1.9
1967	0.8	1.2	-1.2	2.4	-0.2	-1.9	-0.8	-2.0
1968	1.1	1.2	-1.3	2.7	-0.4	-2.1	-0.8	-1.9
1969	0.9	1.4	-1.5	3.1	-0.5	-2.3	-0.6	-1.8
1970	0.0	0.0	0.0	0.0	0.0	0.0	0.0	0.0

Notes: 1. Column Heading Codes: LAT--Latvia; GRG--Georgia; UZB--Uzbekistan; TAD--Tadzhikistan; EST--Estonia; ARM--Armenia; KIR--Kirghizia; KAZ--Kazakhstan. 2. Estimates for Union republics not listed in this table were never revised more than one percent in absolute value.

Sources: Original estimates: *Narkhoz* abstracts; Revised estimates: *Vestnik statistiki* (No. 2, 1971), pp. 85-86.

TABLE 2.1. PERSONS DEPARTING FROM AND ARRIVING AT SIBERIAN CITIES, 1956-59.

Region	Persons departing for region listed at left per 100 persons arriving in Siberian cities
North	100
Northwest	77
Center	73
Volga-Vyatka	48
Central Black-Earth	51
Volga	76
North Caucasus	107
Urals	110
Far East	91
South	135
West	99
Transcaucasus	130
Central Asia	142
Kazakhstan	156

Source: *CDSP*, XIV, No. 26 (July 25, 1962), p. 4.

TABLE 2.2. PERCENTAGE DISTRIBUTION OF REASONS STATED FOR LEAVING WORK.

Reason for leaving	Leningrad	Krasnoyarsk	All-Union
Wages	23.5	17.5	13.8
Work and working conditions	37.5	13.9	17.4
Living conditions	29.9	19.4	15.9
Leaving the region		17.5	25.4
Stopping work			18.3
Education		5.2	
Disciplinary discharge	1.4		
Other	7.8	26.5	9.2

Source: E. C. Brown, *Soviet Trade Unions and Labor Relations* (Cambridge, Mass.: Harvard University Press, 1966), p. 37.

TABLE 2.3. AREA UNDER SPRING WHEAT, MILLIONS OF HECTARES.

	U.S.S.R.	R.S.F.S.R.	Kazakhstan
1950	26.0	19.8	3.7
1959	45.6	27.6	18.5
1960	48.3	30.2	17.3
1961	45.7	28.4	16.8
1962	49.3	30.6	18.2
1963	48.3	30.1	17.5
1964	48.9	30.8	17.5
1965	50.4	31.5	17.9
1966	50.2	32.3	17.3
1967	47.3	30.4	16.3
1968	48.3	30.6	17.3
1969	52.0	32.8	18.7

Source: *Narkhoz* abstracts.

TABLE 2.4. TARGETS OF THE SIXTH FIVE-YEAR PLAN FOR FERROUS METALS IN 1960.

Commodity	Millions of tons	Percentage of 1955 output
Pig iron	53.0	159
Steel	68.3	151
Rolled metal	52.7	152

Source: *CDSP*, VIII, No. 3 (February 29, 1956), p. 3.

TABLE 2.5. INDICATORS OF REGIONAL CONTRIBUTIONS IN FERROUS INDUSTRIAL PRODUCTION.

	1955	1960	1965	1969	1960-69 Percentage increase
Iron ore (millions of metric tons)					
U.S.S.R.	71.9	105.9	153.4	186.1	75.7
European (excluding Urals)	43.0	66.9	103.3	127.7	90.9
Urals and Asian USSR	28.9	39.0	50.1	58.3	49.5
Kazakhstan	0.2	5.8	14.1	18.2	213.8
Siberia	3.6	6.0	8.3	12.5	108.3
Pig iron (millions of metric tons)					
U.S.S.R.	33.3	46.8	66.2	81.6	74.4
European (excluding Urals)	19.0	28.1	40.9	51.1	81.9
Urals and Asian USSR	14.3	18.7	25.3	30.5	63.1
Kazakhstan	0.0	0.3	1.6	1.7	466.7
Siberia	2.4	3.3	4.8	6.9	109.1
Steel (millions of metric tons)					
U.S.S.R.	45.3	65.3	91.0	110.3	68.9
European (excluding Urals)	24.0	37.3	53.1	66.9	79.3
Urals and Asian USSR	21.0	28.0	37.9	44.3	58.2
Kazakhstan	0.2	0.3	1.1	1.3	333.3
Siberia	4.5	5.5	6.7	8.0	45.4

Note: Component figures may not add to U.S.S.R. figures because of rounding.

Sources: *Narkhoz 69*, p. 205; *Narkhoz 68*, p. 191; Theodore Shabad, *Basic Industrial Resources of the U.S.S.R.* (New York: Columbia University Press, 1969), pp. 36-45; Theodore Shabad, "New Notes," *Soviet Geography*, XII (May 1971), pp. 318-19.

TABLE 2.6. PERCENTAGE CONTRIBUTION OF THE AREA OF THIRD METALLURGY COMPLEX (KAZAKHSTAN AND SIBERIA) TO ALL-UNION TOTALS IN 1960 AND 1969.

	1960	1969
Iron ore	11.1	16.5
Pig iron	7.7	10.5
Steel	8.9	8.5

Sources: *Narkhoz 69*, p. 205; *Narkhoz 68*, p. 191; Shabad, *Basic Industrial Resources of the U.S.S.R.*, pp. 36-45; Shabad, "New Notes," pp. 318-19.

TABLE 2.7. PERCENTAGE DISTRIBUTION OF INVESTMENT (1959-67) POPULATION (1965) AND INDUSTRIAL PRODUCTION (1965).

	Capital investment of governmental and cooperative entities excluding collective farms, 1959-1967	Population, Jan. 1, 1965	Gross industrial production, 1965
European U.S.S.R.	71.0	77.2	83.6
East	16.2	10.2	9.9
Kazakhstan	7.5	5.2	3.0
Central Asia	5.2	7.4	3.5

Note: Percentage component figures may not add to 100.0 because of rounding.

Sources: *Narkhoz 64*, p. 12; *Narkhoz 65*, p. 539; *Narkhoz 67*, p. 626.

TABLE 2.8. DATA ON REGIONAL PRODUCTION OF COAL, PETROLEUM, NATURAL GAS, AND ELECTRICITY.

	1960		1969	
	Absolute	Percentage of All-Union total	Absolute	Percentage of All-Union total
Coal (millions of metric tons)				
European U.S.S.R.	330	64.3	347.8	57.4
East	143	27.9	191.9	31.6
Kazakhstan	32	6.2	57.5	9.5
Central Asia	8	1.6	8.6	1.4
Total	513		605.8	
Petroleum (millions of metric tons)				
European U.S.S.R.	136.8	92.5	278.7	84.9
East	1.6	1.1	23.9	7.3
Kazakhstan	1.6	1.1	10.1	3.1
Central Asia	7.4	5.0	16.0	4.9
Total	147.9		328.3	
Natural Gas (billions of cubic meters)				
European U.S.S.R.	44.2	97.6	131.0	72.3
Asian U.S.S.R.	1.1	2.4	50.0	27.6
Total	45.3		181.1	
Hydroelectric Power (billions of kilowatt hours)				
European U.S.S.R.	229	78.4	515.5	74.8
East	44	15.1	118.4	17.2
Kazakhstan	10	3.4	31.0	4.5
Central Asia	9	3.1	24.0	3.5
Total	292		689.0	

Note: Component figures may not add to total figures because of rounding.

Sources: Shabad, *Basic Industrial Resources of the U.S.S.R.*, pp. 11, 14-15, 25; Shabad, "News Notes," pp. 320-32.

TABLE 2.9. THOUSANDS ENROLLED IN SCHOOLS, RELEASED FROM SCHOOLS, AND RELEASED TO LABOR FORCE.

	1964-65 school enrollment	1964 releases from school	Release primarily to labor force
General schools	46,664		
Classes 1-8 and Others	39,797	6,000	Yes, in rural areas
Class 8	4,671		
Classes 9-11	6,867	3,000	No
Trade schools	1,607	943 graduates/ plus others	Yes
Secondary specialized schools	3,326	558 graduates/ plus others	Yes
Higher education	3,608	354 graduates plus others	Yes

Notes: 1. The author's guesses are underlined by double lines and are made naively on the basis of enrollments; 2. The term, "others," is used to denote individuals leaving schools, but not completing curricula.

Sources: *Narkhoz 64*, pp. 568, 667-68, 686, 688; Nigel Grant, *Soviet Education* (Baltimore: Penguin, 1968), p. 64.

TABLE 3.1. PERCENTAGE OF URBAN ARRIVALS FROM SAME UNION REPUBLIC.

Republic	1967	1969
Russia	80	76
Ukraine	68	66
Belorussia	67	67
Uzbekistan	45	48
Kazakhstan	56	56
Georgia	66	68
Azerbaydzhan	58	57
Lithuania	75	75
Moldavia	52	55
Latvia	62	61
Kirghizia	51	50
Tadzhikistan	39	44
Armenia	53	49
Turkmenia	47	43
Estonia	57	52

Sources: *Vestnik statistiki* (No. 10, 1968), pp. 90-91; *Vestnik statistiki* (No. 3, 1971), p. 78.

TABLE 3.2. RURAL-TO-URBAN FLOWS.

A. Net arrivals per thousand urban inhabitants in union republics, 1967

Republic	Rate	Republic	Rate
All-Union	12.4	Lithuania	22.6
Russia	12.3	Moldavia	18.4
Ukraine	12.8	Latvia	9.5
Belorussia	26.4	Kirghizia	17.1
Uzbekistan	8.7	Tadzhikistan	5.8
Kazakhstan	13.2	Armenia	6.7
Georgia	6.7	Turkmenia	2.7
Azerbaydzhan	6.3	Estonia	7.9

B. Groupings in relation to all-union rate.

Very low	Low	High	Very high
Georgia	Uzbekistan	Central Chernozem*	Belorussia
Azerbaydzhan	Latvia	Volga*	Lithuania
Tadzhikistan	Estonia	Southwest*	Moldavia
Armenia	Northwest*		Kirghizia
Turkmenia	Center*		South*

Note: Asterisks indicate the region was classified on the basis of general observations in Soviet discussion, not 1967 data.

Sources: *Vestnik statistiki* (No. 10, 1968), pp. 94-95; *Vestnik statistiki* (No. 2, 1971), pp. 85-86.

TABLE 3.3. STREAMS OF INTERREGIONAL MIGRATION, URBAN ARRIVALS, 1969.

Both directions	Predominantly single direction
Volga and North Caucasus	Northwest to Center
Volga and Urals	Volga-Vyatka to Northwest
North Caucasus and Far East*	Volga-Vyatka to Volga
Urals and West Siberia	Volga-Vyatka to Urals
West Siberia and East Siberia	Central Chernozem to Don-Dnieper
West Siberia and Far East*	North Caucasus to Don-Dnieper
Don-Dnieper and Southwest	Urals to North Caucasus*
Don-Dnieper and South	Urals to East Siberia*
Southwest and South	East Siberia to Far East
Kazakhstan and Central Asia	

Note: Asterisks designate noncontiguous areas.
Source: *Vestnik statistiki* (No. 3, 1971), pp. 78-83.

TABLE 3.4. STREAMS OF URBAN ARRIVALS (NET OF DEPARTURES) EXCEEDING 10,000 PERSONS, 1969.

Stream	Efficiency index
Central Chernozem to Center	1.9
Central Chernozem to Don-Dnieper	1.6
Urals to Volga	1.5
Urals to North Caucasus*	2.0
Urals to Don-Dnieper*	1.9
Don-Dnieper to Southwest	1.4
Don-Dnieper to South	1.4
Southwest to South	1.5
Kazakhstan to East Siberia	1.4

Note: Asterisks designate noncontiguous areas.
Source: *Vestnik statistiki* (No. 3, 1971), pp. 82-83.

TABLE 3.5. OUT-MIGRATION BY NEW SETTLERS IN EASTERN REGIONS.[6]

A. Percentages of persons arriving in 1962-65 at selected cities and then leaving

Leaving during	Divnogorsk[1]	Nazarovo[2]	Barnaul[3]
First year	34	24	18
Second year	21	12	12
Third year	10	16	7

B. Cumulative percentages of persons arriving during years shown and leaving within three years

City and interval	Percentage
Divnogorsk[1] (1962-65)	65
Berdsk[4] (1963-65)	50
Karasuk[5] (1963-65)	45
Barnaul[3] (1962-65)	37

Notes: 1. Divnogorsk was a rapidly growing city in East Siberia involved in hydroelectric power generation and associated activity. Its 1967 population was 21,000. 2. Nazarovo was a new lignite-mining center near Krasnoyarsk with some food industry. 3. Barnaul was a developed center of Altai Krai having a 1967 population of 407,000. 4. Berdsk was a growing satellite city of Novosibirsk. 5. Karasuk was a rapidly growing food-processing center in West Siberia, southwest of Novosibirsk near the Kazakh border. 6. Data taken directly from Soviet source.

Sources: D. I. Valentei et al. (eds.), *Problemy migratsii naseleniia i trudovykh resursov* (Moscow: Statistiki, 1970), pp. 163, 165. Chauncy D. Harris, *Cities of the Soviet Union* (Chicago: Rand-McNally, 1970), pp. 353-56, 366, 387.

TABLE 3.6. POPULATION EXCHANGES OF RURAL SETTLEMENTS OF NOVOSIBIRSK OBLAST WITH OTHER TYPES OF SETTLEMENTS (THROUGHOUT U.S.S.R.), THOUSANDS OF PERSONS, 1962-66.

U.S.S.R. settlements / Rural settlements of Novosibirsk Oblast	Rural settlements	Small cities and worker settlements	Large- and medium-sized cities	Total
Arrivals at	104.4	14.2	93.6	212.2
Departures from	106.0	23.4	187.8	317.2
Net arrivals at	-1.6	-9.2	-94.2	-105.0

Note: Data taken directly from Soviet source.

Source: T. I. Zaslavskaia (ed.), *Migratsiia sel'skogo naseleniia* (Moscow: Mysl', 1970), p. 116.

TABLE 3.7. EFFICIENCY RATIOS OF MIGRATION INTO URBAN SETTLEMENTS, 1967.

Region	Efficiency ratio	Region	Efficiency ratio
Northwest	2.2	Don-Dnieper	1.8
Center	2.3	Southwest	2.0
Volga-Vyatka	2.2	South	1.7
Central Chernozem	2.3	Baltic	2.2
Volga	2.3	Transcaucasia	2.6
North Caucasus	1.5	Central Asia	1.8
Urals	2.1	Kazakhstan	2.0
West Siberia	2.0	Belorussia	2.6
East Siberia	1.9	Moldavia	1.9
Far East	1.8		

Note: The efficiency ratio is defined as the number of arrivals at urban settlements (from rural localities) divided by the number in the counterstreams. Data based on urban registration.

Source: *Vestnik statistiki* (No. 10, 1968), pp. 92-95.

TABLE 3.8. PERCENTAGE OF GRADUATES FROM RURAL SCHOOLS OF NOVOSIBIRSK OBLAST BY SUBSEQUENT EMPLOYMENT, 1964-66.

Subsequent employment	Incomplete secondary (8th class)	Secondary (10th class)	Combined
Additional training or study	53.8	45.6	50.5
Work in urban locality	17.4	18.1	17.7
Work in rural locality	28.5	29.7	29.0
Other employment	0.3	6.6	2.8

Note: Data taken directly from Soviet source.
Source: T. I. Zaslavskaia (ed.), *Migratsiia sel'skogo naseleniia* (Moscow: Mysl', 1970), pp. 250-51.

TABLE 3.9. TYPES OF RURAL-TO-URBAN MIGRANTS, NOVOSIBIRSK OBLAST, 1964-66.

	Percentage of all migrants	Average years of school attendance	Average months special job training	Average family size
Family-man, primary education, skilled	26.8	5.4	4.3	4
Single youth, incomplete-secondary education, low qualification	21.0	7.2	2.3	1
Single, aged women, without education or skill	7.5	0.0	0.0	1
Single youth, primary education, low qualification	6.3	4.0	1.6	1
Small-family-man, middle aged, low qualification	6.0	4.0	1.6	2
Secondary school graduate	5.6	10.3	0.0	1

Note: Data taken directly from Soviet source.
Source: T. I. Zaslavskaia (ed.), *Migratsiia sel'skogo naseleniia* (Moscow: Mysl', 1970), p. 139.

TABLE 4.1. NET MIGRATION INTO UNION REPUBLICS AND MAJOR ECONOMIC REGIONS, 1959-70.

Territory	Thousands of net migrants	Net migrants per thousand of 1959 census population	Relative of net migration to total population increase
	Union Republics		
Russia	-1446	-12.3	- .115
Ukraine	536	12.8	.102
Lithuania	50	18.5	.121
Latvia	157	74.8	.578
Estonia	92	76.7	.577
Georgia	- 81	-19.9	- .125
Azerbaydzhan	- 57	-15.5	- .040
Armenia	153	86.9	.210
Uzbekistan	427	51.6	.115
Kirghizia	159	77.0	.183
Tadzhikistan	150	75.5	.163
Turkmenia	13	8.6	.020
Kazakhstan	819	89.5	.222
Belorussia	- 264	-32.8	- .279
Moldavia	76	26.4	.111
	Economic Regions		
Northwest	253	23.3	.196
Center	108	4.2	.056
Volga-Vyatka	- 819	-99.2	-8.527
Central Chernozem	- 493	-63.5	-2.155
Volga	83	5.2	.035
North Caucasus	935	80.6	.349
Urals	- 871	-61.4	- .870
West Siberia	- 713	-63.4	- .832
East Siberia	- 104	-16.1	- .105
Far East	149	30.9	.158
Don-Dnieper	420	23.7	.184
Southwest	- 572	-30.1	- .344
South	686	135.1	.525
Baltic	320	48.4	.330
Transcaucasia	14	1.5	.005
Central Asia	749	54.2	.122
Kazakhstan	819	89.5	.222
Belorussia	- 264	-32.8	- .279
Moldavia	76	26.4	.111

TABLE 4.2. INTERREGIONAL NET MIGRATION, THOUSANDS OF PERSONS INTO UNION REPUBLICS, 1959-70.

	RSR	UKR	LTH	LAT	EST	GRG	AZR	ARM	UZB	KIR	TAD	TRK	KAZ	BLR	MLD	CHK
1959	-280	58	9	8	5	18	- 7	10	29	10	16	0	193	-45	15	40
1960	-175	46	5	17	6	-15	17	14	34	16	16	2	179	-60	2	104
1961	-122	-80	4	16	7	- 9	2	14	58	18	28	3	180	-38	1	83
1962	- 98	38	0	13	8	- 4	-38	-4	49	7	26	3	174	-25	7	156
1963	- 64	106	2	18	11	- 7	6	11	46	24	15	2	-25	-71	13	87
1964	- 90	42	2	15	11	- 7	- 5	21	27	10	15	1	62	-30	7	83
1965	-147	66	6	16	7	- 9	- 7	19	34	19	11	-3	27	2	16	57
1966	-146	77	8	16	7	-11	1	18	13	17	1	-7	36	11	7	48
1967	-164	84	6	12	5	-14	-13	18	56	17	6	6	31	- 9	10	49
1968	- 91	49	6	14	9	-15	- 5	22	60	15	7	-2	-16	- 7	2	46
1969	- 70	50	4	12	16	- 8	-10	12	21	6	8	8	-20	8	-4	33

Notes: 1. Column Heading Codes:

RSR	Russia	AZR	Azerbaydzhan	TRK	Turkmenia
UKR	Ukraine	ARM	Armenia	KAZ	Kazakhstan
LTH	Lithuania	UZB	Uzbekistan	BLR	Belorussia
LAT	Latvia	KIR	Kirghizia	MLD	Moldavia
EST	Estonia	TAD	Tadzhikistan	CHK	Check
GRG	Georgia				

2. The entries for 1959 do not include migration before January 15, 1959, and those for 1969 do include migration from January 1 through January 14, 1970. 3. CHK entries are summations across each row in the table. In the absence of net migration into the U.S.S.R., errors in data, and errors due to rounding, each entry would be close to zero.

TABLE 4.3. INTERREGIONAL NET MIGRATION, THOUSANDS OF PERSONS INTO MAJOR ECONOMIC REGIONS.

	NRW	CNT	VLV	CNC	VLG	NCC	URL
1959	-29	-142	-96	-49	-9	112	-26
1960	-8	-93	-101	-46	-4	144	-20
1961	29	-112	-102	-64	74	85	-23
1962	12	-52	-121	-24	75	75	-72
1963	46	-61	-78	-48	-44	89	15
1964	43	-6	-69	-65	-6	63	-80
1965	1	19	-75	-47	-11	92	-100
1966	4	-65	-42	-28	46	84	-91
1967	20	-0	-50	-60	-9	86	-87
1968	22	11	-42	-45	6	89	-82
1969	112	609	-43	-17	-35	16	-305
	WSI	ESI	FEA	DON	SOW	SOU	BAL
1959	-9	4	-40	101	-28	-13	28
1960	-23	4	-35	64	-76	57	32
1961	25	0	26	-68	-66	52	16
1962	-7	17	24	62	-63	39	11
1963	-117	1	56	105	-58	60	43
1964	-73	13	82	48	-77	72	35
1965	-24	-18	52	76	-80	71	34
1966	-63	-45	22	81	-64	61	23
1967	-67	-30	37	68	-53	68	16
1968	-85	-30	71	15	-27	58	22
1969	-270	-19	-145	-131	20	161	60
	TRC	CAS	KAZ	BLR	MLD	CHK	
1959	21	56	193	-45	15	43	
1960	16	68	179	-60	2	101	
1961	7	108	180	-38	1	129	
1962	-46	85	174	-25	7	171	
1963	10	88	-25	-71	13	22	
1964	9	53	62	-30	7	80	
1965	3	60	27	2	16	100	
1966	8	23	36	11	7	8	
1967	-10	84	31	-9	10	45	
1968	1	80	-16	-7	2	46	
1969	-6	44	-20	8	-4	35	

Notes: 1. Column Heading Codes:

NRW	Northwest	SOW	Southwest
CNT	Center	SOU	South
VLV	Volga-Vyatka	BAL	Baltic (The)
CNC	Central Chernozem	TRC	Transcaucasia
VLG	Volga	CAS	Central Asia
NCC	North Caucasus	KAZ	Kazakhstan
URL	Urals	BLR	Belorussia
WSI	West Siberia	MLD	Moldavia
ESI	East Siberia	CHK	Check
DON	Don-Dnieper		

TABLE 4.3. CONTINUED.

2. Entries for 1959 do not include migration before January 15, 1959, and 1969 entries do include migration from January 1 through January 14, 1970. 3. CHK entries are summations across each row in the table. In the absence of net migration into the U.S.S.R., errors in data, and errors due to rounding, each entry would be close to zero.

TABLE 4.4. 1962-64 OUTPUT OF GRAIN, MILLIONS OF PHYSICAL TONS.

	1962	1963	1964	1963 as percentage of mean of 1962 and 1964
All-Union	140.2	107.5	152.1	74
Ukraine	28.7	21.9	30.4	74
West Siberia	9.1	4.3	12.5	40
Kazakhstan	15.9	10.6	23.9	53

Source: *Narkhoz 64*, p. 296.

TABLE 4.5. CENSUS-SURVIVAL ESTIMATES OF NET MIGRATION OF PERSONS AGED 9-48 IN 1959.

Union Republic	Thousands of net migrants	Net migrants per thousands of 1959 census population
Russia	-1153	-16.2
Ukraine	300	11.8
Lithuania	34	21.0
Latvia	106	87.6
Estonia	63	92.3
Georgia	-56	-23.0
Azerbaydzhan	-43	-20.7
Armenia	73	72.1
Uzbekistan	127	29.1
Kirghizia	73	64.2
Tadzhikistan	-1	-1.3
Turkmenia	9	10.7
Kazakhstan	551	101.9
Belorussia	-149	-31.5
Moldavia	62	35.8

TABLE 4.6. COMPARISON OF ESTIMATES OF NET MIGRATION.

	A	B	C
	Residual, net migrants per thousand of 1959 census population (all ages 1959)	Census-survival, net migrants per thousand of 1959 census population (aged 9-48 in 1959)	Ratio A/B
Russia	-12.3	-16.2	0.76
Ukraine	12.8	11.8	1.08
Lithuania	18.5	21.0	0.88
Latvia	74.8	87.6	0.85
Estonia	76.7	92.3	0.83
Georgia	-19.9	-23.0	0.87
Azerbaydzhan	-15.5	-20.7	0.74
Armenia	86.9	72.1	1.21
Uzbekistan	51.6	29.1	1.77
Kirghizia	77.0	64.2	1.20
Tadzhikistan	75.5	-1.3	-58.08
Turkmenia	8.6	10.7	.80
Kazakhstan	89.5	101.9	0.88
Belorussia	-32.8	-31.5	1.04
Moldavia	26.4	35.8	0.74

TABLE 4.7. SELECTED MIGRATION STREAMS.

From	To	Migrants	Net migrants	Efficiency index	Gross migration measure
		Union Republics			
Russia	Estonia	21141	7737	1.58	2.60
Uzbekistan	Russia	108337	44119	1.69	4.40
Uzbekistan	Kazakhstan	44334	24409	2.23	5.19
Kazakhstan	Belorussia	18700	9161	1.96	2.61
Tadzhikistan	Russia	29600	11269	1.61	2.47
Turkmenia	Russia	21717	7496	1.53	2.14
Average		13304	0	1.41	1.23
		Economic Regions			
Volga-Vyatka	Northwest	23378	10755	1.85	3.57
Volga-Vyatka	Center	37570	14224	1.61	4.01
Central Chernozem	Center	50257	30230	2.51	4.73
Central Chernozem	Volga	23791	12108	2.04	2.93
Central Chernozem	Don-Dnieper	31105	15849	2.04	3.66
North Caucasus	Center	47258	21660	1.85	3.67
Urals	North Caucasus	47531	26323	2.24	4.67
Urals	East Siberia	27677	9780	1.55	4.28
Urals	Far East	25535	10822	1.74	4.30
Urals	Don-Dnieper	31401	17292	2.23	2.61
Urals	South	15227	9318	2.58	2.15
West Siberia	North Caucasus	37632	18635	1.98	4.31
West Siberia	Far East	36407	12480	1.52	7.21
West Siberia	Don-Dnieper	20289	9201	1.83	2.01
Don-Dnieper	Far East	27632	10525	1.62	4.16
Southwest	Northwest	33747	19523	2.37	3.02
Southwest	Center	45440	32613	3.54	2.44
Southwest	Far East	17581	6800	1.63	2.59
Southwest	South	62766	35211	2.28	7.86
Transcaucasia	North Caucasus	25831	15354	2.47	2.74
Central Asia	Center	49374	37931	4.31	2.60
Central Asia	Volga	37287	14601	1.64	3.15
Central Asia	Kazakhstan	82461	35050	1.74	8.09
Kazakhstan	Northwest	22233	12850	2.37	2.51
Kazakhstan	Center	34843	13757	1.65	2.95
Kazakhstan	North Caucasus	39513	14864	1.60	4.71
Kazakhstan	Far East	20169	10825	2.16	3.40
Kazakhstan	Don-Dnieper	31446	11892	1.61	3.16
Kazakhstan	South	14124	6476	1.85	2.39
Kazakhstan	Belorussia	18700	9161	1.96	2.61
Belorussia	Baltic	12006	6926	2.36	2.18
Average		15520	0	1.17	2.46

TABLE 4.7 (Continued)

Notes: 1. If *Mij* denotes the number of persons enumerated in area *j* on January 15, 1970 who said that they previously during 1968-69 had lived in another area, area *i*, then the column headings take on the following meanings: a. Migrants: *Mij*; b. Net Migrants: *Mij* - *Mji*; c. Efficiency Index: *Mij/Mji*; and, d. Gross Migration Measure *(Mij* + *Mji* . 1000/*(Pi* . *Pj)* ½ where *Pi* and *Pj* are 1970 regional populations. 2. The average figures pertain to all 210 interrepublic and all 342 interregional streams, respectively. 3. The *Mij* figures were taken directly from Census Volume VII.

Source: TsSU, *Itogi vsesoiuznoi perepisi naseleniia 1970 goda*, VII (Moscow: Statistika, 1974), Tables 1-17.

TABLE 4.8. MIGRATION RATES DURING 1968-69 ACCORDING TO 1970 CENSUS.

	A In-migration rate	B Out-migration rate	C Sum (A+B)	D Difference (A-B)
		Union Republics		
Russia	4.5	3.9	8.4	0.7
Ukraine	6.3	5.9	12.2	0.4
Lithuania	4.4	4.0	8.4	0.4
Latvia	9.6	6.6	16.2	3.0
Estonia	13.0	7.3	20.3	5.8
Georgia	2.3	6.2	8.5	-3.9
Azerbaydzhan	2.7	5.4	8.1	-2.8
Armenia	5.3	4.2	9.5	1.1
Uzbekistan	5.1	8.6	13.8	-3.5
Kirghizia	12.4	14.9	27.3	-2.5
Tadzhikistan	6.4	9.6	16.0	-3.2
Turkmenia	7.2	9.7	16.9	-2.5
Kazakhstan	16.3	17.1	33.4	-0.8
Belorussia	7.6	7.4	15.0	0.1
Moldavia	7.1	8.4	15.5	-1.3
		Economic Regions		
Northwest	16.2	11.6	27.8	4.6
Center	10.9	7.8	18.7	3.2
Volga-Vyatka	9.8	13.8	23.5	-4.0
Central Chernozem	8.7	12.7	21.4	-4.0
Volga	12.1	11.0	23.0	1.1
North Caucasus	13.9	12.3	26.3	1.6
Urals	12.6	16.2	28.9	-3.6
West Siberia	13.7	17.6	31.3	-3.9
East Siberia	18.8	17.1	35.9	1.7
Far East	30.2	20.4	50.6	9.8
Don-Dnieper	10.6	9.2	19.8	1.4
Southwest	5.7	8.7	14.4	-3.0
South	21.0	12.9	33.9	8.1
Baltic	7.3	4.9	12.2	2.4
Transcaucasia	2.2	4.6	6.7	-2.4
Central Asia	5.2	8.4	13.5	-3.2
Kazakhstan	16.3	17.1	33.4	-0.9
Belorussia	7.6	7.4	15.0	0.2
Moldavia	7.1	8.4	15.5	-1.4

TABLE 4.8. (Continued)

Notes: 1. The rates of column A are calculated by dividing the reported number of 1968-69 interrepublic in-migrants by 1970 census populations, multiplying by 1000, and finally dividing by 2.0 to yield a quasi-annual rate of migrants per thousand population by year. 2. The rates of column B are similarly derived using 1968-69 interrepublic out-migrants. 3. The Baltic region in the present instance excludes Kaliningrad Oblast. 4. Components may not add totals due to rounding.

Source: Ts.S.U. *Itogi vsesoiuznoi perepisi naseleniia 1970 goda*, VII (Moscow: Statistika, 1974), Tables 1-17.

TABLE 4.9. POPULATION EXCHANGE DUE TO MIGRATION IN EASTERN REGIONS DURING 1968-69.

A. Population Gain Due to Migration

From/To	Urals	West Siberia	Kazakh-stan	East Siberia	Far East	All other regions
Urals	0	14,208	3,514	9,780	10,822	71,491
West Siberia	-14,208	0	23,400	15,105	12,480	55,950
Kazakhstan	-3,514	-23,400	0	4,078	10,825	33,733
East Siberia	-9,780	-15,105	-4,078	0	13,098	-8,714
Far East	-10,822	-12,480	-10,825	-13,098	0	-65,443
All others	-71,491	-55,950	-33,733	8,714	65,443	0

B. Efficiency Index: Ratio of Arrivals to Departures

From/To	West Siberia	Kazakh-stan	East Siberia	Far East	All other regions
Urals	1.35	1.07	1.55	1.74	1.27
West Siberia		1.45	1.34	1.52	1.36
Kazakhstan			1.24	2.16	1.13
East Siberia				1.43	0.94
Far East					0.71

Source: Ts.S.U., *Itogi vsesoiuznoi perepisi naseleniia 1970 goda*, VII (Moscow: Statistika, 1974), Tables 2-17.

TABLE 5.1. VARIABLE LISTING AND ORIGINAL DATA SOURCES.

DIST	Derived air distance between capitals.
EMPLOY	Derived increase in numbers employed, less increase in domestic population of working age during 1959-70 per thousand employed, January 15, 1959. TsSU. *Itogi vsesoiuznoi peripisi naseleniia 1970 goda.*
EMPLOYJ	EMPLOY variable annualized less the number of net urban arrivals from own rural areas per thousand population. *Vestnik statistiki, No. 10, 1968; No. 3, 1971.*
ETHNIC1	Number of Russians per thousand population in 1959; zero for Russia and Russian regions and calculated rates for elsewhere. TsSU. *Vsesoiuznoi perepisi naseleniia 1959 goda* and *Itogi perepisi 1970.*
ETHNIC2	Logarithm of the number of nationality A in republic B plus the number of nationality B in republic A, times 1000, divided by the sum of the two republic populations, all as of the 1959 census. *Itogi perepisi 1959* and *Itogi perepisi 1970.*
EXHORT	Dummy variable taking on the value of one for Kazakhstan and Russia, in republic analysis, and West Siberia, East Siberia, the Far East and Kazakhstan, in regional analysis.
I	Derived estimate of cumulative investment of enterprises and cooperatives, but no kolkhozs, in millions of rubles. TsSU. *Narkhoz*, 1970, p. 488 and TsSU. *Narkhoz RSFSR, 1970*, p. 320.
LS	Estimate of labor supply growth based on EMPLOY and 1959 populations of working age.
MIG	Migrants on net account, 1959-70, pp. 143-57.
MIGR	Logarithm of number of urban arrivals from i to j divided by the product of the population in thousands of republic i and the urban population in thousands of republic j. *Vestnik;* No. 10, 1971, No. 3.
MR	Migrants of net account during 1959-70 per thousand population on January 15, 1959, pp. 143-57.
TEMP	Derived average annual temperature based on *Sovetskii Soiuz* geography series.
TEMP-	Same as TEMP.
TRADE	Retail trade per capita, 1965. *Narkhoz.*
TRADE-	Logarithm of TRADE for correct year. *Narkhoz.*
WAGE	Average annual wage, 1965, derived from average All-Union figure and *ASTE Bulletin*, XVI, No. 2, p. 7.
WAGE-	Logarithm of WAGE.

TABLE 5.2. TEST IA RESULTS FOR ELEVEN-YEAR MIGRATION RATES.

Class	Republics	Regions
Average values		
Labor-surplus	38.6	10.2
Neutral	56.7	7.2
Labor-deficit	21.7	8.0
Analysis of variance		
Explained variation	2869	22
Unexplained variation	24798	63471
Degrees of freedom	2,11	2,16
F statistic	0.64	0.00

TABLE 5.3. TEST IB RESULTS FOR ELEVEN-YEAR MIGRATION LEVELS.

Variables	Republics	Regions
Constant	51654	-238780
Investment level (I)	11.1165 (1.14)	3.18460 (0.37)
Labor supply growth (LS)	-123.215 (-0.57)	362.123 (1.01)
Estimation technique	GLS	OLS
R^2	..	0.08
r	-0.73	0.28

Notes: GLS denotes generalized least squares. The standard deviation of the error term was taken to be proportional to population size. OLS stands for ordinary least squares; the symbol r denotes the correlation between actual and predicted values; the values in parentheses are t statistics.

TABLE 5.4. TEST IIA RESULTS FOR ELEVEN-YEAR MIGRATION RATES.

Variable	OLS	PC-4	Ridge
Republics			
TRADE	-0.011	0.202	0.047
WAGE	-0.321	0.008	0.004
ETHNIC1	0.127	0.516*	0.201
EMPLOY	1.053*	0.290*	0.418*
TEMP	-0.138	-0.041	-0.084
EXHORT	-0.250	-0.127	-0.103
R^2	0.89	..	..
r	0.94	0.79	0.83
Regions			
TRADE	0.225	0.304	0.145
WAGE	0.295	0.064	0.115
ETHNIC1	0.236	0.467*	0.286
EMPLOY	0.382*	0.380*	0.298
TEMP	0.754*	0.311	0.326
EXHORT	0.117	-0.098	-0.006
R^2	0.79	..	..
r	0.89	0.79	0.84

Notes: 1. OLS denotes ordinary least squares; PC-4, principal component estimation based on four components; Ridge, ridge regression. 2. The symbol r denotes the correlation between actual and predicted values. 3. An asterisk indicates statistical significance at the 0.05 level in the case of OLS. In other instances it indicates possible significance on the presumption that the variance of the estimator is smaller than that for OLS and that there is no bias. 4. The numbers are Beta coefficients.

TABLE 5.5. TEST IB RESULTS CONCERNING URBAN ARRIVALS.

Variable	OLS	PC-4	Ridge
1967			
TRADEI	-0.511	0.154	-0.021
TRADEJ	-1.184*	0.065	-0.225
WAGEI	3.884*	-0.217	1.455
WAGEJ	2.839*	0.681	0.550
ETHNIC2	0.069*	0.080*	0.052*
EMPLOYJ	0.006	0.003	0.004
TEMPI	-0.014	-0.033	-0.006
TEMPJ	-0.064*	0.003	-0.012
EXHORT	-0.269	0.139	0.106
DIST	-0.622*	-0.516*	-0.329*
R^2	0.58	..	..
r	0.76	0.71	0.69
1969			
TRADEI	-0.609*	0.043	-0.124
TRADEJ	-0.952*	-0.051	-0.134
WAGEI	2.818*	-0.458	1.050
WAGEJ	4.213*	0.791	1.030
ETHNIC2	0.069*	0.080*	0.055*
EMPLOYJ	-0.003	0.005	0.002
TEMPI	-0.019	-0.027	-0.008
TEMPJ	-0.059*	-0.006	-0.015
EXHORT	-0.354	0.179	0.042
DIST	-0.616*	-0.515*	-0.365*
R^2	0.55	..	..
r	0.74	0.70	0.69

Notes: 1. OLS, PC-4, and Ridge are defined as in Table 5.4. 2. The symbol r denotes the correlation between actual and predicted values. 3. Asterisks have the same meaning as specified in Table 5.4. 4. The dependent variable is expressed as its own logarithm as are TRADEI, TRADEJ, WAGEI, WAGEJ, ETHNIC2, and DIST, respectively. Hence the coefficients for these variables may be interpreted as elasticity estimates.

TABLE 6.1. RATIO OF NET MIGRATION TO TOTAL POPULATION INCREASE, 1959-70.

Union Republics	Ratio	Economic regions	Ratio
Russia	-.115	Northwest	.196
Ukraine	.102	Center	.056
Lithuania	.120	Volga-Vyatka	-8.572
Latvia	.578	Central Chernozem	-2.155
Estonia	.577	Volga	.035
Georgia	-.125	North Caucasus	.349
Azerbaydzhan	-.040	Urals	-.870
Armenia	.210	West Siberia	-.832
Uzbekistan	.115	East Siberia	-.105
Kirghizia	.183	Far East	.158
Tadzhikistan	.163	Don-Dnieper	.184
Turkmenia	.020	Southwest	-.344
Kazakhstan	.222	South	.525
Belorussia	-.279	Baltic	.330
Moldavia	.111	Transcaucasia	.005
		Central Asia	.122
		Kazakhstan	.222
		Belorussia	-.279
		Moldavia	.111

Source: Table 4.1.

TABLE 6.2. PERCENTAGE INCREASE OF POTENTIAL LABOR FORCE DUE TO NET MIGRATION, 1959-70.

Republic	Percentage	Republic	Percentage
Russia	-12	Uzbekistan	8
Ukraine	2	Kirghizia	12
Lithuania	2	Tadzhikistan	11
Latvia	9	Turkmenia	1
Estonia	10	Kazakhstan	13
Georgia	-3	Belorussia	-5
Azerbaydzhan	-2	Moldavia	4
Armenia	12		

Note: Percentages are calculated according to:

$$\text{Net migrants per thousand 1959 census population (Table 4.1.)} \times .1 \times .75 \times \frac{1}{\text{Percentage of 1959 population of working age}}$$

Sources: Table 4.1. A. I. Gozulov and M. G. Grigor'iants, *Narodonaselenie SSSR*, p. 72.

TABLE 6.3. PERCENTAGE INCREASES IN EMPLOYMENT OF SPECIALIZED-SECONDARY SCHOOL AND HIGHER EDUCATION GRADUATES, 1961-66; AND TOTAL POPULATION DUE TO MIGRATION, 1961-1966.

	Increase in employment	Percentage points above All-Union increase in employment	Increase in total population due to migration
All-Union	46	0	
Russia	44	-2	-0.5
Ukraine	50	4	0.6
Lithuania	61	15	0.8
Latvia	50	4	4.2
Estonia	48	2	4.0
Georgia	37	-9	-1.0
Azerbaydzhan	42	-4	-1.0
Armenia	49	3	3.9
Uzbekistan	63	17	2.3
Kirghizia	60	14	3.9
Tadzhikistan	55	9	4.1
Turkmenia	43	-3	0.0
Kazakhstan	59	13	4.1
Belorussia	54	8	-1.8
Moldavia	64	18	1.6

Note: Percentage increases in employment calculated from data with reporting dates of December 1, 1960 and November 15, 1966.

Source: TsSU, *Trud v SSSR*, p. 256.

TABLE 6.4. GRADUATES, EMPLOYMENT GROWTH OF GRADUATES, AND POPULATION GROWTH DUE TO MIGRATION, 1961-66.

	Index of graduates to growth of employment	Number of points below All-Union index	Percentage increase in population due to migration
All-Union	1.33	0.00	
Russia	1.40	-0.07	-0.5
Ukraine	1.27	0.06	0.6
Lithuania	0.72	0.61	0.8
Latvia	1.06	0.27	4.2
Estonia	1.10	0.23	4.0
Georgia	1.32	0.01	-1.0
Azerbaydzhan	1.32	0.01	-1.0
Armenia	0.90	0.43	3.9
Uzbekistan	1.24	0.09	2.3
Kirghizia	0.98	0.35	3.9
Tadzhikistan	1.13	0.20	4.1
Turkmenia	1.33	0.00	0.0
Kazakhstan	1.00	0.33	4.1
Belorussia	1.15	0.18	-1.8
Moldavia	0.91	0.42	1.6

Sources: TsSU, *Trud v SSSR*, p. 256; *Narkhoz 64*, p. 12; *Narkhoz 65*, p. 700; *Vestnik statistiki* (No. 2, 1967), p. 92.

TABLE 6.5. PERCENTAGE INCREASES IN EMPLOYMENT, WAGE LEVEL, AND POPULATION DUE TO MIGRATION.

Union Republic	A 1960-69 employment (blue- and white-collar workers)	B 1960-69 wage level (retail trade per worker)	C 1959-70 population due to migration
Russia	35	33	-1.3
Ukraine	47	29	1.3
Belorussia	56	39	-3.3
Uzbekistan	64	20	5.0
Kazakhstan	55	28	9.6
Georgia	52	15	-1.9
Azerbaydzhan	64	17	-1.5
Lithuania	68	37	1.9
Moldavia	103	18	2.7
Latvia	40	36	7.5
Kirghizia	80	25	7.4
Tadzhikistan	73	22	7.3
Armenia	89	14	8.2
Turkmenia	46	31	0.8
Estonia	33	43	7.7

Correlations	Wage level change	Migration
Employment change	-.66	.20
Wage level change		-.02

Sources: *Narkhoz 69*, pp. 533, 603; Table 4.2.

TABLE 6.6. AGRICULTURAL LAND-LABOR RATIOS IN THE EAST, 1969.

	Hectares per household on collective farms (fishing excluded)	Hectares per workers on state farms
Russia	11.1	11.9
West Siberia	21.9	16.3
East Siberia	18.5	15.3
Far East	18.9	9.3

Source: *R.S.F.S.R. Narkhoz 69*, pp. 250-51, 258-59.

TABLE A.1. UNION REPUBLICS AND MAJOR ECONOMIC REGIONS.

Republic or region	1970 census population (millions)
Russia or Russian SSR (RSR)	130.1
Northwest Region (NRW)	12.2
Center Region (CNT)	27.7
Volga-Vyatka Region (VLV)	8.3
Central Chernozem Region (CNC)	8.0
Volga Region (VLG)	18.4
North Caucasus Region (NCC)	14.3
Urals Region (URL)	15.2
West Siberia Region (WSI)	12.1
East Siberia Region (ESI)	7.5
Far East Region (FEA)	5.8
Kaliningrad Oblast (KOB)	0.7
The Ukraine or Ukrainian SSR (UKR)	47.1
Don-Dnieper Region (DON)	20.1
Southwest Region (SOW)	20.7
South Region (SOU)	6.4
Baltic Region (BAL)	7.6
Lithuania or Lithuanian SSR (LTH)	3.1
Latvia or Latvian SSR (LAT)	2.4
Estonia or Estonian SSR (EST)	1.4
Kaliningrad Oblast (KOB)	0.7
Transcaucasia Region (TRC)	12.3
Georgia or Georgian SSR (GRG)	4.7
Azerbaydzhan or Azerbaydzhan SSR (AZR)	5.1
Armenia or Armenian SSR (ARM)	2.5
Central Asia Region (CAS)	20.0
Uzbekistan or Uzbek SSR (UZB)	12.0
Kirghizia or Kirghiz SSR (KIR)	2.9
Tadzhikistan or Tadzhik SSR (TAD)	2.9
Turkmenia or Turkmen SSR (TRK)	2.2
Kazakhstan or Kazakh SSR and Region (KAZ)	12.9
Belorussia or Belorussian SSR and Region (BLR)	9.0
Moldavia or Moldavian SSR and Region (MLD)	3.8

TABLE C.1. THOUSANDS OF PERSONS ARRIVING AND DEPARTING IN THE TWO YEARS PRIOR TO 1970 CENSUS.

Republic	Arriving from Another Republic	Departing for Another Republic	Difference
Russia	1181.1	1005.1	176.0
Ukraine	589.9	553.0	36.9
Belorussia	136.0	133.5	2.5
Uzbekistan	120.8	203.4	-82.6
Kazakhstan	422.8	444.5	-21.7
Georgia	21.4	57.8	-36.4
Azerbaydzhan	27.1	55.5	-28.4
Lithuania	27.7	25.1	2.6
Moldavia	50.5	60.0	-9.5
Latvia	45.3	31.0	14.3
Kirghizia	72.5	87.2	-14.7
Tadzhikistan	37.0	55.5	-18.5
Armenia	26.3	20.7	5.6
Turkmenia	31.0	41.8	-10.8
Estonia	35.3	19.7	15.6
TOTAL	2824.7	2793.8	30.9

Source: Ts.S.U., *Itogi vsesoiuznoi perepisi naseleniia 1970 goda*, VII (Moscow: Statistika, 1974), Tables 2-17.

TABLE C.2. COMPARISON OF CENSUS AND RESIDUAL ESTIMATES OF NET MIGRATION, 1968-69.

Republic	Thousands		Rate per thousand per year		
	Census	Residual	Census	Residual	Difference
Russia	176.0	-158	0.7	-0.6	1.3
Ukraine	37.0	97	0.4	1.0	-0.6
Belorussia	2.4	1	0.1	0.1	0.1
Uzbekistan	-82.7	79	-3.5	3.3	-6.8
Kazakhstan	-21.7	-35	-0.8	-1.4	0.5
Georgia	-36.3	-23	-3.9	-2.5	-1.4
Azerbaydzhan	-28.5	-15	-2.8	-1.5	-1.3
Lithuania	2.6	10	0.4	1.6	-1.2
Moldavia	-9.5	-2	-1.3	-0.3	-1.1
Latvia	14.2	25	3.0	5.3	-2.3
Kirghizia	-14.6	21	-2.5	3.6	-6.1
Tadzhikistan	-18.5	15	-3.2	2.6	-5.8
Armenia	5.6	33	1.1	6.6	-5.5
Turkmenia	-10.8	6	-2.5	1.4	-3.9
Estonia	15.6	25	5.7	9.2	-3.5
Total	30.8	79			
Average			-0.6	1.9	-2.5
Weighted average			0.1	0.3	-0.2

Sources: Tables 4.2 and C.1.
Note: Components may not add to totals due to rounding.

TABLE C.3. ESTIMATES OF NET INTER-REPUBLIC URBAN ARRIVAL, 1969

Republic	Thousands		Rate per thousand		
	Census	Registration	Census	Registration	Difference
Russia	82.9	40.8	1.0	0.5	0.5
Ukraine	40.6	84.2	1.5	3.3	-1.7
Belorussia	7.9	11.7	2.0	3.0	-1.0
Uzbekistan	-14.8	15.4	-3.4	3.5	-6.9
Kazakhstan	23.5	6.6	3.6	1.0	2.6
Georgia	-13.4	-2.8	-6.0	-1.3	-4.7
Azerbaydzan	-11.4	-4.6	-4.4	-1.8	-2.6
Lithuania	1.1	5.1	0.7	3.3	-2.6
Moldavia	3.2	10.6	2.8	9.4	-6.6
Latvia	4.5	4.0	3.0	2.7	0.3
Kirghizia	-4.6	4.5	-4.2	4.1	-8.3
Tadzhikistan	-4.0	-0.6	-3.7	-0.6	-3.1
Armenia	3.7	8.8	2.5	5.9	-3.4
Turkmenia	-2.3	-0.5	-2.3	-0.5	-1.8
Estonia	4.8	7.7	5.4	8.7	-3.3
Total	121.7	190.9			
Average			-0.1	2.7	-2.8
Weighted average			0.9	1.4	-0.5

Sources: Ts.S.U., *Itogi vsesoiuznoi perepisi naseleniia 1970 goda*, Vol. VII (Moscow: Statistika, 1974), Tables 2-17; *Vestnik statistiki* (No. 3, 1971), p. 80.

Note: Components may not add to totals due to rounding.

TABLE C.4. COMPARISON OF RESULTS: STANDARD ERRORS OF DISCREPANCIES.

	Residual			Population-Registration			Total
	I	II	III	I	II	III	
Census results higher							
Kazakhstan	0.13	0.18	0.69	0.65	1.85	1.72	5.22
Russia	0.39	0.53	1.25	0.13	1.14	0.92	4.36
Latvia	-0.66	-0.91	0.84	0.09	1.08	1.11	1.55
Estonia	-1.01	-1.38	1.14	-0.83	-0.17	0.51	-1.74
Census results lower							
Kirghizia	-1.77	-2.43	-1.35	-2.07	-1.86	-1.78	-11.26
Uzbekistan	-1.89	-2.60	-1.67	-1.72	-1.38	-1.35	-10.61
Tadzhikistan	-1.63	-2.24	-1.38	-0.77	-0.10	-0.48	-6.60
Armenia	-1.48	-2.03	-0.30	-0.85	-0.20	0.16	-4.70
Georgia	-0.44	-0.61	-0.49	-1.17	-0.63	-1.12	-4.46
Turkmenia	-1.14	-1.56	-0.79	-0.45	0.35	-0.01	-3.60
Moldavia	-0.35	0.50	0.16	-1.63	-1.26	-0.54	-3.12
Azerbaydzhan	-0.36	-0.49	-0.17	-0.65	0.07	-0.45	-2.05
Estonia	-1.01	-1.38	1.14	-0.83	-0.17	0.51	-1.74

TABLE C.5. PERCENTAGES BY WHICH CENSUS ESTIMATES FALL SHORT OF POPULATION-REGISTRATION ESTIMATES.

Republics	Arrivals	Departures
Russia	36	45
Ukraine	49	43
Belorussia	43	31
Uzbekistan	48	24
Kazakhstan	31	40
Georgia	46	-16
Azerbaydzhan	55	19
Lithuania	42	20
Moldavia	49	33
Latvia	24	24
Kirghizia	48	32
Tadzhikistan	45	30
Armenia	45	18
Turkmenia	50	41
Estonia	45	47
Average	44	29
Weighted average	41	40

TABLE C.6. PERCENTAGES BY WHICH CENSUS ESTIMATES FALL SHORT OF POPULATION-REGISTRATION ESTIMATES FOR SELECTED STREAMS.

FROM \ TO	RSR	UKR	KAZ	UZB	KIR	TAD	TRK
RSR	..	..	..	51	47	49	55
UKR	..	..	..	53	57	57	60
KAZ	..	..	..	44	45	44	49
UZB	20	28	-7	..	..	..	..
KIR	34	24	4	..	..	..	..
TAD	23	28	-10	..	..	..	..
TRK	14	38	-7	..	..	..	..

Notes: Abbreviations used for republics: RSR - Russia; KIR - Kirghizia; UKR - Ukraine; TAD - Tadzhikistan; KAZ - Kazakhstan; TRK - Turkmenia; UZB - Uzbekistan. Movement from all points in the area of origin to urban points in the area of destination constituted the streams.

TABLE C.7. NATURAL INCREASE ERRORS IMPLIED BY CENSUS-ESTIMATES OF NET MIGRATION.

			Natural increase		Percentage bias in reported		
Republic	Reported Population Increase	Census Net Migration	Implied	Reported	Natural increase	Births	Deaths
Census rates higher							
KAZ	418	-22	440	446	1	..	-3
RSR	1383	180	1203	1529	27	..	-18
Census rates lower							
KIR	156	-15	171	134	-22	-17	..
UZB	735	-84	819	648	-21	-17	..
TAD	185	-19	204	168	-18	-15	..

Notes: 1. Abbreviations used for republics: KAZ - Kazakhstan; RSR - Russia; KIR - Kirghizia; USB - Uzbekistan; TAD - Tadzhikistan. 2. The data in the first four columns represent thousands of persons.

APPENDIX A
TERRITORIAL DIVISIONS AND UNITS OF ANALYSIS

During 1959–70, fifteen Union republics and eighteen major economic regions separately constituted the U.S.S.R. The relationship between the two partitions is shown in Table A.1 and Figures A.1 and A.2.

Figure A.1.
Union Republics
See Table A.1. for Abbreviations.

Figure A.2.
Major Economic Regions
See Table A.1. for Abbreviations.

Moldavia is not considered to be a major economic region in Soviet usage. It is regarded as one in this study. Republics do not share major economic regions, and major economic regions do not share republics, with the single exception being Kaliningrad Oblast which is part of both the Russian republic and the Baltic region. The political division of the U.S.S.R. into republics is much more important in the affairs of Soviet administration than the division into major economic regions. The latter scheme is valuable to students of U.S.S.R. regional matters because it partitions the vast Russian republic.

Each of the republics is divided into major political units; "major political units" is used here for entities known as krais, autonomous republics, oblasts, and autonomous oblasts. All autonomous republics and krais are major political units, but oblasts are not when they are subsumed under an autonomous republic or a krai. The administrative structure is indicated in Figure A.3.

The major economic region divisions do not split any major political unit between two regions. There are 209 major political units, so that in 1970 an approximate average population for them was 1.2 million people. The range of populations was, of course, great, and the geographical size of these units varied even more. The composition of the major political units down to *raiony* and cities is also shown in Figure A.3. The most common divisions for *raiony* are *sel'sovety* (rural councils) and *sovety* (councils) of settlements of urban-type; most cities have divisions into city *raiony*. *Geography of the USSR* and *The Delenie (Divisions) of the Soviet Union* provide additional information.[1]

1. Paul Lydolph, *Geography of the USSR* (New York: Wiley, 1970) and *SSSR Administrativno-territorial'noe delenie soiuz respublik* (Moscow: Izvestiia).

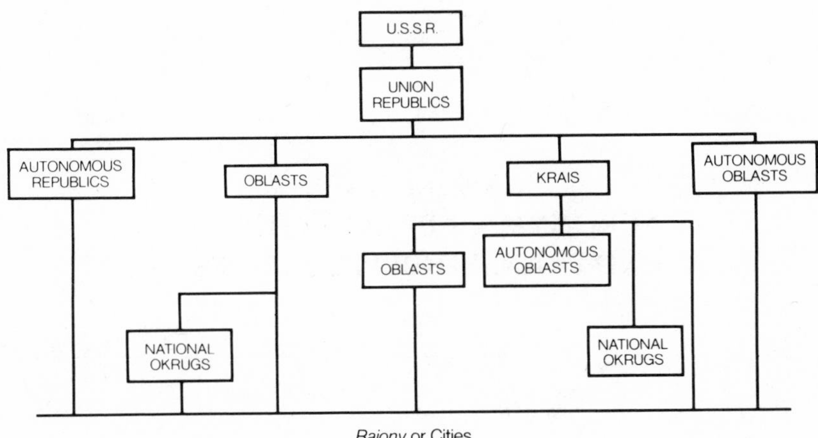

Figure A.3.
Scheme of Administrative Relationships

Appendix B
ACRONYMS, ABBREVIATIONS, AND TRANSLITERATED TITLES

CDSP *The Current Digest of the Soviet Press*

GOSPLAN State Planning Commission

Narkhoz *(Narodnoe khoziaistvo)* *The National Economy,* the annual statistical yearbook

TsSU (Tsentral'noe Stasticheskoe Upravlenie) Central Statistical Administration

Z.A.G.S. (Zapis' Aktov Grazhdanskogo Sostoianiia) Civil Records Registry Office

Appendix C
1970 CENSUS RESULTS CONCERNING INTERREPUBLIC NET MIGRATION

Census data on population migration[1] conflict with conclusions reached by Western and Soviet researchers concerning interrepublic population movement during the 1960s. For example, according to the census, Russia gained population during the last two years of the 1960s while Central Asia lost population; it had been widely thought that exactly the opposite occurred.

In the 1970 census Soviet adults were asked how long they and their families had lived continuously in their present location. If their response indicated less than two years, previous place of permanent residence was sought and recorded. These data provide, among other things, some measures of interrepublic movement during 1968–69. Table C.1 shows census returns on most recent moves into and out of various republics. By subtracting departures to other republics from arrivals from other republics one gets a rough indication of migration balances. In the case of Russia, we subtract 1005.1 from 1181.1 and get 176.0, indicating very approximately that on net balance 176,000 persons moved into Russia between January 16, 1968, and January 15, 1970. The "very approximately" qualification is appropriate since persons who moved more than once, let us say from republic A to republic B to republic C, would have been recorded as going from B to C when in fact the A to B to C sequence means that on net balance A lost population, B neither gained nor lost, and C gained.

These census estimates may be compared with the results from two other schemes for determining the number of migrants on net account during 1968–69.[2] They may be examined in their relation to the residual estimates of chapter 4, and their urban component may be scrutinized in relation to the net urban arrival flows reported by the Central Statistical Administration for 1969.[3] These last data derive from the registration of persons arriving and departing

1. TsSU, *Itogi vsesoiuznoi perepisi naseleniia 1970 goda,* Vol. VII Moscow, Statistika, 1974), Tables 1–18.
2. As in chapter 4, 1968–69 denotes the period from January 15, 1968, through January 14, 1970.
3. *Vestnik statistiki* (No. 3, 1971), pp. 73–83.

from urban-type settlements. These two comparions will first be made to reveal inconsistencies and then various influences that could have produced the discrepancies will be examined.

INCONSISTENCY WITH OTHER ESTIMATES

Western investigators estimated net migration for republics during 1968–69 by eliminating known natural increase (birth less deaths) from total population increase and using the residual as an estimate of net migration. They utilized postcensal estimates of population (for January 1, 1968; January 1, 1969; and January 15, 1970) and reported rates of natural increase.[4] Their results generally agree.

Table C.2 compares the census results of Table C.1 with the residual estimates of Table 4.2 modified slightly to cover a time period beginning January 15, 1968, rather than January 1, 1968.[5] Whether one focuses on numbers of migrants on net account or on rates of net migration per thousand population, it is obvious that the two series diverge. Of course, it could not be expected that they would correspond exactly due to the problem of multiple movements noted above. The negative entries in the last column indicate that in the majority of instances the census rates fall short of the residual rates. A notable exception is provided by the case of Russia; for the Central Asian republics, the census rates are far below the residual rates. The Western work estimates net in-migration to Central Asia and net out-migration from Russia, a finding corroborated by Soviet research for the period of the early and mid-1960s[6] and apparently continuing into 1968 and 1969.[7] The census data contradict earlier thinking.

The pattern of divergences may be examined somewhat more formally. Let *CAR* designate the census rate and *RAR*, the residual rate. The degree of linear relationship between the estimates may be judged according to how well the formula $CAR = a + (b \,.\, RAR)$ fits the data. Three cases may be distinguished:

Case I: The value of a is constrained to 0.0 and the value of b, to 1.0;

Case II: The value of a is fitted according to least squares, but the value of b is constrained to be 1.0; and,

Case III: Both a and b are fitted according to least squares.

4. *Vestnik statistiki* (No. 2, 1971), pp. 85–87.

5. For example, Table 4.2 reports that net arrivals in Russia for 1968 and for 1969 (covering the period through January 14, 1970) were −104 and −70 thousand, respectively. The absolute value of the total of the two was lowered by 2.0 percent (yielding −170), reflecting the shorter time period of 2 years rather than 2 years, 15 days.

6. P. P. Litviakov (ed.), *Demograficheskie problemy zaniatosti* (Moscow: Ekonomika, 1969), p. 160; D. I. Valentei et al. (eds.), *Narodonaselenie i ekonomika* (Moscow: Ekonomika, 1967), p. 103; and V. V. Pokshishevskii, "Migration of U.S.S.R. Population Discussed" in U.S. Joint Publications Research Service, *Translations on U.S.S.R. Resources*, JPRS 49279 (November 19, 1969), p. 56.

7. V. I. Perevedentsev, "Migratsiia naseleniia i ispol'zovanie trudovykh resursov," *Voprosy ekonomiki* (No. 9, 1970), pp. 40–41; and, Radio Free Europe, *Migration Against the Plan?* (September 1, 1970), research report.

The first case corresponds to an informal examination of whether the various pairs of rates agree. It suggests that *CAR* equals *RAR* on the hypothesis of perfect overall consistency. The second case allows the data to define a nonzero intercept term presumably reflecting the generally lower level of the census rates. The third allows the data by themselves to determine the relationship. The results obtained, with standard errors of coefficients indicated in parentheses, with coefficients of determination,[8] R^2, and with standard errors of the estimates, *S.E.*, are:

Case I: $CAR = RAR$ $\quad R^2 = -0.90 \quad S.E. = 3.53$

Case II: $\underset{(0.67)}{CAR = -2.50} + RAR$ $\quad R^2 = 0.05 \quad S.E. = 2.58$

Case III: $CAR = \underset{(0.64)}{-1.58} + \underset{(0.17)}{0.52}\,RAR$ $\quad R^2 = 0.04 \quad S.E. = 2.13$

In both cases in which the intercept term is unconstrained, it is statistically less than 0.0, confirming the informal judgment that *CAR* rates are lower.

Greatest interest arises, however, in identifying instances of extraordinary discrepancy between rates; this may be accomplished by listing cases where the actual *CAR* rates are more than one standard error away from fitted *CAR* rates. Instances of actual values more than one standard error above the fitted values occurred as follows:

Case I	Case II	Case III
(none)	Russia	Russia
	Kazakhstan	Estonia

Instances of values more than one standard error below were:

Case I	Case II	Case III
Uzbekistan	Uzbekistan	Uzbekistan
Kirghizia	Kirghizia	Kirghizia
Tadzhikistan	Tadzhikistan	Tadzhikistan
Armenia	Armenia	
Turkmenia		

On the basis of these comparisons it appears that the census rates may be higher for Russia and definitely lower for Uzbekistan, Kirghizia, Tadzhikistan, and perhaps for Armenia.

A second comparison may be made by examining the census estimates of arrival on net account at urban settlements in relation to the same reports emanating from the system of registering persons upon their arrival and departure from urban places.[9] The census returns pertain to 1968–69; unfortunately registration data on urban arrivals and departures were published only for the year 1969. The present comparison assumes that the experience of 1969 was

8. $R^2 = 1 -$ (unexplained variation/total variation) and is bounded below by zero only in the case of unconstrained ordinary least squares.

9. *Vestnik statistiki* (No. 3, 1971), p. 80.

similar to that of 1968–69. The levels and rates of migration are expressed on an annual basis. The results appear in Table C.3. The table seems to show a pattern similar to the one observed in the previous comparison. According to the census, Kazakhstan and Russia and also Latvia gained more persons and all the other republics lost most persons than the registration system indicates. The census estimates appear to be much lower for Kirghizia and Uzbekistan in Central Asia and for Moldavia.

Again it is possible to proceed more formally. Let *CUAR* designate the census arrival rates and *PUAR*, the population-registration arrival rates. The same three cases of linear relationship are of interest; results obtained were:

Case I: $CUAR = PUAR \qquad R^2 = -0.37 \qquad S.E. = 4.02$

Case II: $\underset{}{CUAR} = \underset{(0.76)}{-\,2.83} + PUAR \qquad R^2 = 0.31 \qquad S.E. = 2.95$

Case III: $CUAR = \underset{(0.96)}{-\,1.94} + \underset{(0.22)}{0.67}\,PUAR \qquad R^2 = 0.41 \qquad S.E. = 2.89$

It is interesting to note that the last two fits again imply that the census values are usually lower than the registration estimates. Instances of actual values lying more than one standard error above the fitted values included:

Case I	Case II	Case III
(none)	Kazakhstan	Kazakhstan
	Russia	Latvia
	Latvia	

Instances of the opposite circumstance were:

Case I	Case II	Case III
Kirghizia	Kirghizia	Kirghizia
Uzbekistan	Uzbekistan	Uzbekistan
Moldavia	Moldavia	Georgia
Georgia		

On the basis of these results it appears that census results were probably higher for Kazakhstan and definitely lower for Kirghizia and Uzbekistan and probably lower for Moldavia and Georgia.

Two comparisons have been made, one between residual and census results and the other between population-registration and census estimates of net urban arrival. In each comparison three criteria were employed. Instances of extraordinary discrepancy were noted by listing observations for which the actual census estimates were more than one standard error from their predicted values. Table C.4 lists the number of standard errors above or below predicted values that actual values were. The data seem to indicate that no matter what standards are used the census estimates are always substantially lower for Kirghizia and Uzbekistan. Tadzhikistan usually appears much lower, too. Perhaps Armenia and Georgia are also lower. The data tend to show that census estimates perhaps for Kazakhstan and Russia may be higher, but they are not conclusive in this regard.

ANALYSIS OF THE DIVERGENCES

Why do these divergences occur? Various combinations of circumstances could have produced the results or a single, exceptional circumstance could have been responsible. Several "pure" or single-cause possibilities may be examined.

Inaccurate Census Responses

A noteworthy characteristic of the division of Union republics into areas for which the census estimates appear to be higher (Kazakhstan and Russia) and for which they definitely are lower (Kirghizia and Uzbekistan, perhaps along with Tadzhikistan, Armenia, and Georgia) is that the former areas are ones into which the state encouraged net interrepublic in-migration and that the latter are regions for which the state discouraged it. If the census results are accurate, the state redistributed labor force and population during 1968–69 more successfully than practically all observers had previously realized. On the other hand, it may be asked what kind of influences could have worked during the 1970 census to yield a possibly erroneous picture of substantial net out-migration from labor-surplus areas. Consider the case of migration between Russia and Central Asia. It had been thought that the first area was losing population and the second gaining, owing in part to movement from Russia to Central Asia. What kinds of misstatement by census respondents at the time of the census would have raised the Russian balance or lowered the Central Asian balance? Most obviously, if an individual had moved from Russia to Central Asia during 1968–69, but at the time of the census simply replied that he had lived continuously in Central Asia, then the indicated effect would have resulted. The number of moves into Central Asia and out of Russia would both have been too low.

This possibility appears somewhat likely. It is probable that the enumerator recorded whatever the respondent stated. Migration from the western and northern parts of the U.S.S.R. to Central Asia received unfavorable commentary and publicity. The state discouraged such movement, yet individual enterprises stood to gain from recruiting trained workers from outside the region. Despite state efforts, skilled migrants probably came.[10] In view of this, newcomers undoubtedly preferred to lose their distinctive status as migrants as quickly as possible. Thus, it is easy to imagine recent arrivals merely replying that their present location had been a permanent place of residence for the last two years, especially if the respondent knew (as was likely) that subsequent questions dealt with area of previous residence and reason for leaving. There appears to have been nothing to prevent this possibility. There is no evidence to suggest that individual responses were checked by any extraordinary measures such as requests by enumerators to see domestic passports for notations con-

10. I. R. Mulliadzhanov, *Narodonaselenie Uzbekskoi SSR* (Tashkent: Uzbekistan, 1967), p. 127; Litviakov, *Demograficheskie problemy*, p. 158; and, A. G. Volkov, *Statistika migratsiia naseleniia* (Moscow: Statistika, 1973), p. 230.

cerning former residences. In addition, it would have been impossible to search through collective-farm rolls and territorial-administrative records for previous residences of respondents.

Of all the questions asked in the 1959 and 1970 censuses these migration questions are among the few seeking retrospective information. Students of survey methods and population statistics know recollections can be faulty or inaccurate, and that often there is no way of checking their accuracy. Perhaps framers of the question failed to anticipate this problem in the present instance. The history of censuses is replete with questions that failed to yield accurate information. The latest U.S. example concerns question 41b of the 1970 census which asks the extent of receipt of welfare or public assistance payments. When the responses for all New York City residents were totaled, the sum was approximately half of what it should have been according to state and city records.[11]

It is possible, in at least a rough fashion, to check this hypothesis of respondent bias. The census reports on arrivals at urban points during 1968–69 can be compared with those deriving from the population-registration system for 1969.[12] As above, to obtain data that are commensurate, the census results are divided by 2.0 to yield annual levels of arrival, and it is assumed that the experiences of 1968–69 and of 1969 were similar.

The reports from the registration system concerning urban areas should be reasonably accurate, and they may serve as a standard of accuracy. Upon arriving in an urban area, civil law required that an individual present his domestic passport and register his presence. Typically, workers at offices of housing management recorded the arrival and departure of persons in books of address forms having detachable portions which served as the source documents for migration statistics in this system. Failure to register implied that one was in violation of the civil code and could not legally obtain housing or secure employment. A person's continued presence in an area increased the likelihood that his migration into the area would eventually be discovered. It would thus appear that in most instances it was very much in the individual's interest to register.

There are two reasons to expect that the census estimates will generally fall short of the registration levels. The census data are retrospective, a circumstance which suggests that they would likely have a downward bias due to the failure of some respondents to remember or state at the time of the census that they had changed place of residence in the last two years. It is difficult to imagine an individual becoming entangled with the authorities in this regard, for, as has been previously noted, there is no evidence of any kind of special checking for accuracy, and once the census questions were asked and the answers recorded, the enumerator went away. A second circumstance that likely worked to the same end stems from the way multiple moves were treated

11. "Current Reading," *The Public Interest*, No. 32 (Summer 1973), pp. 113–14.
12. *Vestnik statistiki* (No. 3, 1971), p. 78.

in the census. The census recorded persons who moved, no matter how many times during 1968–69, simply as persons who changed place of residence. Multiple moves are not fully reflected in the census data. In short, the census counted the number of persons who moved and the registration system, the number of moves. This circumstance lowers the census rates in relation to the registration rates to whatever extent persons moving more than once accounted for the total number of changes in residence during 1968–69.

The number of interrepublic migrants arriving in cities was 1,731,878 according to the registration system and 1,020,073 according to the census,[13] implying that the latter falls short of the former by 41 percent. The number of persons leaving urban areas was 1,514,521 according to the registration system and 912,121 according to the census, indicating a short-fall of 40 percent.

The data for the 210 (15 × 14) point-to-point interrepublic streams can be aggregated to provide information on the overall levels of arrival and departure for the various republics, and the percentage discrepancies can be calculated for arrival and depatures estimates in each republic. The percentages are displayed in Table C.5. Two aspects of the data are of special interest. Looking at pairs of percentages for republics, one notes that the usual circumstance is that the arrival discrepancy exceed the departure error, implying, if it is assumed the registration data are accurate, that the census undersetimates levels of urban arrival on net account for most republics. Looking down the columns, one observes that there is substantial variation in the levels of shortfall between republics. The data, in this regard, are consistent with the hypothesis that respondent bias occurred, at least in part, according to whether the state desired or did not desire net migration into republics. The shortfall levels in arrivals for Russia and Kazakhstan and also for Latvia are noticeably low, and the measure for departures is especially low for practically all the Transcaucasian and Central Asian republics.

In the case of Russia, several streams from Central Asia are estimated by the census to have been at levels close to those reported by the population-registration system. The former are less than the latter to the following extents: Uzbekistan to Russia, 20 percent; Tadzhikistan to Russia, 23 percent; Kirghizia to Russia, 34 percent; and Turkmenia to Russia, 14 percent. The shortfalls in the case of Central Asia to Kazakhstan streams actually disappeared, that is, were negative, and therefore were excesses, in three instances: Uzbekistan to Kazakhstan, -7 percent; Kirghizia to Kazakhstan, 4 percent; Tadzhikistan to Kazakhstan, -10 percent; and Turkmenia to Kazakhstan, -7 percent. These results in all likelihood indicate an ability and willingness by respondents to recall that they had moved to labor-deficient republics, an action of which the state generally approved.

For the Central Asian republics, Table C.5 indicates relatively low arrival counts and high departure counts according to the census; both influences work

13. These totals come from summing the numbers of point-to-point interrepublic migrants and do not include migrants whose point of origin was not known.

to produce census estimates of *net* urban arrival much lower than the population-registration estimates. The exact pattern of the differences in discrepancies is shown in Table C.6. All of the entries in the upper right-hand corner of the table, representing streams from Russia, the Ukraine and Kazakhstan to the labor-surplus points of Central Asia are relatively large probably indicating that many persons who made such moves failed to recall them at the time of the census. All the entries in the lower left, representing movement from labor-surplus areas to urban points elsewhere, are relatively small probably demonstrating a willingness by respondents during the census to reveal changes of residence of which the state presumably approved. This is especially true with regard to moves to and from Kazakhstan. On those from Central Asia to Kazakhstan, the census and population-registration estimates are approximately equal. But on moves in the other direction, the census estimates fall short of the population-registration estimates by 44 to 49 percent.

This reading of the evidence suggests that respondent bias was present in answers to the migration questions of the 1970 census. People failed to remember or concealed moves from labor-deficient to labor-surplus areas with great frequency. Although the comparisons are quite clear in this regard, this conclusion must be qualified in several respects. First, the two sets of data were not identical in coverage with regard to time and measure of migration. It was asumed that the experiences of 1968–69 and 1969 could be deemed as essentially the same and that multiple movements occurred to the same extent in different regions. Second, it was hypothesized that the population-registration system, as it functioned in urban areas, produced accurate data; if evidence is uncovered that it did not do so during the year 1969, the present analysis is undermined. Third, the sizes of the overall discrepancies between the registration and census estimates of total interrepublic arrivals and departures are so large as to make one somewhat uneasy about making inferences about the situation in particular republics.

Inaccurate Birth and Death Rates

If the census reports on interrepublic migration are correct, it is possible that the Western residual estimates of migration err because the reported rates of natural increase are inaccurate. If births had been substantially underreported in some regions, then the reported levels of natural increase for 1968–69 would have been too low, thereby imputing too much of the observed population increase to the residual category of net migration. While it seems likely that this mechanism was at work at least to some extent, it cannot explain the second set of discrepancies between the census and registration rates of net interrepublic urban arrival, since neither estimating scheme uses the reported levels of birth or deaths.

Nevertheless, it is worthwhile to see whether the phenomenon could explain the first set of discrepancies between the census and residual rates. Usually, births and deaths, if not accurately registered, are underregistered. If both are underregistered, then the biases in the reported rates tend to offset each other. That is, a death rate which is too low when subtracted from a birth rate which is too low yields a natural increase rate having less bias than at least one of the other rates. Thus between January 1, 1968 and January 15, 1970, total population increase in Russia was reported to have been approximately 1,383 (thousands);[14] census-estimated increase due to migration was approximately 180 (thousands),[15] thereby implying that natural increase was somewhere near 1,203 (thousands), obtained by subtracting the second number from the first. Reported natural increase was approximately 1,544. Based on an assumption that the census migration returns are accurate, this circumstance implies that reported natural increase may have been something on the order of 27 percent too high.

The formula, [NR/NC)−1] × 100, where *NR* stands for the reported natural increase and *NC*, the natural increase implied by the census estimates of net migration, may be used to calculate the hypothetical percentage biases in reported natural increase rates, $BIAS_{NR}$. Furthermore, if it is assumed, in general, that reported births, *BR*, and reported deaths, *DR*, are never overregistered and in specific instances that reported levels of either births or deaths are accurate, then the biases in the other component of natural increase can also be derived. In the case of accurate reports of births, the bias in the death rates, $BIAS_{DR}$, can be derived and can be calculated according to:

$$BIAS_{DR} = BIAS_{NR} \quad \frac{NC}{NC - BR}$$

In the case of accurate registration of deaths, the bias in the reported number of births, $BIAS_{BR}$, is:

$$BIAS_{BR} = BIAS_{NR} \quad \frac{NC}{NC + DR}$$

To the extent that the prior assumption about the accuracy of either births or deaths is incorrect; that is, that both components of natural increase are in fact underregistered, then the derived bias must be farther from zero. Thus, the absolute values of biases for either births or deaths are minimum absolute values.

With these three formulas, the results presented in Table C.7 were obtained. They indicate in several instances that the implied levels of underreporting of vital events would have to have been very high for the census data on migration to represent the true state of affairs. Deaths in the Russian republic would had to have been underregistered by somewhere in the neighborhood of 18 percent as births would had to have been in the listed Central Asia republics. It is

14. Derived by applying the reported rate of increase for 1968 to the mid-year population of that year and applying the rate for 1969 to the mid-interval population between January 1, 1969, and January 15, 1970, raised by a factor of 1.04 to reflect the longer time period.

15. The value of 176.0 is raised by a factor of 1.02 to take account of the slightly longer time period commencing January 1, 1968, rather than January 15.

difficult to imagine how registered deaths could be almost 20 percent too low in the Russian republic. With regard to births it will be remembered that an estimated 3 percent of all births were not reflected in published reports in the late 1960s. To the extent that the all-Union reports were too low, one would certainly anticipate that Central Asia could have been the source of much of the inaccuracy. But the required level of underregistration of births would had to have been even greater.

On the basis of comparisons between census and residual estimates of migration, it appears that the implied biases in reported rates of natural increase would have to have been very large for the census estimates of net migration to be judged accurate. Any such biases can offer only a partial explanation of the observed discrepancies. Furthermore, they cannot account for similar discrepancies noted in the net urban arrival comparison, since natural increase plays no part in the census and population-registraton schemes of estimation. Therefore, they by themselves, cannot explain the observed discrepancies.

Errors in Population Numbers

If the census migration estimates are correct and the residual estimates are calculated by:

$$\text{Net Migration} = \begin{matrix}\text{Closing}\\\text{Population}\end{matrix} - \begin{matrix}\text{Opening}\\\text{Population}\end{matrix} - (\text{Births} - \text{Deaths}),$$

then it is possible that errors derive from inaccurate population numbers. If biases are uniform through time, the real variable of interest, population increase, may, however, be relatively free from bias. In this connection, the 1968 and 1969 population numbers used by the Western authors were issued by the Central Statistical Administration after the census was taken. As such, they represent revisions of intercensal estimates in light of subsequent information; the revised estimates and the census are consistent and fit a pattern of even population growth during the late 1960s. It is possible that the population estimates could have varied in special ways to produce the observed discrepancies, but again the similar discrepancies between census and population-registration urban arrival rates cannot be explained by such circumstances.

CONCLUSIONS

Census data on population migration conflict with conclusions reached by other methods of analysis. Most notably they do not agree with various residual estimates of net migration made by Soviet and Western investigators. Specifically, it has been found that the census estimates of net migration are generally lower and are especially so for Kirghizia and Uzbekistan. They also appear to be lower for Tadzihikistan, Armenia, and Georgia. They may be higher for Kazakhstan and Russia.

Two examinations led to these conclusions. Census rates were compared to residual rates for the years 1968–69. Practically all the census rates were lower than the residual rates. Then, 1969 rates of interrepublic net urban arrival as estimated from census data and from population-registration data were contrasted. Levels of net arrival were higher for Kazakhstan, Russia, and Latvia according to the census and lower for most of the Central Asian and Transcaucasian republics and for Moldavia.

Three possible explanations for the divergences were discussed. It was concluded that respondent misstatement accounts at least in part for the observed discrepancies. Persons questioned at the time of the 1970 census informed enumerators more often of moves from labor-surplus to labor-deficient areas than of changes of residence of a contrary nature. It was found that moves from Central Asia to Russia and from Central Asia to Kazakhstan were relatively completely reported, but that moves in the opposite direction were not. The effect was to lower estimated net migration rates into Central Asia and to raise them for Russia and Kazakhstan. Other explanations having to do with errors in natural increase and in population numbers could also explain some of the discrepancies. But inasmuch as natural increase and population numbers played no part in either of the estimates for the second comparison, they cannot provide a complete explanation. It is likely that the residual estimates are too high in some instances due to the natural increase figures that are too low.

BIBLIOGRAPHY

SOVIET BOOKS

Aleksandrov, N. G., et al., eds. *Trudovoe pravo*. Moscow: Sovetskaia Entsiklopediia, 1969.

Arutiunian, L. A. *Sotsialisticheskii zakon narodonaseleniia*. Moscow: Nauka, 1975

Antosenkov, E. G., ed. *Opyt issledovaniia peremeny truda v promyshlennosti*. Novosibirsk: Nauka, 1969.

Ashimbaev, T. A., ed. *Naselenie i trudovye resursy gorodov Severnogo Kazakhstana*. Alma-Ata: Nauka, 1970.

Bagrii, P. I., et al., eds. *Voprosy demografii*. Kiev: Statistika, 1968.

Broner, D. L., and Venetskii, I. G., eds. *Problemy demografii* Moscow: Statistika, 1971.

Danilevich, V. G. *Spravochnik po zarabotnoi plate*. Minsk: Nauka i Tekhnika, 1970.

Goluzov, A. I., and Grigor'iants, M. G. *Narodonaselenie SSSR*. Moscow: Statistika, 1969.

Khorev, B. S., ed., *Malyi gorod*. Moscow: Izdatel'stvo Moskovskogo Universiteta, 1972.

———, and Moiseenko, V. M., eds. *Migratsionnaia podvizhnost' naseleniia v SSSR*. Moscow: Statistika, 1974.

Kostakov, V. G., and Litviakov, P. P. *Balans truda*. Moscow: Ekonomika, 1970.

Lavrishchev, A. *Economic Geography of the U.S.S.R.* Moscow: Progress, 1969.

Litviakov, P. P., ed. *Demograficheskie problemy zaniatosti*. Moscow: Ekonomika, 1969.

Maikov, A. Z., ed., *Migratsiia naseleniia RSFSR*. Moscow: Statistika, 1973.

Manevich, E. *Problemy obshchestvennogo truda*. Moscow: Ekonomika, 1966.

Moskovskii Institut Narodnogo Khoziaistva. *Ekonomicheskie raiony S.S.S.R.* Moscow: Ekonomika, 1969.

Mulliadzhanov, I. R. *Narodonaselenie Uzbekskoi SSR*. Tashkent: Uzbekistan, 1967.

Onikienko, V. V., and Popovkin, V. A. *Kompleksnoe issledovanie migratsionnykh protsessov: Analiz migratsii naseleniia USSR*. Moscow: Statistika, 1973.

Perevedentsev, V. I. *Methody izucheniia migratsii naseleniia*. Moscow: Nauka, 1975.

———. *Migratsiia naseleniia i trudovye prohlemy Sibiri*. Novosibirsk: Nauka, 1966.

Rusanov, E. S. *Raspredelenie i ispol'zovanie trudovykh resursov SSSR*. Moscow: Ekonomika, 1971.

Rybakovskii, L. L. *Regional'nyi analiz migratsii*. Moscow: Statistika, 1973.

———, ed. *Vosproizvodstvo trudovykh resursov Dal'nego Vostoka*. Moscow: Nauka, 1969.

Telepko, L. N. *Urovni ekonomicheskogo razvitiia raionov SSSR*. Moscow: Ekonomika, 1971.

Topilin, A. V. *Territorial'noe pereraspredelenie trudovykh resursov v SSSR*. Moscow: Ekonomika, 1975.

TsSU. *Itogi vsesoiuznoi perepisi naseleniia 1959 goda*. 16 vols. Moscow: Gosstatizdat, 1962.

———, *Itogi vsesoiuznoi perepisi naseleniia 1970 goda*. 7 vols. Moscow: Statistika, 1972–74.

———, *Narodnoe khoziaistvo*. Moscow: Statistika, 1960-70.

———, *Posobie po statistike dlia raionnykh i gorodskikh inspekturov*. Moscow: Statistika, 1970.

———, *Trud v SSSR*. Moscow: Statistika, 1968.

Valentei, D. I., et al., eds. *Narodonaselenie i ekonomika*. Moscow: Ekonomika, 1967.

———. *Problemy migratsii naseleniia i trudovykh resursov*. Moscow: Statistika, 1970.

Volkov, A. G., ed. *Statistika migratsii naseleniia*. Moscow: Statistika, 1973.

———, et al., eds. *Voprosy demografii*. Moscow: Statistika, 1970.

Zaionchkovskaia, Zh. A. *Novosely v gorodakh*. Moscow: Statistika, 1972.

Zaslavskaia, T. I., ed. *Migratsiia sel'skogo naseleniia*. Moscow: Mysl', 1970.

SOVIET MONOGRAPHS AND PRESS ARTICLES

Al'tman, L. P. "Economic Regionalization of the U.S.S.R. and New Methods of Economic-Geographic Research." *Soviet Geography*, VI, No. 9 (November 1965), 48–56.

Baibakov, N. "Progress sovetskoi ekonomiki," *Pravda*, August 12, 1967, p. 2.

Bulochnikova, L. "Sel'skaia migratsiia i puti ee regulirovaniia." *Planovoe khoziaistvo*, No. 8, 1968, pp. 70–77.

Current Digest of Soviet Press, 1959–72.

Ladenkov, V. N. "Studies of Migration of Skilled Personnel in Agriculture," *Problems of Economics*, XV, No. 10 (February 1973), 62–80.

Mel'nikov, N. "Milliardy ekonomii." *Pravda*, January 16, 1967, p. 2.

"Naselenie nashei strany." *Pravda*, April 17, 1971, pp. 1ff.

Nekrasov, N. N. "Man, Industry and Nature." *Soviet Union*, No. 1, 1971, pp. 5-7.

———. "Ot Moskvy do samykh do okrain." *Pravda*, December 31, 1970, p. 2.

———. "Scientific Principles for a General Long-Range Scheme of Location of the Productive Forces of the U.S.S.R." *Soviet Geography*, V, No. 9 (November 1964), 13–18.

Perevedentsev, V. I. "Migratsiia naseleniia i ispol'zovanie trudovykh resursov." *Voprosy ekonomiki*, No. 9, 1970, pp. 33–43.

———. "Novaia literatura po migratsii naseleniia v SSSR." *Voprosy ekonomiki*, No. 10, 1974, pp. 144–52.

———. Sovremennaia migratsiia naseleniia." *Voprosy ekonomiki*, No. 5, 1973, pp. 128–37.

Pokshishevskii, V. V. "Migration of Population, U.S.S.R.," in U.S., Joint Publications Research Service, *Translations on U.S.S.R. Resources*, JPRS 49279 (November 19, 1969), pp. 51–66.

———, et al. "On Basic Migration Patterns." *Population Geography: A Reader*. Edited by G. Demko et al. New York: McGraw Hill, 1970, pp. 318–31.

Smulevich, B. "O sovremennom Mal'tuzianstve." *Vestnik statistiki*, No. 6, 1971, pp. 35–43.

Vechkanov, G. "Raising the Effectiveness of the Territorial Redistribution of Labor Resources." *Problems of Economics*, XII (October 1969), 58–67.

Vestnik statistiki, 1962–72.

Vilenskii, M. "Determining the Efficiency of Territorial Distribution of Production." *Contemporary Soviet Economics*. Edited by Murray Yanowitch. White Plains, N.Y., International Arts and Sciences Press, 1969, pp. 117–28.

Yanovskiy, V. "Men in the North," in U.S., Joint Publications Research Service, *Translations on U.S.S.R. Labor*, JPRS 46794 (November 4, 1968), pp. 1–15.

WESTERN BOOKS

Brown, Emily C. *Soviet Trade Unions and Labor Relations*. Cambridge, Mass.: Harvard University Press, 1966.

Gregory, James S. *Russian Land Soviet People*. New York: Pegasus, 1968.

Hunter, H. *Soviet Transportation Policy*. Cambridge, Mass.: Harvard University Press, 1957.

Karcz, Jerzy, ed. *Soviet and East European Agriculture*. Berkeley: University of California Press, 1967.

Lowry, Ira S. *Migration and Metropolitan Growth: Two Analytical Models*. San Francisco: Chandler, 1966.

Nove, Alec. *An Economic History of the U.S.S.R.* London: Penguin Press, 1970.

Rogers, Andrei. *Matrix Analysis of Interregional Population Growth and Distribution*. Berkeley: University of California Press, 1968.

Salisbury, Harrison E. *War Between Russia and China*. New York: W. W. Norton, 1969.

Shabad, Theodore. *Basic Industrial Resources of the U.S.S.R.* New York: Columbia University Press, 1969.

Shaw, R. Paul. *Migration Theory and Fact: A Review and Bibliography of Current Literature*. Philadelphia: Regional Science Research Institute, 1975.

Treml, Vladimir G., and Hardt, John P., eds. *Soviet Economic Statistics*. Durham, N.C.: Duke University Press, 1972.

U.S. Bureau of the Census. *Projections of the Population of the U.S.S.R., by Age and Sex: 1964–1985*. International Population Reports, Series P-91, No. 13. Washington, D.C.: U.S. Government Printing Office, 1964.

———. *Projections of the Population of the U.S.S.R., by Age and Sex: 1969 to 1990*. International Population Reports, Series P-91, No. 19. Washington, D.C.: U.S. Government Printing Office, 1969.

U.S. Congress. Joint Economic Committee. *Dimensions of Soviet Economic Power*. Washington, D.C.: U.S. Government Printing Office, 1962.

———. *Economic Performance and the Military Burden in the Soviet Union*. Washington, D.C.: U.S. Government Printing Office, 1970.

———. *New Directions in the Soviet Economy*. Part III. Washington, D.C.: U.S. Government Printing Office, 1966.

———. *Soviet Economic Prospects for the Seventies*. Washington, D.C.: U.S. Government Printing Office, 1973.

———. *Soviet Economy in a New Perspective*. Washington, D.C.: U.S. Government Printing Office, 1976.

U.S. Department of Commerce. *Estimates and Projections of the Population of the U.S.S.R., by Age and Sex: 1950 to 2000*. International Population Reports, Series P-91, No. 23. Washington, D.C.: U.S. Government Printing Office, 1973.

WESTERN MONOGRAPHS AND PRESS ARTICLES

Beaucourt, Chantal. ''Les Methods de la plantification regionale en U.R.S.S.'' *Economies et Societes,* I, No. 3 (March 1967), 201-16.

Feshbach, Murray. ''Observations on the Soviet Census.'' *Problems of Communism,* XIX (May-June 1970), 58–64.

Greenwood, Micheal J. ''Research on Internal Migration in the United States: A Survey.'' *The Journal of Economic Literature,* XIII, No. 2 (June, 1975), 397–433.

Harris, Chauncy D. ''Urbanization and Population Growth in the Soviet Union, 1959–1970.'' *Geographical Review,* LXI, No. 1 (January 1971), 102–24.

Hart, R. A. ''Interregional Economic Migration: Some Theoretical Considerations.'' *Journal of Regional Science,* XV, Nos. 2–3 (1975), 127–38, 289–305.

Hawrylyshyn, Oli. ''Internal Migration in Yugoslavia After World War II.'' Institute for Economic Research Discussion Paper No. 32, Queen's University. Kingston, Ontario: ca. 1970.

Koropeckyj, Iwan S. ''The Development of Soviet Location Theory before the Second World War: I and II.'' *Soviet Studies,* XIX (July and October 1967), 1–28, 232–45.

Lee, Everett S. ''A Theory of Migration.'' *Readings on Population.* Edited by David Heer. Englewood Cliffs, N.J.: Prentice-Hall, 1968, pp. 181–93.

Mazur, D. Peter. ''Expectancy of Life at Birth in 36 Nationalities of the Soviet Union: 1958–60.'' *Population Studies,* XXIII, No. 2 (July 1969), 225–46.

Radio Free Europe. ''Migration Against Plan.'' September 1, 1970.

Ravenstein, E. G. ''The Laws of Migration.'' *Journal of the Royal Statistical Society,* XLVIII, pt. 2 (June 1885), 167–222.

Rottenberg, Simon. ''On Choice in Labour Markets.'' *The Labour Market:* Edited by B. J. McCormick and E. O. Smith. Baltimore: Penguin, 1968, pp. 49–74.

Salisbury, Harrison E. ''Russians Going to Area China Claims.'' *New York Times,* March 22, 1963, p. 8.

Shabad, Theodore. ''News Notes.'' *Soviet Geography,* 1960–71.

INDEX

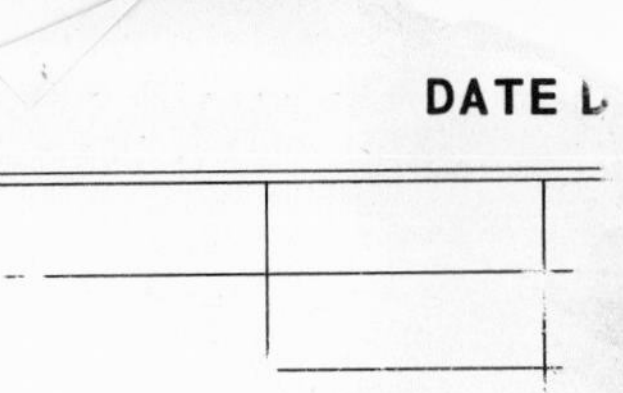